D0794164

Date Due

Japanese Consumer Dynamics

Also by Parissa Haghirian

CASE STUDIES IN JAPANESE MANAGEMENT

INNOVATION AND CHANGE IN JAPAN MANAGEMENT

J-MANAGEMENT: Fresh Perspectives on the Japanese Firm in the 21st Century

MARKTEINTRITT IN JAPAN

SUCCESSFUL CROSS-CULTURAL MANAGEMENT: A Guide for International Managers

UNDERSTANDING JAPANESE MANAGEMENT PRACTICES

Japanese Consumer Dynamics

Edited by

Parissa Haghirian
Associate Professor of International Management, Sophia University

First published 2011 by
PALGRAVE MACMILLAN

Palgrave Macmillan in the UK is an imprint of Macmillan Publishers Limited, registered in England, company number 785998, of Houndmills, Basingstoke, Hampshire RG21 6XS.

Palgrave Macmillan in the US is a division of St Martin's Press LLC, 175 Fifth Avenue, New York, NY 10010.

Palgrave Macmillan is the global academic imprint of the above companies and has companies and representatives throughout the world.

Palgrave® and Macmillan® are registered trademarks in the United States, the United Kingdom, Europe and other countries.

ISBN: 978–0–230–24286–9 hardback

This book is printed on paper suitable for recycling and made from fully managed and sustained forest sources. Logging, pulping and manufacturing processes are expected to conform to the environmental regulations of the country of origin.

A catalogue record for this book is available from the British Library.

A catalog record for this book is available from the Library of Congress.

10   9   8   7   6   5   4   3   2   1
20 19 18 17 16 15 14 13 12 11

Printed and bound in Great Britain by
CPI Antony Rowe, Chippenham and Eastbourne

Contents

Part III   Consumer Trends in Japan

Tables

Figures

Preface

Japanese consumers have always posed a challenge for Western market-ers and market researchers. In contrast to consumers in other developed markets, the Japanese have always shown very particular patterns of consumption. They spent excessively in the 1980s, yet became cost-conscious in the 1990s; they indulged heavily in luxury brands over the last decade, but decided only a few years ago that expensive brands were out of fashion. As well as this, they are still extremely quality-oriented – especially when consuming services – and show great affinity for new and innovative technologies and cutting-edge design.

Underlying these contradictory messages are a number of major shifts in Japanese society, which have not only changed consumers' attitudes and behaviour, but have led to the emergence of whole new consumer groups. The most widely discussed of these new groups is the elderly – the baby boomer generation. As Japan's elderly population rapidly expands, the question of how to address the 'silver' market has emerged as a major issue for Japanese companies. Another very influen-tial consumer group is single people. The number of single households is growing in Japan, a trend that is also observed in other industrialized countries. One more Japanese consumer trend is the high number of affluent consumers, a group which shows interest not only in luxury products but also in luxury experiences. All these groups have a strong influence on Japanese markets and evoke significant reactions among media and marketers. And, since all three groups are growing in signifi-cance in other industrialized countries, the Japanese consumer market holds valuable insights for marketers and market researchers focused on the West as well.

In recent years I have published a number of articles on how the Japanese consumer market has changed and how this has influenced Western corporations in Japan. Living and working in Japan, I was able to access Japanese media and research reports on these trends, but found a scarcity of relevant results published in Western languages. It became obvious that most publications in this field dated from the 1990s, and therefore that the major changes observed today were receiving insuffi-cient coverage; despite their massive purchasing power and the fact that they play a dominant role in the world economy, Japanese consumers are under-investigated. The reasons for this neglect are not quite clear, but are presumably linked to the difficulties that Western researchers experience in managing cultural and linguistic barriers. There are a number of comparative studies in which Western surveys have been repeated in Japan, but the particularities of Japanese consumer behaviour have not been investigated since the beginning of the new millennium. Thus, contemporary trends among Japanese consumers, as well as the consumer groups that have emerged in the past few years, have not received significant coverage outside Japan.

The lack of accessible data on the topic led me to the idea of editing a book on the state of the Japanese consumer market today, on trends in Japanese consumer behaviour and the recently emerged consumer groups.

Japanese Consumer Dynamics provides an overview on the Japanese consumer market. All the chapters have been written by authors with many years of experience of working, living, consuming and researching in various disciplines in Japan. The book is divided into three parts. The first part consists of an overview on the historical development of Japanese consumers, their particular consumer behaviour and consumer rights in Japan. The second part then introduces new consumer groups, such as the baby boomers, the single market, *otaku* consumers and young men, who have only recently attracted the interest of Japanese corporations. The final part of the book discusses new trends in the Japanese consumer market, such as changes in food consumption and retail, American TV series and their influence on Japanese consumers, and mobile consumerism in Japan.

The first part of the book presents an overview of Japanese consumers themselves. In Chapter 1, I give an overview of the development of Japanese consumerism since World War II. The evolution of Japanese consumerism goes hand in hand with Japan's economic development. Alongside the rapid expansion of manufacturing and exports in Japan, Japanese people took on a new role and changed from producers to avid consumers who are significant drivers in global markets today.

Chapter 2 discusses the particularities of Japanese consumers. Japanese consumers are not only among the richest consumers in the world: they also show very special behaviour when purchasing or searching for product information. First of all, Japanese consumers seem to have a very high affinity for brand products. Product safety plays an important role when addressing Japanese consumers; other aspects are a high orientation towards technology, and zero tolerance for product defects. All these attitudes often differentiate Japanese consumers from

Western consumers. The issue of price sensitivity has also generated a lot of interest in and outside Japan: Japanese consumers were traditionally considered to show lower levels of price sensitivity and seemed to prefer high-price products that communicated quality over cheaper or discounted goods. But this has now changed, and it is becoming more widely acceptable to buy cheaper products.

In Chapter 3, Luke Nottage discusses Japanese consumer rights. Such rights are well entrenched in Japanese society, and many gaps in Japanese consumer protection law were filled during the 1990s. Nottage provides a historical overview of Japanese consumer rights protection, focusing on product safety, consumer contracts and consumer loans, which are the most controversial aspects of Japanese consumer law.

The second part of the book presents Japan's new consumer groups, with an eye to the signals these groups may send regarding the development of markets in the West and in industrialized countries more generally. Chapter 4 investigates the most prominent Japanese consumer group, the baby boomers or the so-called 'silver' market. In this chapter, Emmanuel J. Chéron sets out how Japanese retirees have become the most interesting consumer group for Japanese marketers in recent years. Chéron discusses the market structure of elderly consumers in Japan, and the segmentation and positioning of this group. The chapter closes with an overview of how corporations can successfully address baby boomers and the silver market.

Kristie Collins discusses another very interesting new Japanese consumer group in Chapter 5: the single consumer, or consumers who live alone. This group has not only taken on great importance worldwide, but will also have a significant economic impact on the Japanese consumer market in the future. The number of people living in single households in Japan is increasing, and Japanese consumers living alone span different age groups. Starting with young singles still living with their parents ('parasite singles'), and ranging from ARAFO ('around 40') singles to retired consumers, Collins shows how influential all three groups are and sets out how companies will need to anticipate and address the product and service needs of this critical market segment.

Japan's new rich consumers are the focus of Chapter 6. Japan is widely known as the only 'mass luxury market' in the world. In this chapter I describe just how affluent Japanese consumers have become and how they have developed their wealth. The phrase the 'new rich' – as Japan's wealthy consumers are called – refers to consumers who have more than 100 million yen in financial assets. The most affluent group consists of consumers who have more than 500 million yen in assets, and in Japan there are more than 52,000 households in this category. The large number of affluent consumers has also created a major interest in luxury products; since 2008, however, interest in luxury has been changing, and purchasing cheaper and less fashionable brands has become more acceptable. The chapter sets out this and other recent developments in the purchasing behaviour of Japan's super-rich.

In Chapter 7, Aaron Toussaint presents research results on a consumer group that has only become a topic of discussion since 2009, namely Japanese men. Traditionally, Japanese men were less involved in purchasing decisions than Japanese women, and were mainly seen as providers of financial assets for their families. Their buying decisions mainly involved products like beer and cars. Changes in Japanese society and business, including an increasing unemployment rate, lower levels of job security and more women in the workforce, have changed the role of Japanese men in society and as breadwinners. Their interests seem to be shifting from taking care of their families to taking care of themselves: the Japanese media even call these new male consumers 'grass eaters'. The fact that these men are breaking out of their traditional roles has a strong effect on how they purchase products, and Toussaint discusses the factors that have influenced these developments and how male consumption in Japan has changed in recent years.

Chapter 8 focuses on another topic that has occupied the Japanese media and public during the last decade: the *otaku* (enthusiastic consumer) market. Here, Patrick W. Galbraith presents a definition of *otaku* and developments in fandom and interest in certain product groups such as manga and anime. He shows that *otaku* are not only a profitable market for Japanese corporations, but are also integrated into product development procedures and market research.

The third part of the book investigates the new trends that can be observed in the Japanese market. In Chapter 9, Stephanie Assmann discusses the Japanese food market. Japanese consumers have traditionally spent more money on food than consumers in other cultures. Food is the second highest expense after housing for Japanese families, because most food sold in Japan is produced overseas and needs to be imported. The food market has also undergone big changes: after a number of food scandals, safety issues have come to dominate consumer attitudes, and food retail has also undergone a transformation.

Chapter 10 presents a discussion of how the Western media has influenced Japanese attitudes and purchasing behaviour with respect to fashion. Aiko Yoshioka examines how the successful American TV series and film *Sex and the City* was portrayed in Japanese fashion magazines.

Whereas the TV series is mostly seen as a lifestyle influence in many Western countries, in Japan it had more influence on Japanese fashion, and was presented as a fashion example for many women.

In Chapter 11, Benjamin Hentschel examines mobile consumption in Japan. Japanese consumers have had access to mobile Internet since 2000. Mobile phones have become everyday devices, used not only to talk to other people, but also to send messages, to purchase products, and to make payments in shops. The chapter provides an overview of the development of mobile consumption, mobile commerce and consumer behaviour on the mobile Internet. The chapter also discusses the ways in which Japanese companies have developed innovative products and services that integrate into the life of the mobile consumer.

DR PARISSA HAGHIRIAN
Sophia University
Tokyo, Japan

Contributors

Stephanie Assmann is a lecturer at the Center for the Advancement of Higher Education at Tohoku University in Sendai. She received a PhD in Japanese Studies from the University of Hamburg, Germany in 2003 after being awarded a fellowship by the Japanese Ministry of Education for research at Doshisha University in Kyoto. Stephanie has obtained professional experience through working for Citizen Watch Europe and the Consulate General of Japan in Hamburg. Her research interests include gender equality in the workplace and consumer behaviour with an emphasis on food. Together with Eric C. Rath she is co-editing a collection of essays entitled *Japanese Foodways: Past and Present* (University of Illinois Press).

Emmanuel J. Chéron is Professor of Marketing in the International Business and Economics Group at the Faculty of Liberal Arts, Sophia University in Tokyo. He has an MBA from Queen's University, Kingston, Ontario and a PhD from Laval University, Quebec City, Canada. Dr Chéron was previously affiliated with the School of Business at Laval University and at the University of Quebec in Montreal. He has been invited as visiting professor at Kansai University, Osaka, and Keio University, Tokyo, Japan as well as at the Business Institute of Management of Paris 1 Panthéon-Sorbonne. He is, furthermore, visiting professor at the School of Marketing Sorbonne-Assas, France. His present research interests focus on marketing in Japan, international marketing, strategic marketing and marketing of services, with a strong emphasis on quantitative methods applied to marketing decision-making. He has co-authored two books and computer software. He has published in numerous journals including *Transportation Research*, *Journal of International Consumer Marketing*, *International Journal of Research in Marketing*, *Canadian Journal of Administrative Sciences*, *Asian Journal of Marketing*, *Japanese Psychological Research*, *Recherche et Applications en Marketing* and *Décisions Marketing*. He has also published in many conference proceedings, including those of the American Marketing Association, the Academy of Marketing Science, the Association for Consumer Research, the Administrative Science Association of Canada, the European Marketing Academy and the French Marketing Association. He serves on the Editorial Review Board of two academic journals. He has also had the opportunity to consult for Crown corporations, public and private companies.

Kristie Collins is an Assistant Professor in the Department of Modern Languages and Modern Cultures at the University of Tsukuba. She received a Bilingual Honours Bachelor's degree in Canadian Studies and Theatre from York University (1996) and a Master's degree in Teaching English as a Foreign/Second Language from the University of Birmingham (1999), and recently completed a PhD in Interdisciplinary Studies from the University of Tsukuba (2010). Kristie has taught Gender Studies, Cultural Studies, Intercultural Communication, and English as a Foreign Language in Canada, Poland, England, Turkey, Finland and Japan, and is developing a course on 'Gender and Communication in the International Workplace' for Aalto University to be delivered in 2011. She is currently national co-chair of the GALE (Gender Awareness in Language Education) group in Japan, and regularly presents papers in Japan and abroad. Her research interests include mediated and lived experiences of female singleness, identity construction and stigma management, and gender and intercultural communication.

Patrick W. Galbraith is a PhD candidate in the Graduate School of Interdisciplinary Information Studies at the University of Tokyo. His research focus is *otaku*, or the emergence of a new mode of social existence in relation to shifts in capitalism and the rise of information-consumer society. He has worked as a freelance journalist specializing in Japanese pop-culture since 2004, and founded a non-profit tour and news service in Akihabara. He is the author of the *Otaku Encyclopedia*. Recent publications include '*Moe:* Exploring Virtual Potential in Post-Millennial Japan', 'Akihabara: Conditioning a Public *Otaku* Image' and '*Fujoshi:* Girls and Women Exploring Transgressive Intimacy in Contemporary Japan'.

Parissa Haghirian is Associate Professor of International Management at the Faculty of Liberal Arts at Sophia University in Tokyo, Japan. She is, furthermore, a visiting professor at Groupe HEC in Paris, Aalto University and Keio Business School, and an adjunct professor at Temple University in Tokyo. Dr Haghirian holds a Master's degree in Japanese Anthropology (University of Vienna, Austria) and a Master's degree and a PhD in International Management (Vienna University of Business, Austria). Since joining Sophia University Dr Haghirian has researched numerous aspects of Japanese business practices, published several books and many articles on the topic, and organized conferences and speeches on Japanese management in Europe and Japan. She is the editor of *'J-Management: Fresh Perspectives on the Japanese Firm in the 21st Century'* (iUniverse Star) and *'Innovation and Change in Japanese Management'* (Palgrave Macmillan) and the author of *Understanding Japanese Management Practices* (Business Expert Press) and *Multinationals and Cross-cultural Management: The Transfer of Knowledge Within Multinational Corporations* (Routledge International Business in Asia). Dr Haghirian has taught undergraduate, graduate and MBA level classes on the subject of Japanese business practices and consulted with numerous Western and Japanese companies in Tokyo. Her research interests include Japanese management, Japanese consumer behaviour and cross-cultural business communication.

Benjamin Hentschel is a Master Student in the Graduate School of Global Studies (majoring in International Business and Development Studies) at Sophia University in Tokyo. After a semester at Ryukoku University in Kyoto (2006) and several internships related to German–Japanese business relations in Tokyo (2006/07) and Düsseldorf (2007/08), he returned to Tokyo in 2008 to do extensive research for his diploma thesis. In 2009, he obtained a Diploma Degree in East Asian Regional Studies from Duisburg-Essen University, Germany. His research interests include knowledge management, the contemporary Japanese firm and economy, intercultural communication and management, as well as new media and technology.

Luke Nottage is Associate Professor at Sydney Law School, a founding Co-Director of the Australian Network for Japanese Law (www.law.usyd. edu.au/anjel) and Director of Japanese Law Links Pty Ltd (http://members.optusnet.com.au/~kimono2005/Japanese_Law_Links_Pty_Ltd/). He specializes in comparative and transnational consumer and commercial law, especially regarding Japan. He has consulted on consumer law issues for lawyers in Japan and worldwide, as well as for the Japanese Cabinet Office, the OECD and the European Commission. Luke has also made multiple submissions, often drawing on Japanese and international law developments, for the Australian government's reviews of consumer law since 2006.

Aaron Toussaint is currently Research Manager at *Five by Fifty*, a Tokyo-based trend forecasting and ethnographic marketing research agency. In 2005, after obtaining his BA in philosophy with a minor in Asian Studies from St John's University in the US state of Minnesota, Aaron moved to Japan. In 2008 he entered Sophia University, where he completed his MA in International Business and Development Studies. While at Sophia, Aaron researched the effect of cultural factors on brand loyalty (2009), cross-cultural market entry problems in Japan (2008), and the economic impact of US military bases in Okinawa (2008). His research on market entry problems was transformed into a highly successful teaching case study presented at Temple University in Japan, Hosei University, and Sophia University, among others, and will be featured in the first edition of a forthcoming global marketing textbook by Ilan Alon and Eugene Jaffe. Aaron's current research interests include the effect of consumer ethnocentrism on product evaluation, as well as trends in Japan's FMCG (fast moving consumer goods) markets, especially alcoholic beverages.

Aiko Yoshioka lectures in ethnic issues at Aoyama Gakuin University and English at Sophia University in Tokyo. She received her MA in Women's Studies from the University of Adelaide (1998) and her PhD in Cinema Studies from La Trobe University in Australia (2004). She has written several essays on the representation of race, ethnicity and gender in film and TV. She has worked for a research project on clothing and body funded by the Japan Society for the Promotion of Science (JSPS) from 2006 to 2009 and focused on fashion, consumption and *Sex and the City*. Her current interests are identity formation and societies, media and popular culture.

Part I
Japanese Consumers Today

1
The Historical Development of Japanese Consumerism

Parissa Haghirian

Introduction

Japan is the second-largest consumer market in the world, and Japanese consumers have the second-highest purchasing power. Japanese cities – and, above all, Tokyo – offer every good imaginable, and even today, in the midst of the global economic crisis, they are still a powerful attraction for Japanese consumers.

This chapter looks at the historical development of Japanese consumption after World War II. By way of synopsis, the history of Japanese consumption shows rapid periods of expansion powered by underlying economic growth, and quick adaptation to crisis. Consumption has both driven, and been driven by, fundamental social change. As the chapter describes in more detail, Japanese consumers experienced their first boom during the Korean War, and started to show interest in consumer products in the 1950s, at a time when economic growth rates were as high as 10 per cent. In the 1960s, consumption became a widespread phenomenon: *mai kâ* (my car) and *mai hômu* (my home) became synonyms for wealth and success. At the beginning of the 1970s the first post-war generation came of age: the *shinjinrui*, as they were called, showed signs of increasing hedonism in their patterns of consumption, and began to manifest a preference for Western products over Japanese – a preference which was noted by Western manufacturers, who began to take a greater interest in the Japanese market. The 1980s were dominated by the bubble economy, during which consumption became a lifestyle. When the bubble burst, however, rising unemployment and the collapse of numerous Japanese corporations threatened the national sense of security, and consumers started to make more risk-free and price-oriented buying decisions. The Japanese economy showed signs of recovery at the beginning of this millennium, and consumption once more increased. The latest economic crisis, however, has had a new impact on Japanese purchasing behaviour, and at the moment it is not clear whether Japanese consumers will react to the crisis very differently from their Western counterparts. Despite this, Japan and its consumers continue to provoke great interest among foreign manufacturers, and Japanese consumers still play a dominant role in the economic state of the nation.

The post-war years

Consumption and consumers have always been 'an integral part of economic life' in Japan (Francks, 2009, p. 1). Even in the nineteenth century the Japanese were able to choose from a wide variety of goods on offer from domestic producers. The foundation of contemporary Japanese consumer culture, however, was laid during the interwar years. It was in this period that the migration of country workers to the cities led to strong urbanization and the emergence of a new middle class. As Francks notes:

> By the inter-war period, Japan was experiencing the development of many of the infrastructure features taken to characterize 'modern life' in the West – commuter suburbs, department stores, the system of mass advertising and so on. In many respects these features provided the framework within which a growing urban middle class sought to obtain and accommodate new consumer goods derived from the West and the lifestyle embodied in them. (Francks, 2009, pp. 109ff.)

However, the years following World War II were marked by poverty. Partner (1999, p. 139) points out that 'In the early 1950s, consumption had more to do with putting rice on the table than with pursuit of pleasure. ... Caloric intake in Japan remained far below that of affluent Western countries.' With the military forces demobilized, the overall number of jobless people reached 13.1 million. As well as unemployment, Japan faced food shortages: the rice harvest in 1945 was two-thirds of the average (Nakamura, 1995).

This period of acute shortage, however, was also the period of the American occupation, during which many Japanese first became acquainted with Western products and consumer culture. As Dower comments (2000, p. 136): 'In those years of acute hunger and scarcity, the material comfort of the American was simply staggering to behold.' During the war years, consumption and indulgence in extravagances had not been considered appropriate: 'extravagance is an enemy' had been a wartime slogan (Dower, 2000, p. 137) and the focus had been on survival and support for the country.

The period of shortage lasted for a few years after the war ended, and only the Korean War led to the first rise in living standards. Starting in 1950, US military procurement for its operations in Korea created a large demand in the Japanese market and so pushed the Japanese economy forward. This led not only to effective demand within the Japanese market, but also to an increase in foreign exchange and subsequently to an increase in material imports and an expansion in production capacity (Saito, 2000, p. 221). Exports rose in response to the rise in international prices, stimulating production, employment and profits: the Japanese economy thus surged forward into its first post-war boom (Nakamura, 1995).

As a result of this boom, from 1951 onwards the foundations were being laid for the enormous success of the Japanese economy (Saito, 2000, p. 221). In 1952 the Bank of Japan and the Ministry of Finance founded the Central Council for Savings Promotion (Garon, 2006). As incomes increased, Japanese households were increasingly able to spend and save at the same time (Horioka, 2006). The famous Jimmu boom of 1955–6 led to major changes in Japanese consumption and rates of saving. Whereas an average urban working family saved only 2 per cent of its income in 1951, this had risen to 12.5 per cent by 1957 (Shinohara, 1959). At the same time Japanese people started to enjoy consumption and the purchase of newly available consumer goods (Saito, 2000). In 1955 Japan regained the productivity levels of the pre-war years. During the rapid growth period from 1955 to 1973, Japan had an average rate of growth of 9.1 per cent, whereas Europe had a growth rate of 5–6 per cent and the US a rate of only 3 per cent. Over this period, investment in industrial facilities increased 16.5 per cent and production capacity expanded 15.7 times. Other factors influencing the rapid growth were a rise in exports and increasing domestic demand, which was due to the popularization of consumer durables (Gakken, 2002). At the same time, an increasing number of Japanese workers were leaving the agricultural sector and going to work in construction and manufacturing. This trend continued into the 1970s. Nakamura (1995) reports that in 1955 there were 6.9 million workers in the manufacturing industry, whereas in 1970 there were already 13.5 million. In the 1960s this trend also led to a high number of workers entering into tertiary industries such as commerce and service trades. Japan developed into an industrialized economy.

These economic changes led not only to an increase in income but also to an increase in spending among Japanese consumers, who started to manifest their enjoyment of their new-found wealth by purchasing consumer goods. Partner (1999, p. 138) observes that the 'apparently spontaneous, even festive nature of these purchases is captured by the slogans attached to successive waves of consumption: the "three sacred treasures" of the 1950s (television, electric washing machine, and refrigerator).' These treasures, although very expensive, entered Japanese homes with great rapidity. In 1955, 4 per cent of households had a washing machine, and ownership of televisions and refrigerators stood at less than 1 per cent. By 1960, 45 per cent of Japanese households owned a washing machine, 54 per cent a TV set and 15 per cent a refrigerator. By 1970, more than 90 per cent of Japanese households owned all three items (Yoshimi, 2006). Historians often point to the rapidity with which Japanese filled their homes with the accoutrements of affluence after the war, even when incomes were low (Partner, 1999). Nakamura considers the wish to 'keep up with the Joneses' a major factor for the rapid diffusion of these new goods, coupled with high rates of saving (Nakamura, 1995, p. 105).

The 1960s

During the 1960s Japan continued to prosper. The longest boom (the Izanagi boom) began in October 1965 and lasted for 57 months. Japanese GDP increased by over 10 per cent annually in the five consecutive years from 1966 to 1970, and consumers reacted to this by buying even more consumer products. The favourite combination of products at that time was 'the 3Cs' – car, cooler and colour TV (Saito, 2000, p. 224). The increasing diffusion of television also exposed the majority of Japanese people to commercials (Ballon, 1973), giving them even more information about consumer products. Manufacturers provided markets with an endless supply of new and popular products, and huge public works projects were constantly under way, such as the development of the bullet train, expressways, bridges linking Honshu and Shikoku, and the Honshu–Hokkaido underwater tunnel (Sawa, 2010).

The increases in incomes and savings led to social and economic changes, as well as changes in the structure of Japanese society – particularly the structure of the family (Partner, 1999, p. 143). As Thomas (2007, p. 75) observes: 'In the 1960s and 1970s, the Japanese economy flourished, giving birth to a newly flush middle class that wanted to live a more ostentatious life.' The Western family model became popular in Japan: women who had previously held jobs and actively supported their families started to retreat from working life and become full-time mothers and housewives. American electrical goods companies, like their Japanese counterparts, promoted idealized images of young, pretty housewives effortlessly performing housework (Partner, 1999, p. 152). This trend is most strongly reflected in the *mai-hômu* (my home) trend, which can be interpreted as the Japanese version of 'My home is my castle' (Ortmanns, 1994, p. 285). *Mai hômu* and *mai kâ* (my car) became keywords of Japanese consumption in the 1960s: owning a house and a car was seen as a marker of success. As the number of individual cars increased, *mai kâ* became the most popular middle-class item. However, despite this appetite for consumption, rates of saving remained high, and many people preferred to pay for consumer goods with their savings rather than pay interest on instalment plans (JETRO, 1985).

As consumption became a lifestyle, the nature of Japanese consumers also changed. The first generation of post-war Japanese were very different from their elders, and started to follow new trends. In Japanese, this new generation is called *shinjinrui*, which can be translated as 'the New Breed'. These new consumers 'did not think or act like Japanese' (De Mente, 2004, p. 263) and they differentiated themselves from the older generation through their consumer behaviour. As Yoshimi observes (2006, p. 210), 'They began to enjoy consuming many types of styles and cultures as completely modified artifacts,' and America 'had by then become…an artifact which people would repeatedly consume'. Sand (2006, p. 88) describes the attitude of the new generation in more fundamental terms: 'Thanks to Japan's transition from production-led industrial society to consumption-led postindustrialism, Japanese were at last free subjects…defining themselves through consumption, while capitalism was their servant, compelled to deliver ever-new opportunities for their pleasure.' However, the *shinjinrui*, with their non-traditional attitudes, had a cumulative effect on Japan's society and economy, and also influenced the Japanese consumer market. Their consumer behaviour was not predictable, and manufacturers started to develop new approaches in market research and advertising to keep up with them (De Mente, 2004, p. 264).

The increasing interest in consumer products also had significant effects at the level of legislation. In 1968, the Japanese government responded to demands for a comprehensive system of consumer-protection policymaking and administration that accorded consumer advocates opportunities to represent the consumer interest at the national level (Maclachlan, 1997). The Consumer Protection Basic Law (*Shôshisha hogo kihon hô*) was the first law to uphold consumer protection as a governmental objective. 'It specified the regulatory responsibilities of all levels of government toward consumers, the responsibilities of firms to improve the quality of their products and services and to respond to consumer claims, and the obligations of consumers themselves to acquire the knowledge for making rational purchasing decisions' (Nishimura, 2006, p. 273).

The 1970s

The oil crisis, hitting in October 1973, put an end to the period of rapid economic growth, and in the following year the Japanese economy experienced its first negative rate of growth since the end of World War II; after 1975, however, the economy resumed growing at 4–5 per cent a year (Sawa, 2009).

Japanese consumers' priorities began to change during the 1970s, and patterns of consumption shifted accordingly. Japanese consumers started to spend their money on items which could increase satisfaction in their lives. The World Exposition held in Osaka in 1970 led to a huge increase in tourism (JETRO, 1985). By the end of the 1970s more than four million Japanese had travelled overseas (Jansen, 2000). The quality of goods and services became more important than their price – a big change from the consumer demands of the 1950s and 1960s (JETRO, 1985).

The Japanese consumer market became increasingly interesting to domestic firms during the 1970s. From the 1970s onwards, the range of choice in the products available to consumers expanded markedly. These changes were most obvious in the case of the Japanese diet: whereas more than 50 per cent of calorie intake had been from rice in the 1950s, this figure fell to only 25 per cent in the 1990s. At the same time, the share of Japanese household expenditure devoted to food decreased, from 50 per cent in the 1940s to 25 per cent by the beginning of the 1990s. Hand in hand with this development, the Japanese diet began to include more Western elements, and Japan became the greatest food importer worldwide (Francks, 2009, p. 194). Today, Japan obtains 60 per cent of its food supply from overseas sources (see Chapter 9 in this book).

The 1980s

In the latter half of the 1980s private consumption became a motor of economic development (Kokumin seikatsu sentâ, 1997, p. 166; cited in Meyer-Ohle and Fuess, 1997). The so-called bubble saw a further boom in consumption. Salaries continued to improve, and, with many jobs available, a large-scale market for expensive imported products developed. Foreign travel became even more fashionable, with the number of Japanese travelling overseas rising to 10 million per year (Jansen, 2000). Ninety per cent of Japanese people considered themselves 'middle class' (JETRO, 1985).

During these boom times, European brand manufacturers began their successful entry into the Japanese market. First and most successful was Louis Vuitton, which entered the market in the mid-1980s. The shopping boom was not restricted to Japanese end-consumers only; it also affected Japanese corporate investors, who bought Western companies (e.g. Sony's purchase of Columbia Pictures), and individual investors, who bought an increasing quantity of Western artworks (Thomas, 2007).

Japanese consumption became more conspicuous in the late 1980s, moving away from conformist-oriented consumption and becoming more focused on status-seeking (Schütte and Ciarliante, 1998). A new category of lifestyle-oriented consumers emerged who had a strong desire to assert their independence from surrounding society (Laserre and Schütte, 1998). Rapid growth of consumption could be found in the areas of dining out, private transportation or personal cars, education, medical and health care, recreation and entertainment (JETRO, 1985). The three new fixations of the 1980s were the 'three Js' (Partner, 1999, p. 138) – jewels, jet travel and *jutaku* (home ownership). But the bubble economy also created the first distinctively Japanese consumer stereotype: unmarried university-educated women, aged 25 to 34, who worked in well-paying jobs and still lived with their parents, and who were known as 'parasite singles' (Thomas, 2007). By the beginning of the 1990s, Japan had developed into a post-industrial consumer society.

The bursting of the bubble and the lost decade of the 1990s

The bursting of the bubble at the beginning of the 1990s changed all this. The crash led to bankruptcies, rising unemployment, and banks being left with their notorious 'bad' loans, and all this affected the attitudes and behaviour of Japanese consumers – their lust to spend in particular. Schütte and Ciarliante (1998) observed that, following the speculative bubble and the conspicuous consumption of the late 1980s, there appeared to be a shift in Japanese values in the 1990s.

Consumption in the 1990s was influenced by two principal factors, the economic recession and the processes of deregulation, and these had a profound influence on the retail market, which had been based on a traditional and highly complex distribution system already in existence before Japan opened up to the West. This system was challenged by the change of the traditional retail stores law (*daiten hô*). The law on large-scale retail was amended in 1990, leading to a rush of new large stores and shopping centres in the suburbs (Gakken, 2002). It became easier to open a business, and, at the same time, competition increased.

Many Japanese companies were forced to restructure. One major cost-driver in Japanese firms was their distinctive distribution structure, which traditionally involved many layers of intermediaries and middle-men. The traditional distribution system proved to be too expensive, and new and more consumer-oriented models were developed, while new retailing styles appeared (Gakken, 2002). Direct imports – conducted by companies such as Uniqlo or Zoff – allowed good quality at lower prices (Chen, 2003). Outlet malls for leftover products offered merchandise at a 30–70 per cent discount on the regular price. '100 yen' stores became a frequent sight in Japanese cities. These new styles of consumption proved to be more in tune with the pessimistic consumer attitudes of the times, and they also forced certain traditional corporations, such as the Sogo department store, out of business (Gakken, 2002).

Japanese consumers had changed their attitudes and developed more cost-oriented patterns of consumer behaviour. Schütte and Ciarlante (1998, p. 73) wrote, 'This consumer is highly aware of the price–value relationship…. is focused on individualistic satisfaction and is willing to search for value.' Consumers seemed to be less conscious of images of status and luxury and high fashion. As Okahashi *et al.* (1998, p. 341) remark, 'it is clear that consumer values have changed significantly since the recession took hold, and not all of these changes are merely a product of the tightening of purse-strings to weather the recession. Some of the changes are in fact due to the greater maturity and experience of Japanese consumers.'

The new millennium

As the new millennium began, Japanese society had clearly undergone a tremendous change since the bursting of the bubble 10 years earlier. Not only was the economic situation more stressful for many Japanese, but many myths of the Japanese economic miracle – such as lifetime employment or the unbeatable stability of the Japanese corporation – had been thrown into doubt. Japanese society itself had changed:

> Japanese consumers went through a huge and lasting emotional adjustment during the 13-some-odd years of economic stagnation throughout the 1990s and early 2000s. Throughout this period, Japanese consumers were forced to adapt to a new reality, having faced a number of dramatic 'psyche changing' events such as the end of lifetime employment and the uncertainty related to company and government pensions. In the years since, many have had to find new ways to make a living, including part-time jobs and entrepreneurial activity (Howard, 2009b, p. 29).

The number of women entering the workforce increased, part-time work became more common and Japanese baby boomers started to retire; the younger generation, then, faced an insecure future.

The first decade of the new millennium was also a time of product and food scandals, which left Japanese consumers with concerns about the safety and ethics of their, so far highly admired, firms. Japan has had its share of scandals, with Livedoor doing the same in Japan as Enron did in the US; and the list continues, with scandals of various forms emanating from Snow Brand Foods, Tokyo Electric Co., Nippon Meat Packers, and Matsushita, all of which led to higher levels of concern among Japanese consumers regarding customer service and good management practices (*BusinessWorld*, 2003; cited in Tsalikis and Seaton, 2008). It is, therefore, not surprising that Japanese consumers were sending very mixed messages to marketers at the beginning of this century. In his longitudinal study on Japanese consumer behaviour, McHardy Reid (2007, p. 97) observed that 'Consumers shop around more rationally and include more options in their portfolio of alternatives (e.g., 100-yen stores, all night auctions) and are now prepared to purchase previously owned apparel and other items, something that was anathema during the boom years.' He further observed a shift away from the hedonism of the bubble years to an increasing interest in health and health-promoting products such as organic food, and also a rise in consumer spending in adult education. But Japanese consumers continue to express their individuality through creative choices among desirable brands seen as high quality, reputable and prestigious. While these

consumers want to express their individuality, they also want to maintain social norms (Knight and Kim, 2007). Thus, despite the scandals
and the aftermath of the bubble, luxury consumption boomed in the
first decade of this century.

All these changes led to stronger segmentation within the Japanese
market and the formation of influential new consumer groups. Next
to the parasite singles who dominated earlier discussions of Japanese
consumption, the Japanese baby boomers grew in influence. These
groups, the first generation to be born after World War II, are the
classic Japanese salarymen, the backbone of the Japanese economic
miracle. And since Japan has the highest percentage of elderly citizens in the world and they receive very generous remunerations when
leaving companies, often after more than 30 years of service, they
became the most sought-after consumer group in Japan, holding
80 per cent of Japanese financial assets (see also Chapter 4). Working
and single women are the next target group discussed in Japanese
media. As the marriage age in Japan is increasing and the number of
single households is on the rise, the number of women controlling their
own income is rising as well. In the first decade of this century their
influence has become obvious even to very traditional Japanese corporations – Japanese banks, for instance, began giving loans to single
women only in the 1990s, and even then reluctantly, expecting them
to get married, become housewives and lose their regular income. Over
the past decade many banks have recognized the financial power of
single Japanese women and have developed new products that allow
them to buy property more easily (Haghirian, 2007). Both groups –
baby boomers and single women with income – fall into the category
of the 'new rich' consumer, a phrase which refers to consumers with
more than 10 million yen in financial assets. The so called *nyuu richi*
and their interest in high-quality and luxury products has also led
to an increase in entries by Western luxury brands into the Japanese
market. Even in 2008, the love for expensive goods led to overall
retail sales of an estimated 135 trillion yen (US$1.48 trillion), second
only to the United States (Salsberg, 2010). Another widely discussed
group are the *otaku*, the enthusiastic consumers, who are often considered obsessives, occupied only with their hobbies. However, their
purchasing power and creativity have also stimulated significant reactions among Japanese marketing firms. Japanese companies were and
are famous for segmenting their consumer groups very carefully and
reacting to their wishes very promptly by developing new services and
products.

The economic crisis of 2008 and its effects on Japanese consumer behaviour

There is no doubt that the 2008 economic crisis has changed Japanese consumer behaviour. At the time of writing – the beginning of 2010 – consumption in Japan is weak (*Nikkei Shimbun*, 2010) and consumer attitudes and behaviour are once more showing dramatic shifts (Salsberg, 2010). One obvious sign is the closure of 11 department stores in 2010, which reminds many Japanese of the year 2000, in which the Sogo department store closed. In comparison to the year 2000, however, overall spending in Japan has decreased by 8 per cent (*Nikkei Shimbun*, 2010). After decades of differing from consumers in industrialized countries, eschewing low prices and preferring to shop at the high end, Japanese consumers seem to be becoming more similar to their Western counterparts in seeking out value and attempting to entertain themselves at a reasonable cost. Japanese consumers are reducing costs, and 37 per cent of them claim to have cut overall spending. One way of doing this is to stay at home instead of going out. A new term was coined for this trend: *sugomori*, or 'chicks in the nest' (Salsberg, 2010).

The reason for this dramatic change is the shrinkage of the middle class in Japan. The number of households holding an 8–9 million yen budget per year shrank 18 per cent, the over 15 million yen class of households shrank 30 per cent, and the 10–15 million yen class shrank 19 per cent. At the same time wages have not increased at the rate they used to. The seniority-based payment system is still in place, but the wage differential between employees in their twenties and employees in their fifties is only 83 per cent. In 1985, the earnings of 50-year-old men were 122 per cent higher than those of employees in their twenties. All these changes are strongly reflected in patterns of spending. Younger consumers are reluctant to spend money on cars or loans, being unsure about their future income. Older consumers are reluctant because they worry about outliving their money after retirement (*Nikkei Shimbun*, 2010). Most recently, another new consumer group has also become more prominent: this comprises young men who do not purchase in the way their fathers did – the so-called *soushoku danshi* (grass eaters). These consumers do not purchase classic male goods such as cars and alcohol, but show more cost-oriented consumer behaviour and a taste for things such as beauty products.

Outlooks on the future of Japanese consumption are pessimistic. Sawa (2010) writes that 'Although government fiscal expenditures may increase families' disposable income, the marginal propensity to consume – the proportion of additional disposable income that actually goes to consumption – is expected to remain low'; at the same time:

> medical and health care expenditures are bound to rise as the population ages. Younger families are spending more money out of pocket to look after parents. The decreasing number of children and the rising number of elderly will undoubtedly reduce spending on goods and services, except in the medical and health care fields. (Sawa, 2010, p. 14)

However, very wealthy consumers have neither changed their consumer behaviour nor lost any of their lust for luxury. Even if they have also reported cuts in income due to the economic crisis since 2008, they still spend on expensive luxury and brand products (*Nikkei Shimbun*, 2009).

Conclusion

In view of all these mixed messages, the question of how Japanese consumption and consumer behaviour will develop in the future has become a topic widely discussed by the Japanese media and researchers. Since the bursting of the bubble Japanese consumers have adapted 'admirably' to the new circumstances 'and continue to do so' (Howard, 2009a). They have faced a number of attitude-altering events, such as decreasing job security and dramatic changes in society, and face a more uncertain future than ever before. Howard (2009a) regards this as the reason for consumers to engage in deeper deliberation when it comes to large-scale purchases, but also '[for] a tendency to take higher stakes such as the election in 2009, in which the Liberal Democratic Party was removed from power after decades'. Howard continues that 'throwing out the old' and 'giv[ing] the new and unproven a chance' may also be observed in future Japanese consumer behaviour.

At this point we can only speculate on how the Japanese consumer market will develop, even over the short term. Nevertheless, it seems safe to assume that the Japanese market will continue to resemble other Western markets in respect of the presence of visible class differences. As the number of middle-class consumers decreases, the Japanese consumer market may come to be marked by a clear distinction between wealthy consumers and consumers of lower income. And, as in other industrialized markets, there is a tendency to ethnocentric purchases when it comes to food and safety-related products, such as hygienic and medical products. Brands will still play an important role, even if it becomes more socially acceptable to buy cheaper fashion items.

In any event, the Japanese consumer market will remain one of the most important consumer markets in the world and will continue to inspire innovative and creative products. Japanese consumers will, whether they become more like Western consumers or maintain their particular habits, still be one of the world's most influential consumer groups.

References

Ballon, R. (1973), *Marketing in Japan*, Tokyo: Sophia University in cooperation with Kodansha International Ltd.

BusinessWorld (2003), 'Japan Beefs Up Corporate Ethics after Series of Scams' (31 January), p. 1.

Chen, M. (2003), *Asian Management Systems*, London: Thompson Learning.

De Mente, B. (2004), *Japan's Cultural Code Words: Key Terms That Explain the Attitudes and Behavior of the Japanese*, Tokyo: Tuttle Publishing.

Dower, J. W. (2000), *Embracing Defeat: Japan in the Wake of World War II*, New York: W.W. Norton & Company.

Francks, P. (2009), *The Japanese Consumer: The Alternative Economic History of Modern Japan*, Cambridge: Cambridge University Press.

Gakken (2002), *Japan As It Is: A Bilingual Guide*, Tokyo: Gakken Corporation.

Garon, S. (2006), 'The Transnational Promotion of Saving in Asia: "Asian Values" or "Japanese Model?" ', in Garon, S. and Maclachlan, P. L. (eds), *The Ambivalent Consumer: Questioning Consumption in East Asia and the West*, London: Cornell University Press, pp. 163–88.

Haghirian, P. (2007), 'Innovative Marketingstrategien japanischer Unternehmen (Japanese Companies Develop Innovative Marketing Strategies)', *Japan Markt*, August: 8–10.

Horioka, C. Y. (2006), 'Are the Japanese Unique? An Analysis of Consumption and Saving Behavior in Japan', in Garon, S. and Maclachlan, P. L. (eds), *The Ambivalent Consumer: Questioning Consumption in East Asia and the West*, London: Cornell University Press, pp. 113–36.

Howard, D. (2009a), 'Japan's Consumers Choose Change – So Much for Old Stereotypes', *Nikkei Weekly* (28 September).

Howard, D. (2009b), 'How Are Post-crisis Consumers Adjusting? Pretty Well Actually', *Nikkei Weekly* (2 November).

Jansen, M. B. (2000), *The Making of Modern Japan*, Cambridge, MA: Harvard University Press.

JETRO (1985), *Selling in Japan: The World's Second Largest Market*, Tokyo: Japan External Trade Organization (JETRO).

Knight, D. K. and Kim, E. Y. (2007), 'Japanese Consumers' Need for Uniqueness: Effects on Brand Perceptions and Purchase Intention', *Journal of Fashion Marketing and Management*, 11(2): 270–80.

Kokumin seikatsu sentâ (1997), *Sengo shôshisha undôsha [History of Post-war Consumer Movement]*, Tokyo: Ôkurashô Insatsukyoku.

Laserre, P. and Schütte, H. (1998), *Strategy and Management in Asia Pacific*, London: McGraw-Hill Publishing.

McHardy Reid, D. (2007), 'Consumer Change in Japan: A Longitudinal Study', *Thunderbird International Business Review*, 49(1): 77–101.

Maclachlan, P. (1997),'The Seikatsusha and the Fight for Consumer Rights: Consumer Movement Activism in Postwar Japanese Society', in Meyer-Ohle, H. and Fuess, H. (eds), *Japanstudien 9, Dienstleistung und Konsum in the 1990er Jahren*, Munich: Iudicium Verlag, pp. 113–28.

Manzenreiter, W. (1998/99), 'Konsum und Freizeit in nach der Bubble: Trends der neunziger Jahre', in Linhart, S. (ed.), *Angewandte Sozialforschung*, 21(1–2): 73–96.

Meyer-Ohle, H. and Fuess, H. (1997), 'Konsum und Dienstleistung im Japan der 1990er Jahre: Einleitung', in Meyer-Ohle, H. and Fuess, H. (eds), *Japanstudien 9, Dienstleistung und Konsum in the 1990er Jahren*, Munich: Iudicium Verlag, pp. 15–23.

Nakamura, T. (1995), *The Postwar Japanese Economy: Its Development and Structure, 1937–1994*, Tokyo: University of Tokyo Press.

Nikkei Shimbun (2009), 'Rich Classes Still Want to Spend: Despite Economic Downturn, Moneyed Consumers Still Looking for Luxury', Tokyo: *Nikkei Shimbunsha* (14 December).

Nikkei Shimbun (2010), 'Shrinkage of Middle Class Hits Consumption', Tokyo: *Nikkei Shimbunsha* (10 May).

Nishimura, T. (2006), 'Household Debt and Consumer Education in Postwar Japan', in Garon, S. and Maclachlan, P. L. (eds), *The Ambivalent Consumer: Questioning Consumption in East Asia and the West*, London: Cornell University Press, pp. 260–80.

Okahashi, T., Gary, N. C. and Cornish-Ward, S. (1998), 'Japan: High Noon for the Rising Sun–New Realities and Forces of Change in a Mature Consumer Market', in Pecotich, A. and Shultz, Clifford J., II (eds), *Marketing and Consumer Behavior in East and South-East Asia*, Sydney: McGraw-Hill Companies, pp. 315–70.

Ortmanns, A. (1994), 'Rollenbilder im Wandel; Mann und Frau in japanischen Sozialkundebüchern von 1945 bis 1993', in Gössmann, H. and Waldenberger, F. (eds), *Japanstudien 5*, Munich: Iudicium Verlag, pp. 281–309.

Partner, S. (1999), 'Assembled in Japan: Electrical Goods and the Making of the Japanese Consumer' (Study of the East Asian Institute, Columbia University), Berkeley: University of California Press.

Saito, M. (2000), 'The Japanese Economy', Singapore: World Scientific Publications. .

Salsberg, B. (2010), 'The New Japanese Consumer', *McKinsey Quarterly* (March).

Sand, J. (2006), 'The Ambivalence of the New Breed: Nostalgic Consumerism in 1980s and 1990s Japan', in Garon, S. and Maclachlan, P. L. (eds), *The Ambivalent Consumer: Questioning Consumption in East Asia and the West*, London: Cornell University Press, pp. 85–104.

Sawa, T. (2009), 'Consumption amid Constraints', *Japan Times* (10 February).

Sawa, T. (2010), 'Japan's Economy Will Grow on Eco-consumption, Immigration', *Japan Times* (9 February).

Schütte, H. and Ciarliante, D. (1998), *Consumer Behavior in Asia*, London: Palgrave Macmillan.

Shinohara, M. (1959), 'The Structure of Saving and the Consumption Function in Postwar Japan', *Journal of Political Economy*, 67(6): 589–603.

Skov, L. and Moeran, B. (1996), *Women, Media, and Consumption in Japan* (Consumasian), Honolulu: University of Hawai'i Press.

Thomas, D. (2007), *Deluxe: How Luxury Lost Its Luster*, London: Penguin Books.

Tsalikis, J. and Seaton, B. (2008), 'The International Business Ethics Index: Japan', *Journal of Business Ethics*, 80: 379–85.

Yoshimi, S. (2006), 'Consuming America, Producing Japan', in Garon, S. and Maclachlan, P. L. (eds), *The Ambivalent Consumer: Questioning Consumption in East Asia and the West*, London: Cornell University Press, pp. 63–84.

2
Japanese Consumer Behaviour

Parissa Haghirian and Aaron Toussaint

Introduction

In general terms, consumer behaviour is strongly related to the national culture of the consumer group in question (Schütte and Ciarliante, 1998). Culture is defined as the set of values, beliefs and activities which are communicated from elders to younger people (Adler, 2001), or 'patterns of thought and manners which are widely shared' (Child and Kieser, 1977, quoted in Usunier, 2000). It is reasonable to expect, then, that consumer behaviour in Japan would be strongly related to Japanese culture; and, indeed, Japanese consumers have displayed very particular patterns of consumer behaviour. The Japanese predilection for brand products and European luxury goods is particularly well known in the West; what is perhaps less well known, but is nonetheless of significant interest, is the Japanese attitude towards product prices, which has in recent years changed from a preference for high prices to a wider acceptance of cheaper products.

This chapter gives an overview of Japanese buying habits and consumer preferences. It describes aspects of the typical behaviour patterns of Japanese consumers, such as the predilection for new products, the great interest in brands and the high standards that are demanded with respect to quality and service. The chapter also discusses the recent changes in Japanese consumer behaviour that have been prompted by the prolonged recession and the economic crisis.

Group-oriented or not?

The most widely discussed question in studies of Japanese consumer behaviour concerns whether the Japanese make group-oriented or individualistic purchasing decisions. In collectivist-oriented cultures, product and brand preferences are more likely to express attitudes arising from social norms than from internal drives or motives (Haghirian, 2010). Loyalty is a key concept in collectivist cultures, and Asian consumers tend to 'rely more on information found in their reference group' and tend to 'follow the group consensus until there is significant evidence showing that the new product is better' (Usunier, 2000). Further, Japan's unique Shinto-based culture places an emphasis on the individual's responsibility to the group, including family, co-workers, employer and society at large (Erffmeyer *et al.*, 1999). Japanese consumers are thus seen as collectivistic consumers, basing their purchasing decisions on whether they will thereby find acceptance among their peers, and seeking to integrate into their social group by buying products which strengthen their positions within it.

One collectivistic feature often observed in Japanese consumer behaviour is the fad, which is 'an innovation that represents a relatively unimportant aspect of culture, which diffuses very rapidly, mainly for status reasons, and then is rapidly discontinued' (Rogers, 1995, p. 214). Schütte and Ciarliante (1998, pp. 107, 108) describe this tendency towards faddism as 'pack consumerism', and locate it squarely within the Japanese tendency towards conformism: 'instilled from childhood, reinforced by the educational system and solidified by peer pressure, the desire to conform is the engine behind the faddism to which the Japanese are particularly prone' (pp. 106, 107). Panic-oriented consumer behaviour is the opposite of the fad, and the history of the last 50 years of Japanese consumerism offers plenty of examples of both. Francks (2009, p. 178), for instance, describes the 'Panda craze' in 1972, when two pandas from China arrived in Japan, and the panic buys during the oil crisis in 1973. More recent examples include negative reactions to the food scandal regarding poisoned *gyoza* (dumplings) from China, which led to a rising interest in locally produced food.

Brand consumers who show low brand loyalty

Japanese consumers certainly do show some traits of collectivistic consumer behaviour, but it is notable that the concept of collectivistic purchasing behaviour is mostly used in the context of explaining why the Japanese buy expensive luxury products. Chadha and Husband (2008), for instance, use the concept in their writings on the development of the luxury market in Japan: 'Soon a large enough chunk of the population were carrying their status markers, and now the overriding need was to conform to this new set of rules about how to express your status' (p. 44).

In any event, brands play an important role in the Japanese consumer market. Japanese consumers have a high affinity for brands, and Japan is often said to possess the world's only luxury mass market. The economic crisis of recent years has posed a marginal challenge to these attitudes, but nevertheless expensive brand products remain important in signalling status and success in Japanese society. The term *burando* (brand) only refers to luxury products such as bags and fashion, and does not apply to products that can be consumed less overtly, such as skin care or other products, even if they are themselves 'branded' (Haghirian, 2010).

Traditionally, Japanese consumers have tended to choose mostly large, well-known companies when purchasing products, and Japanese corporations have decades of experience in brand development and communication. Consumers believed that they could avoid making the wrong decision or buying an inferior product by always sticking to the same company – since purchasing a new brand from an unknown company might result in dissatisfaction (Schneidewind, 1998). Thus, Japanese advertisements often focus more on the company than on the product (Saga and Nishida, 2009). As Schütte and Ciarlante (1998) point out, image-building in Japan is not limited to a brand but is in most cases linked with the corporate image. The company and its reputation have a major influence in the decision to buy, and at the end of TV advertising spots the company producing the product is mentioned.

The reason for the strong belief in brand names is, according to Schütte and Ciarliante, again to be found in the collectivistic orientation of Japanese culture. Product or brand preferences, they write, 'represent expressions of what is considered socially acceptable rather than individual preferences' (p. 71). Japanese consumers, like other Asian consumers, show a propensity towards avoidance of uncertainty and risk, which often results in consumer behaviour exhibiting high brand-name consciousness, a greater insistence on quality, and the active use of reference groups, opinion leaders and group shopping (Schütte and Ciarliante, 1998). 'The focus on quality and brand-name consciousness [...] is partly a reflection of risk aversion as a recognised brand name serves as a proxy for quality' (Schütte and Ciarliante, 1998, p. 75). In Japan, buying and wearing luxury goods has become a 'way of life', and there is no going back unless the consumers simply cannot afford them anymore (Chadha and Husband, 2008). Thus, Japan has become the only mass luxury market in the world (see Chapter 6) and because of this Japanese consumers have become highly selective in their brand purchases (Schütte and Ciarliante, 1998).

Despite their love for brands and the enormous amounts of money spent on Western luxury goods, Japanese consumers show little brand loyalty. Japanese consumers do not necessarily stay with the same brand for a long time, attaching priority to – once again – service, product quality, and technology (Melville, 1999; Schneidewind, 1998). Not all researchers in the field agree, however, that the Japanese have low levels of brand loyalty. 'As younger Japanese move towards greater individuality, change has been accompanied by the belief that an individual's personal identity can be expressed through his other consumption choices [...] Thus brand loyalty in the case of status-seeking consumption is very high but is established in line with the normative standards set by the reference group or the aspirational reference group' (Schütte and Ciarliante, 1998, p. 74).

What about individualism?

Collectivism in consumer behaviour was being treated as a significant topic of study as early as the 1960s, a period marked by a rapid increase in consumption, when 'keeping up with the Joneses' was given as one explanation for the rapid diffusion of new consumer products among Japanese households (Nakamura, 1995, p. 105). But showing off newly achieved economic wealth is not, however, a phenomenon only observed in Japan; rather, it seems reasonable to assume that consumers in other post-war societies (even very individualistic ones) act from similar motives.

In fact, Francks (2009) regards the purchases of consumer goods during the 1960s as a sign of increasing individualism. Japanese family entertainment, which was traditionally very strongly connected to the local community, became more individualistic precisely because of these newly acquired consumer goods. Thanks to the increase in the number of modern household products, instead of going as a group to the local public bath, one could stay at home watching TV and enjoying greater leisure time. And even if the 1970s was characterized by mass market phenomena such as fads and panic (phenomena which can still be observed today), Francks writes, 'beneath this surface homogenisation, Japanese consumers continued to find ways to differentiate themselves as members of a wider society' (Francks, 2009, p. 178) – even though this differentiation may have been based more on gender and age than on class or family status. The development of the so-called *shinjinrui* or 'the new breed' that followed in the 1970s supported this attitude (see Chapter 1). Especially purchase behaviour during bubble times was considered highly individualistic (Erffmeyer *et al.*, 1999). These observations seem to be supported by the enormous number of Japanese and foreign corporations offering products in the Japanese market and the great variety of products being successfully marketed in Japan even today.

Love for new products

The collectivistic attitude of consumers is also seen as an explanation for the high rate of diffusion of new products in the Japanese market. Once a brand has gained acceptance among early adopters, the rate of diffusion proceeds rapidly in societies with homogeneous cultural and socio-economic backgrounds, such as Japan. The interest in new and exciting products makes Japanese consumers willing to pay a lot of money for them (Haghirian, 2010), and Japanese companies have developed great expertise in responding to this expectation. They react by constantly launching new products: new products are labelled *shin-hatsubai*, a term which corresponds to the English 'New Improved, Now On Sale', and Japanese consumers show marked preference for such products. The word *shinhatsubai* is composed of the character for 'new' (*shin*), followed by a character with a dynamic meaning, that of 'discharge, start, leave' (*hatsu*); the last character means 'sell' (*bai*). The expression conveys a sense of a new movement of goods into the market place (Henschall, 1988, cited in Watts, 1998). Not all of these products, however, are real and radical innovations, nor do they offer new value for the customer; often, these 'new and improved' products are simply new flavours or the same product in different packaging.

Another particular feature of Japanese products are the *gentei* (special editions), which are product adaptations that are only sold for a limited period of time. Many *gentei* are only on sale for a month and usually reflect the time of the year. Most *gentei* can be found within the sphere of food products, and every year Japanese consumers are surprised by various entertaining flavours of famous brands. Even brands that are not Japanese have adopted this trend: most famous for its *gentei* is the Kitkat, the famous chocolate bar, which has been released seemingly in every flavour imaginable – apple, passion fruit, and pumpkin or mango pudding, green tea, apple vinegar and vegetable. Other Western brands have followed suit: Coca Cola, for instance, offers a 'cool summer edition' every year (e.g. blue Hawaii, or *Shiso*, a herb used to flavour raw fish) (Haghirian, 2010).

Japanese consumers are also very technology- and gadget-oriented (Maamria, 2001), preferring products which are technologically state-of-the-art (Maamria, 2001). Moreover, due to competitive pressures, new product launches in Japan far outnumber those in other developed markets in many categories (Laserre and Schütte, 1998). Japanese consumers do not only expect high-quality products and services, but also demand that the technology be cutting-edge as well. Japanese people are clearly very curious about and attracted by innovation and recent developments in technology. They have an affinity for new products, especially when these offer new functions or features. The turnover rate for electronic appliances is very high and Japanese people tend to throw away gadgets like TVs and VCRs even when they are still working, in order to replace them with a newer product (Low, 1999; Melville, 1999).

Quality obsession

One of the most important issues – indeed, probably the most important issue in selling to the Japanese – is quality (Melville, 1999, p. 67). JETRO reported already in the 1980s: 'Consumers do expect to pay more for innovative, well-made and fashionable products, and demand for these goods has been rising.' And even today Japanese consumers are obsessed with quality. *Quality* in Japan is a property that must permeate every aspect of a product, including continuous attention to improvement. If Japanese customers are satisfied with the quality of the product a company is offering they might buy from this company again. However, if the Japanese customers are dissatisfied with the quality then they will usually never again buy a product from this company, and the reputation of the firm could be spoiled for years (Haghirian, 2010).

The same attitude can be found towards services. Japanese corporations have traditionally been very process and detail-oriented and have perfectionalized all their customer-oriented procedures (Haghirian, 2010). Customer service, product quality and after-sales service are the three pillars of marketing and selling in Japan (Kotler, 1999). In Japan, customers are called O-kyaku-sama. The word Kyaku means guest or customer, and the prefix O and the suffix sama are honorific expressions showing politeness and respect to a potential client (Haghirian, 2010). The relationship between buyer and seller is therefore a hierarchical one, in which the customer holds all the power (Schütte and Ciarlante, 1998). For the Japanese, service is related to the

concept of giri, reflecting the sense of obligation that the seller has to
the buyer (Kotler, 1999; Schütte and Ciarlante, 1998). In a Japanese
firm, customer needs always come first and professional friendliness
is expected of all employees. After entering the firm, each new hire
will receive extensive training on how to communicate with customers. The rules for such interactions are often very detailed, explaining
exactly how to bow and how to exchange name cards. It might seem
like simple common sense that offering good service is an essential
factor in selling a product and in building a good reputation for a
company and its products. However, even when comparing what is
considered good service in Japan and in the West, big differences can
be observed (Usunier, 2000). In Japan, service first of all means being
friendly and treating customers correctly: 'Japanese salespeople are
taught that they must show a cheerful, healthy appearance as well
as willingness and enthusiasm' (Schütte and Ciarlante, 1998). Service
also means offering support, (product-related) information, repair/
maintenance etc., and offering it readily and on time (Schneidewind,
1998). First-rate service is expected as part of the purchase, including
after-sales attention (Morgan and Morgan, 1991).

Japanese consumers generally expect the best service in the world,
and the concept of service in Japan differs greatly from that in the West.
In Japan, *good service* means that customers' wishes are taken care of in
every possible way. When entering a Japanese shop one will be greeted
by at least one shop clerk, possibly two, making preliminary inquiries as
to whether the customer would like to find information on the product
or actually wants to purchase. Waiting times, unless there are really
big crowds, are virtually nil. Every interaction with a customer will be
extensively trained for and is invested with great importance. Japanese
consumers react to 'bad service' very quickly: brand loyalty is low, and
once a shop or product has failed to fulfil basic requirements it is swiftly
abandoned (Haghirian, 2010).

Price sensitivity

Another way in which Japanese consumers are supposed to be different from consumers in other industrialized markets is in their attitudes towards product prices. Japanese consumers are said to show no
price sensitivity: if service, quality and technology meet the expectations of the Japanese consumer, he or she is willing to pay a high price
(Melville, 1999). Price, in fact, is perceived as an indicator of quality,

and Laserre and Schütte (1998) note that the longstanding emphasis in Japan is on service rather than price. The reliance on price as an indicator of quality is most critical in the case of purchases of products that affect the standing of the individual within the peer group. Since the customer's association of higher prices with higher quality is apparently quite strong in Japan, this might be one explanation for lack of price sensitivity (Schütte and Ciarlante, 1998). The consumers of the bubble economy (which ended at the beginning of the 1990s) were known for caring little about prices; however, as the recession of the 1990s wore on, Japanese consumers became more and more price-conscious. The economic downturn after the bursting of the bubble meant that Japanese consumers 'were now being forced towards practicality even for status items', while before they had only been 'price-conscious in personal-use purchases' (Schütte and Ciarliante, 1998). This led to 'an increasing focus on lifestyle resources such as personal capital and assets and an increasing conservatism in consumption. In effect, Japanese consumers have become more price sensitive, exhibit much higher tendencies toward purchasing restraint, and are generally leaning toward more consumptive downscaling' (Kobayashi, 1994). At the same time many retailers started to change their distribution systems, and companies like Uniqlo and Zoff began a trend towards more cost-sensitive – while still at the same time quality-oriented – attitudes towards products among Japanese consumers. Japanese consumers developed a taste for cheaper products. However, this did not include all kinds of products; designer and luxury products could still be sold for a high price.

Given the consumers' newfound concern with value for money, one might expect that the post-bubble climate would militate against designer products. However, the evidence tells a different story – the major labels, such as the designer brand Chanel, continue to maintain strong distribution presences. Major international luxury brands continue to invest in Japan (McHardy Reid, 2007). 'At the same time consumers resist price increases for daily necessities. Housewives still tend to shop almost daily for fresh foods, and they buy smaller quantities to fit in the limited storage space of Japanese homes. They are therefore constantly aware of prices and price changes' (JETRO, 1985). It is therefore not surprising that, in some instances, the very same consumer who shops in the 100-yen store or patronizes the all-night auctions will also make high-value and apparently price-insensitive luxury purchases (McHardy Reid, 2007). Dentsu Advertising calls these two different attitudes towards prices 'Petite Luxury consumption'. Japanese consumers were willing to pay a high price for luxury items such as designer bags or fashion items, but at the same time would show a preference for a generic product (e.g. washing powder) which was 100 yen (1US$) cheaper than its nearest competitor (Haghirian,2007). The propensity towards Petite Luxury consumption, and the fact that luxury items such as designer bags have become favourite products of the Japanese middle class, was another reason why Japan was seen as the world's first luxury mass market (see Chapter 6). By 2008, however, the attitude towards prices had changed again. Purchasing cheaper fashion products had become socially more acceptable and had led to successful entries into the Japanese market by so-called 'Fast fashion' brands, such as H&M and Zara (*Nikkei Shimbun*, 2009a). New types of discount shops, such as for groceries which started to increase since 2009, are highly successful (*The Nikkei Weekly*, 2009).

Ethnocentrism

Another question which is investigated in studies of Japanese consumer behaviour is whether they prefer to buy Japanese products rather than foreign imports. *Consumer ethnocentrism* refers to a certain type of consumer behaviour in which consumers are prone to evaluate products from their home market more favourably than imports, and in which certain consumer groups actually display hostility to the idea of purchasing imported goods. A number of factors lead consumers to be more ethnocentric – or, in other words, to be more hostile to imported goods. Typically, older consumers, less well-educated consumers, consumers who are economically less well off, and – perhaps surprisingly – women are more likely to be ethnocentric (Sharma *et al.*, 1995, p. 27). Consumers in more collectivist cultures are more likely to be ethnocentric (Gurhan-Canli and Maheswaran, 2000, p. 200). It has further been shown that small nations are often disposed to be more hostile to imports from larger or more influential neighbours (Nijssen and Douglas, 2003). Feeling that one's economic livelihood is threatened by foreign competition (e.g. Japanese rice farmers) makes consumers more disposed to buy domestic goods (Nijssen and Douglas, 2004; Sharma *et al.*, 1995; Shimp and Sharma, 1987).

Several studies have been conducted on Japanese consumers and their reaction to imports as opposed to Japanese goods (Gurhan-Canli and Maheswaran, 2000; Kamins and Nagashima, 1995; Nagashima, 1970, 1977). In most developed countries, domestic products generally enjoy a more favourable evaluation than foreign-made products. This strong preference for domestic products has been clearly evidenced for the US, British, and French markets and the European market in general, and is also seen among Japanese consumers (Usunier, 2000, p. 157). Japanese consumers generally assume that the quality of Japanese products is higher than that of Western products, and are willing to pay higher prices for them. One reason for this is the high level of after-sale service, which is a common feature for Japanese companies but often not expected or received when purchasing foreign products. In Japan, therefore, quality permeates every aspect of a product and involves continuous attention to improvement (Melville, 1999).

Despite the preference for local products, products with a high perceived level of need are not affected by ethnocentric tendencies. It is, perhaps, intuitively obvious that this would be the case, since if consumers need to buy a product they are unlikely to engage in an internal debate over whether or not it would be harmful to their country to import it. In other words, necessity trumps ethnocentrism. Conversely, however, when a product is perceived as unnecessary it is more likely to be affected by ethnocentric tendencies; and, perhaps more importantly, when an industry or nation perceives an import to be a threat to its economic livelihood, ethnocentrism is expected to be strong (Sharma *et al.*, 1995). It should be noted that in Japan many of the areas where foreign firms succeed are areas in which Japan has typically not been competitive; certain agricultural products – for instance, wine or cheese from Europe – and high fashion brands spring to mind. In these areas, Japanese consumers are unlikely to perceive a threat and are therefore more likely to accept imports. Many otherwise ethnocentric consumers are also often conscious of the role of imported items as status symbols, and are therefore more likely to buy them (Rice and Wongtada, 2007). When it comes to televisions and other electronics, as well as cars, foreign products are more likely to be seen as threatening and are therefore eschewed unless they fall into the luxury category and are desired status symbols. Threatening goods being imported from neighbouring countries are even more likely to elicit a negative response – for example Korean TVs or Chinese computers (Nijssen and Douglas, 2004).

Japanese consumer behaviour in the new millennium

Discussions of Japanese consumer behaviour have been fuelled in recent months by the continuing economic crisis: in particular, the sensitivities of Japanese consumers have seemingly undergone significant change. And, yes, since the economic crisis of 2008 impacted Japan's economy, Japanese consumers have changed in many respects. 'A very different type of consumer has emerged: one that is more self-responsible, more independent and even more individualistic. At the same time, these changes are manifesting themselves in a more confident, more demanding and more fickle consumer' (Howard, 2009).

In recent years, it has been observed that ethnocentrism is increasing. After a number of food scandals, trust in food products has notably decreased. And, even though the majority of Japanese food products continue to be imported into Japan, *kokusan* (locally produced) food products are generating increased interest among Japanese consumers. This attitude, however, is mainly reserved for agricultural products and is not affecting other product groups.

Japanese consumers, furthermore, seem to show greater price sensitivity and have shifted their interest away from purchasing luxury products to more cheaply priced fashion products. Suddenly, it is socially acceptable to buy cheaper products. Atsmon *et al.* (2009) even propose that Japanese consumers, after years of 'otherness', are now behaving like consumers in other industrialized countries. At the same time, however, the new rich still show a lust for luxury and keep spending large amounts on expensive brand products (*Nikkei Shimbun*, 2009b).

Once again, we can see that Japanese consumers manifest wide variety in their attitudes and interests. They are more than willing to change their attitudes towards consumption in regard to economic and social changes, and indeed do so with alacrity. It is, therefore, difficult to predict the evolution of post-recession behaviour in Japan.

References

Adler, N. (2001), *International Dimensions of Organizational Behavior*, Cincinnati, Ohio: South-Western College Pub.

Atsmon, Y., Salsberg, B. and Yamanashi, H. (2009), *Luxury Goods in Japan: Momentary Sigh or Long Sayonara? How Luxury Companies Can Succeed in a Changing Market*, McKinsey Asia Consumer and Retail (ed.), available at http://csia.mckinsey.com/~/media/Extranets/Consumer%20Shopper%20Insights/Reports/LUXURY_GOODS_IN_JAPAN.ashx (accessed 14 December 2009).

Chadha, R. and Husband, P. (2008), *The Cult of the Luxury Brand: Inside Asia's Love Affair with Luxury*, London: Nicolas Brealey International.

Child, J. and Kieser, A. (1977), 'Contrast in British and West German Management Practices: Are Recipes of Success Culture Bound?', Paper presented at the Conference on Cross-cultural Studies on Organizational Functioning, Hawaii.

Erffmeyer, R. C., Keillor, B. D. and LeClair, D. T. (1999), 'An Empirical Investigation of Japanese Consumer Ethics', *Journal of Business Ethics*, 18: 35–50.

Francks, P. (2009), *The Japanese Consumer: The Alternative Economic History of Modern Japan*, Cambridge: Cambridge University Press.

Gurhan-Canli, Z. and Maheswaran, D. (2000), 'Cultural Variations in Country of Origin', *Journal of Marketing Research*, 37, p. 200, pp. 309–17.

'H&M and Forever 21 Take On Japan', available at http://www.cocoperez.com/2009-11-12-hm-and-forever-21-take-on-japan#ixzz0Xajr9eUW (accessed 12 November 2009).

Haghirian, P. (2007), *Markteintritt in Japan*, Vienna: LexisNexis.

Haghirian, P. (2010), *Understanding Japanese Business Practices*, New York: Business Expert Press.

Henschall, K. G. (1988), *A Guide to Remembering Japanese Characters*, Tokyo: Tuttle.

Howard, D. (2009), 'Japan's Consumers Chose Change – So Much for Old Stereotypes', *Nikkei Weekly* (28 September).

JETRO (1985), *Selling in Japan: The World's Second Largest Market*, Tokyo: Japan External Trade Organization (JETRO).

Kamins, M. A. and Nagashima, A. (1995), 'Perceptions of Products Made in Japan Versus Those Made in the United States Among Japanese and American Executives: A Longitudinal Perspective', *Asia Pacific Journal of Management*, 12(1): 49–68.

Kobayashi, F., 'Changing Lifestyles', in Yamaguchi, Y. (ed.), *Japan 1994 Marketing and Advertising Yearbook*, Tokyo: Dentsu, Inc.

Kotler, Philip, Swee Hoon Ang, Siew Meng Leong (1998), *Marketing Management: An Asian Perspective*, Singapore: Prentice Hall.

Laserre, P. and Schütte, H. (1998), *Strategy and Management in Asia Pacific*, London: McGraw-Hill Publishing.

Low, M., Nakayama, S. and Yoshioka, H. (1999), *Science, Technology and Society in Contemporary Japan*, Cambridge: Cambridge University Press.

Maamria, K. (2001), 'Made in Japan', *Telecommunications*, International Edition, 35(2): 90–4.

McCreery, J. (2000), *Japanese Consumer Behaviour: From Worker Bees to Wary Shoppers* (Consumasian), Honolulu: University of Hawaii Press.

McHardy Reid, D. (2007), 'Consumer Change in Japan: A Longitudinal Study', *Thunderbird International Business Review*, 49(1): 77–101.

Melville, I. (1999), *Marketing in Japan*. Oxford: Butterworth-Heinemann.

Morgan, J. C. and Morgan J. J. (1991), *Cracking the Japanese Market: Strategies for Success in the New Global Economy*, New York: The Free Press.

Nagashima, A. (1970), 'A Comparison of Japanese and U.S. Attitudes Toward Foreign Products', *Journal of Marketing* (January), 34: 68–77.

Nagashima, A. (1977), 'A Comparative "Made in" Product Image Survey Among Japanese Businessmen', *Journal of Marketing* (July), pp. 95–100.

Nakamura, T. (1995), *The Postwar Japanese Economy: Its Development and Structure, 1937–1994*, Tokyo: University of Tokyo Press.

Nikkei Shimbun (2009a), 'Bargain Hunt in Harajuku: "Fast Fashion" Chains Offer Stylish Apparel at Affordable Prices', Tokyo: *Nikkei Shimbun* (15 June).

Nikkei Shimbun (2009b), 'Rich Classes Still Want to Spend: Despite Economic Downturn, Moneyed Consumers Still Looking for Luxury', Tokyo: *Nikkei Shimbun* (14 December).

Nikkei Weekly (2009), 'Supermarkets' Experiments Paying Off', Tokyo: *The Nikkei Weekly* (28 September), p. 21.

Nijssen, E. J. and Douglas, S. P. (2004), 'Examining the Animosity Model in a Country with a High Level of Foreign Trade', *International Journal of Research in Marketing*, 21: 23–38.

Rice, G. and Wongtada, N. (2007), 'Conceptualizing Inter-Attitudinal Conflict in Consumer Response to Foreign Brands', *Journal of International Consumer Marketing*, 20(1): 31–65.

Rogers, E. M. (1995), *Diffusion of Innovations*, New York: Free Press.

Saga, A. and Nishida, J. (2009), 'Marketing', in Haghirian, P. (ed.) *J-Management: Fresh Perspectives on the Japanese Firm in the 21st Century*, New York; Bloomington: iUniverse, Inc.

Schneidewind, D. (1998), *Shinhatsubai*, Munich: Beck.

Schütte, H. and Ciarlante, D. (1998), *Consumer Behavior in Asia*, London: Palgrave Macmillan.

Sharma, S., Shimp, T. A. and Shin, J. (1995), 'Consumer Ethnocentrism: A Test of Antecedents and Moderators', *Journal of the Academy of Marketing Science*, 23(1): 26–37.

Shimp, T. A. and Sharma, S. (1987), 'Consumer Ethnocentrism: Construction and Validation of the CETSCALE', *Journal of Marketing Research* 24 (August): 280–9.

Skov, L. and Moeran, B. (1996), *Women, Media, and Consumption in Japan* (Consumasian), Honolulu: University of Hawaii Press.

Usunier, J.-C. (2000), *Marketing Across Cultures*, Harlow: Pearson Education Limited.

Watts, J. (1998), 'Soccer Shinhatsubai: What Are Japanese Consumers Making of the J. League?', in D. P. Martinez (ed.), *The Worlds of Japanese Popular Cultures: Gender, Shifting Boundaries and Global Cultures*, Cambridge: Cambridge University Press, pp. 181–201.

3
Consumer Rights in Japan
Luke Nottage

Introduction

The discourse and practice of consumer rights protection are well entrenched in contemporary Japanese society. Japanese consumers have long been known for their exacting standards regarding quality, but they also now increasingly expect diversity and price-competitiveness, with much more access to imported goods and foreign services providers. The consumer voice is expressed not only through what is and is not purchased, but also via claims for redress (for example, for unsafe or non-performing goods) or to terminate contracts (especially for burgeoning types and volumes of services transactions), and through demands for better substantive and procedural law frameworks to operate within. There has been a shift towards boosting private law protections, premised on individual consumers taking the initiative to terminate or withdraw from contracts and – increasingly – to sue for injunctions or damages. This is part of a broader 'third wave' of judicial sector reform underway since 2001, aimed at completing the transplantation of a modern Western legal system first begun following the Meiji Restoration of 1868, and boosted by Occupation-era reforms during 1945–51 (Foote [ed.], 2007).

Yet Japanese consumers, quite realistically, also still expect much from the state in order to enforce their rights. Expectations for intervention range from accreditation of consumer representative organizations – now entitled to seek injunctions against firms using unfair contract terms – through to active criminal law prosecution of those suspected of professional negligence causing death (which can also facilitate consumers seeking private law damages), and even measures to strengthen regulatory frameworks directly policed by government officials. This has culminated in the inauguration in 2009 of a new Consumer Affairs Agency linked to the increasingly powerful Cabinet Office, centralizing many aspects of consumer law enforcement and policy development.[1] That field had traditionally been dominated by consumer law divisions competing for influence within other powerful parts of the government with their own broader agendas, such as the Ministry of the Economy, Trade and Industry (METI, known as MITI until 2001).

This tendency could be seen as evidence of a neo-communitarian reaction or persistent traditionalism within Japanese society, politics and law. It certainly means that Japan's present consumer rights system differs from the ideal – if not always the practice – promoted by one version of American liberalism (Tanase, 2010). But the combination of private and public law aspects leaves Japan with an impressively comprehensive consumer rights system that is particularly comparable in its scope and trajectory with that found in the European Union (EU).[2] It also demonstrates parallels with the systems found in other post-industrial democracies such as Australia, especially now that the latter has re-embarked on major consumer law reform after almost a decade of relative neglect (Nottage, 2009).

Space precludes coverage of all aspects of Japanese consumer law and their many developments, particularly since the 'lost decade' of economic stagnation during the 1990s, which has prompted so much law reform in many other fields as well. Instead, this chapter first offers a brief comparative history of Japanese consumer rights protection. It then turns to legislative and judicial innovations regarding, in turn, product safety, consumer contracts generally, and consumer lending. These represent three of the most controversial, high-profile, yet representative areas for consumer disputing and policy development in contemporary Japan.[3] They have also caused problems in other countries, and it is important to examine how Japan has drawn on some of those experiences – and also generated proposed solutions that can, or do, now influence responses worldwide.[4]

Comparative historical development and scope of consumer protection law and practice[5]

Japanese consumers, producers and policymakers

One conventional view sees Japan as a 'developmental state' dominated by bureaucrats (Johnson, 1982), or a state where their influence is roughly shared with conservative Liberal Democratic Party (LDP) politicians and big business interests (the 'iron triangle': Kerbo and McKinstry, 1995). A corollary of these perspectives has been to down-play the power of consumers as independent actors in the policymaking arena. To be sure, economic recovery was an urgent priority for Japan's leaders after the devastation of World War II, and developing the mar-ket for production of household appliances (especially the 'three sacred treasures': television, washing machine and refrigerator) became a key component of this strategy during the 1950s (Low *et al.*, 1999, pp. 81–9). Yet, while the initially dire economic straits may have encouraged incip-ient consumer activists to cooperate with the government (Maclachlan, 2002, pp. 77–8), this was precisely to rein in attempts by suppliers to manipulate prices or compromise food safety. Further, the tight eco-nomic circumstances continuing into the 1950s would have made them choose their goods as carefully as possible. Nonetheless, Japan's subse-quent 'income doubling plan', followed by growing calls over the 1980s – particularly from the US – for more consumption in relation to savings in order to reduce its ballooning trade deficits (Schoppa, 1997, pp. 11–12), led to the patterns of conspicuous consumption and other features still often associated with Japanese consumers. By the 1990s, these features had prompted sharp critiques of wastefulness, and more generally of the 'emptiness of Japanese affluence' (McCormack, 2001, pp. 78–92).

'Price destruction' since the 1990s, however, suggests at least that Japanese consumers are not psychologically or institutionally driven to indiscriminately purchase high-price goods (Schoppa, 1997), and per-haps appreciate at least some benefits of ongoing deregulation (com-pare Vogel, 1999). As emphasized by one anthropologist, drawing on experience and research in the advertising industry during the 1980s and 1990s, Japan's 'consumers' are now very diverse. For example, the serious 'Baby Boomers', born soon after World War II and reach-ing their peak in the 1970s and 1980s, now compete with the spend-thrift 'New Breed' of the 1980s and early 1990s and the resigned 'Baby Boomer Juniors' entering the workforce during the recessionary 1990s (McCreery, 2000, pp. 6–7).

The emergence of such subgroups reinforces a societal shift from tra-ditional to individualistic values through to the 1970s and especially a subsequent fragmentation of Japan's 'value universe' (Moehwald, 2000), although some argue that its socio-legal system still retains a more com-munitarian orientation in comparison to the US at least (Tanase, 2010). One sociologist observes from further survey data that: 'Paradoxically, the conservatives' emphasis on economic growth has created an affluent society that has become more demanding on quality of life issues and critical of the LDP's support for producer interests' (Lam, 1999, p. 94). Overall, another anthropologist remarks that:

> Today the oligopolistic character of Japanese capitalism and its interests in the efficiency of production and the 'rights' of producers is becoming challenged by the power of consumers, who may not be politicized in any traditional sense, but are extremely well informed, high educated and increasingly internationalized. (Clammer, 1997, p. 65)

In addition, Japanese citizens have long been fastidious about certain aspects of cleanliness, especially regarding foodstuffs (Jussaume and Judson, 1992) – so much so that they may be endangering their health by lowering natural resistance.

For their part, from the 1950s Japanese companies began developing the 'total quality control' approach to industrial production (Low *et al.*, 1999, pp. 54–7). Although a major objective was simply to minimize interruptions to the production line, the system also depended on accurate feedback about defects after delivery, and the continuous search for product improvements. Such systems may have worked better in tight manufacturing and distribution chains limited to commercial entities, but it would have been odd if such techniques and the overall ethos of improving quality had not also benefited consumers. Indeed, Japanese quality control systems were lauded in the West during the 1980s. Yet the assessments of Japanese manufacturing capabilities shifted markedly during the 1990s. Although Asian perceptions of Japanese product quality remain high (Dentsu Institute for Human Studies, 2001, pp. 37–8), some Western commentators proclaim 'the myths of Japanese product quality' and accuse us of 'cognitive dissonance' – developing high expectations of Japanese product quality and then blaming ourselves for failures rather than revising expectations (Eberts and Eberts, 1995, p. 55).

Conscious of such conflicting perspectives, Patricia Maclachlan (2002) has provided the first monograph in Western languages on consumer advocacy and its impact in Japan. Like other recent scholarship, she broadens her analysis beyond a comparison of just Japan and the US. As in the UK, significant consumerism in the US is shown to be quite a recent phenomenon, emerging in the 1960s, driven more by charismatic leaders than from the grass roots, and subjected to growing challenges from deregulatory initiatives since the 1980s. However, consumerism in the US recorded some remarkable successes due to a more decentralized policymaking structure. In Britain's more central-ized polity, consumer interests became more systematically integrated into government decision-making, achieving less dramatic victories but more sustained input and broad protection. From this vantage point, Japanese consumer advocates are perceived to have developed even closer organizational links to the central government, yet their voice has not been heard as systematically in policymaking. Nonetheless, Maclachlan emphasizes that they have maintained a more powerful influence over local governments, drawing on the mass media and other forces to mark considerable gains since the 1960s, especially whenever there has been fragmentation of the iron triangle or 'ruling triad' (Broadbent, 1998).

In 1968, for example, the Consumer Protection Basic Law (No. 78 of 1968) was enacted as a (then rare) private member's bill with multiparty support, after the LDP faced 'mounting citizen activism at the grass-roots level directed at both environmental and consumer issues, and the threat to conservative government rule posed by the rise of progressive local governments' (Maclachlan, 2002, p. 112).[6] In 1977, again before a significant election, the LDP finally agreed to amendments to the Anti-Monopoly Law strengthening restrictions on cartels. In 1983, however, widespread protests were insufficient to prevent deregulation of 11 syn-thetic food additives and safety checks on imported foodstuffs, although these and 67 others were then required to be identified by name and – for all except five of the total – by function (Vogel, 1992, p. 128). With few opponents in this business sector in Japan, regulatory reform initia-tives from the early 1980s combined with more powerful deregulatory ideology under the Reagan administration in the US, seemingly creat-ing an early example of domestic pressure (*naiatsu*) joining with foreign pressure (*gaiatsu*) to encourage policy change in Japan (see, generally, Schoppa, 1997). By 1994, however, accelerating deregulation and trade liberalization helped prompt enactment of Japan's product liability (PL) law, at least offering the chance of indirect control of product safety through more prominent civil remedies arising from defective goods. Enactment also benefited from the LDP's unprecedented loss of power in the Lower House, and the mobilization of a diverse group of interests at local and national levels.

Maclachlan (2002, pp. 242–53) concludes by reviewing subsequent changes in the institutional context of Japanese consumer protec-tion policymaking, and the impact of consumer advocacy, which should further open the processes to pluralist pressures from below.

These include the ongoing recession, more openings for consumer-ism in central government politics, and ongoing deregulation (which consumer groups now see as inevitable, focusing instead on securing other legal protections). Such developments are prompting more open-ness in bureaucratic decision-making, bolstered by the Administrative Procedures Law of 1993, the 'public comment' procedure required for new regulations, and the Official Information Disclosure Law of 1999 (Kadomatsu, 1999). They have underpinned renewed efforts by local government Consumer Lifestyle Centres (CLCs) to provide consumers with resources to decide matters for themselves. Consumer groups have drawn also on readier access to information and further networking opportunities offered by new technologies like the Internet.[7] Consumer interests began placing more emphasis on lobbying, possibly represent-ing more legislative influence, especially at the national level. They have gained more leverage at the agenda-setting and policy-formulation stages, and played greater watchdog functions vis-à-vis firms and the bureaucracy.

In short, joining a newer wave of scholarship directed at Japan, Maclachlan (2002, p. 6) shows convincingly how:

> The story of consumer politics in postwar Japan is replete with exam-ples of how the politically disadvantaged can leverage small but sig-nificant concessions from state and economic interests, that is, how diffuse societal interests are incorporated into Japan's pro-producer polity. Accordingly, [her] study identifies new and innovative ways in which those interests can influence the outcomes of Japan's poli-cymaking process, paying particular attention to local opportunities for citizen activism. In the process, it depicts a style of public-inter-est policymaking that, though rooted in corporatist arrangements encompassing state and economic interests, is more vulnerable to pluralist pressures from below than previously thought.

The legal system and consumer law in Japan

However, her fine study tends to underestimate the multifari-ous effects of consumer law in Japan, particularly Product Liability (PL) law and safety regulation, but also more recently in other fields such as consumer contracts and credit regulation (all explained fur-ther below). A broader neglect of the role of law in Japanese soci-ety is also found among others trained in social sciences rather than law. At one extreme, for example, Karel van Wolferen (1989), a journalist now turned professor of political economy who saw 'the enigma of Japanese power' as lying in its elusive and irresponsible dispersion among the ruling triad, was almost totally dismissive of the legal system (Mosher, 1998). But other commentators, especially from abroad, have also long questioned whether 'law matters' in Japan.[8]

A central debate has concerned its low per capita civil litigation rates compared with other similar economies, especially in Europe and the US. An older 'culturalist' theory explains this on the basis that 'the Japanese don't like law' (Noda, 1976, p. 104), due primarily to the legacy of a Confucian tradition – emphasizing harmonious and hierarchical social relationships (Kawashima, 1963). 'Institutional barriers' theory instead argued that 'the Japanese can't like law' (Haley, 1978). Access to justice is restricted by limited numbers of legal professionals and problems in court proceedings, so claimants cannot afford to sue and thus do not obtain the outcomes nominally prescribed by the law. 'Social management' theory suggested that 'the Japanese are made not to like law.' Institutional barriers are maintained, particularly by social elites, to resolve social problems outside the courts, which might lead society in unpredictable directions. Often, alternative dispute resolution (ADR) procedures and resources are inaugurated to facilitate this approach. Some of the theorists adopting this perspective, especially in its earlier incarnations, have been sceptical about this management of social problems (Upham, 1987). But others suggest that it may be justified under more communitarian approaches to contemporary democracy (Tanase, 2010).

By contrast, 'rationalist' theory asserts that 'the Japanese do like law,' acting in its shadow (Ramseyer and Nakazoto, 1999). Despite high barriers to bringing suit, Japanese law is predictable – at least in some areas, and compared with countries such as the US – so claimants do not even need to file suits to be able to obtain favourable settlements out of court. Much rationalist theory also relies on quantitative social science, particularly econometrics. However, more recent 'hybrid' theory combines more qualitative methodology, and takes a more eclectic and nuanced approach to show how 'the Japanese sometimes like law, but sometimes don't' (Milhaupt and West, 2004; Nottage *et al.* (eds), 2008).

In the field of consumer law, periods of economic confusion (1945–54) and growing awareness of consumer issues (1955–67) led to an era of 'indictment' (*kokuhatsu*, 1968–79), spreading notably from the political to the judicial arena (Omura, 1998, pp. 5–7). Regulatory reform initiatives then forced consumer law advocates onto the defensive during the 1980s, but deregulation during the 1990s has highlighted the challenges and opportunities for consumers in policymaking. Although Maclachlan emphasizes the role of local authorities, and the Local Government Law was certainly amended in 1969 to require them to address consumer protection issues, Article 6 of the Consumer Protection Basic Law of 1968 also urged legislative initiatives by the central government. On the one hand, the consumer protection element was identified or strengthened in several pre-existing laws, notably the Instalment Sales Law (*Kappu Hanbai Ho*, No. 159 of 1961) as amended in 1972 to recognize 'protection' of 'the interests of buyers', to strengthen disclosure regulation and to introduce a cooling-off period allowing buyers to terminate contracts and return goods. Other important amendments were made to the Food Hygiene Law of 1947, the Travel Agency Law of 1952, the Building Lots and Transactions Business Law of 1954, and the Pharmaceutical Affairs Law of 1960. On the other hand, many new laws were enacted to address new consumer issues, beginning with the 'three safety laws' in 1973: the Consumer Product Safety Law (No. 31 of 1973), the Law for the Control of Household Products Containing Harmful Substances, and the Law on Regulating Inspections and Manufacturing of Chemical Substances.

These have been followed by legislation on side effects from pharmaceuticals (in 1979) and the Product Liability Law ('PL Law', No. 85 of 1994). Also, reflecting a shift over the 1990s towards transactions and complaints involving services (Taylor, 1997), there has been a burgeoning amount of legislation to protect consumers' economic interests. These include the Specified Commercial Transactions Law of 2000 (replacing the Door-to-Door Sales Law of 1976); the Housing Quality Promotion Law of 1999, providing for a 10-year guarantee; the Financial Products Sales Law of 2000, imposing damages for specified non-disclosure of information; and the Consumer Contracts Law (No. 61 of 2000), striking out certain unfair terms and allowing termination for misrepresentations or harassment).[9] Although the pace has accelerated since the mid-1990s, consumer legislation has thus accumulated steadily over more than three decades, quite comprehensively dealing with the safety of products and services (both prevention of danger and compensation for harm), the protection of consumers' economic interests, and promotion of fair competition, labelling and standards (Matsumoto, 2002, pp. 4–11).

Since the mid-1970s, moreover, there has been a sudden rise in consumer disputes decided by the courts, especially in civil proceedings (Omura, 1998, pp. 8–9). These rulings have mostly supplemented pre-existing law, such as the venerable Civil Code of 1898. Courts have focused on the structural weaknesses of consumers when dealing with businesses to free them from onerous contracts (even without duress or fraud in the orthodox sense), or to impose high duties of care regarding product safety. They have also taken regulatory requirements, such as disclosure obligations backed by administrative sanctions, and given them some effect in private law. Some judgments have been precursors to legislation, as with the 1984 amendments to the Instalment Sales Act following judgments relating to credit transactions, and quite numerous judgments concerning unsafe products prior to the PL Law of 1994.

As pointed out by Omura (1998, pp. 9–11), this has prompted legal scholars from more and more fields to grapple with the growing set of norms and underlying principles. Administrative and competition lawyers became involved from the 1960s and 1970s, when product safety was a primary concern, followed by a growing number of civil and commercial lawyers as contract law issues also became prominent. From the mid-1970s, problems involved in small claims and group actions attracted attention from civil procedure scholars and legal sociologists. From the mid-1980s, competition law dimensions gained renewed attention, and the expansion of 'economic crimes' brought criminal lawyers into the consumer law arena. Reflecting on this expanding set of perspectives and underlying problems, Omura suggests that Japanese consumer law's perception of consumers themselves has shifted from 'groups (receiving the benefits of regulation)', to 'individuals', to 'groups (pro-actively achieving legal outcomes)'. He also argues that views of the issues facing consumers have moved from substantive to procedural law, and from structure to process. Since the late 1990s, these trends have been reinforced by broader shifts in Japan combining ongoing deregulation with widespread civil justice reforms proposed by the Prime Minister's Judicial Reform Council in June 2001 (Kitagawa and Nottage, 2007).

In short, law in general does matter in Japan, and consumer law is now a well-established field. Legislative initiatives have not only emerged at the local level, occasionally filtering through into central government laws, as argued by Maclachlan (2002); they also form a large body of norms, interacting continuously with the court system and a broad array of legal academics now interested in consumer issues. These developments should help overcome remaining problems with gaps and inconsistencies, and in extracting underlying guiding principles, particularly as the type of hot issues and the frameworks for interpreting Japanese society and its law continue to shift both within and outside Japan. Such problems also remain apparent in the European Union (EU), where some urge the belated enactment of a Consumer Code or other means to comprehensively proclaim the consumer interest in legal terms, as opposed to a general 'European Civil Code' or other restatement of private law, which could be overly dominated by liberal nineteenth-century notions (Nottage, 2004b). Japan's Consumer (Protection) Basic Law, government leaders and policymaking bodies did not spell out consumers' rights to 'choice, safety, redress and to be heard' as explicitly as President Kennedy did in the US in 1962. However, Maclachlan's study, supplemented by more recent work on the role of Japanese law generally, and the contours of contemporary consumer law in particular, suggests considerable 'functional equivalence' (cf. Zweigert and Kötz, 1998) – and even some ideological equivalence – in Japan.

Product liability and safety regulation[10]

PL law first gained prominence in Japan only in the late 1960s. Until then, there had only been 11 reported cases claiming civil liability for defective products since World War II, and these attracted little commentary. By the early 1970s, however, four PL mass injury cases were attracting particular social concern and media attention.[11] These piggy-backed on the even more controversial 'Big Four' environmental pollution cases around that time (Gresser *et al.*, 1981). Also significant was the uncovering of potentially widespread defects in automobiles. However, the latter generated collective action problems and more complex issues for legal doctrine at the time, so that social movement ultimately stalled.

Other causes also lay behind this 'stillbirth' of PL in Japan compared with Australia, the EU, and especially the US during the 1970s. Judicial innovation faltered. This may have been due to more general conservative reactions within Japan's judicial administration, as well as an economy and society afflicted by the Oil Shocks. However, case law development of PL law in Japan also slowed because compensation schemes were established to address the injuries identified by the 'Big Four' PL cases. More generally, legislators and bureaucrats strengthened some product safety regulations, enacting, for example, the Consumer Product Safety Law (No. 31 of 1973), while industries introduced some improved product safety measures. In addition, intensive legal scholarship was initiated in the late 1960s and early 1970s, which then carried through to the late 1980s. Specific law reform proposals died away, but also left much to rebuild from quite rapidly over the 1990s.

This 'rebirth' of PL in Japan was again underpinned by a variety of external and internal factors. Reports of product defects emerged in the late 1980s, and in 1993 the conservative LDP lost its virtual monopoly on political power since 1955. Consumer groups and the Japan Federation of Bar Associations (*Nichibenren*) mobilized to keep enactment of the PL Law on the legislative agenda. Legal scholarship blossomed again, looking particularly closely at the European Community's PL Directive of 1985,[12] which had proved popular even beyond Europe (for example in Australia, when Part VA was added to the Trade Practices Act 1974 – the TPA – in 1992), despite PL's retrenchment in the US (reflected and further cemented by the *Restatement Third – Products Liability* promulgated in 1998). The Directive also, therefore, provided a politically palatable compromise 'global standard', as trade liberalization accelerated in Japan over the 1990s. Amidst all this, the Osaka District Court pushed along the debate by ruling that a defective 'Panasonic' brand TV set produced by Matsushita attracted liability even under the article 709 of the Civil Code, which required the plaintiff to prove negligence on the part of the manufacturer.[13] This was important in signalling that the Japanese judiciary was agreeable to the law developing stricter standards even for one-off claims, especially for the more complex household goods that are often considered 'typical' for contemporary PL litigation (Matsuura, 2001, pp. 143–5 and 167–72). Hitherto, the courts had sometimes been quite activist, but only for some mass-torts scenarios addressed in the late 1960s and early 1970s.

Some 3 months after the Matsushita judgment, on 22 June 1994, Japan enacted its PL Law, modelled on the Directive and adding a new strict-liability cause of action to the Civil Code's tort regime. The scope of liability under the PL Law is quite broad. Sometimes, this is true even relative to the US, especially as further reined in by 'tort reforms' through state legislation – a more general phenomenon also in Australia since 2002. Japan's expansive tendency has been advanced by most judgments there since 1999, which has happened quite quickly compared with the 'lead-in' time for the Directive in Europe or a variant adopted in 1992 by Australia.

For example, in the snapper case the Tokyo District Court (13 December 2002, reported in 1033 Hanji 54) found that *sashimi* (sliced raw fish) constituted a 'processed' movable falling within the scope of Article 2 of the PL Law. Compared with Australian law under Part VA, the Court also took a narrower view of the 'development risks' defence under Article 5, which applies when a producer is unable to detect the defect given the current state of technological or scientific knowledge.

In the McDonalds orange juice case, the Nagoya District Court (30 June 1999, 1682 Hanji 106) acknowledged that the consumer bore the burden of proving the existence of a defect (defined broadly under Article 2 as the lack of safety that consumers expect), which had caused the injury. But it did not require the plaintiff to identify the precise cause within the orange juice that she had partially consumed, but the rest of which had been inadvertently thrown away at the hospital. Also as in US law, and unlike the EC Directive regime, under Article 3 of the PL Law plaintiffs can claim for consequential loss not only to 'consumer' goods but also goods used for business purposes (for further comparisons, see also Nottage and Kano, 2009).

Overall, therefore, the comparative trajectory of Japan's substantive PL law (especially legislation and case law) can be seen as becoming noticeably more 'pro-consumer' first in the late 1960s and early 1970s, and then again from the early 1990s. In the EU, moves towards the 1985 Directive, along with case law interpreting it and related legislation in member states, have tended to work in favour of consumers in a more consistent manner. By contrast, substantive PL law in the US was most favourable to consumers (and even commercial parties) harmed by defective products during the 1970s, but has become less so since the 1980s, a reaction confirmed by the R3d. Likewise, although Australian PL law largely tracked developments in the EU, it has been hemmed in by broader 'tort law reform' since 2002.[14] In the early years of the twenty-first century, PL law in Japan continues to develop – slowly but quite steadily – a more pro-consumer orientation, albeit perhaps less so than the EU. As Australia and especially US case law goes in the other (more pro-defendant) direction, reflecting and hemmed in by broader 'tort reforms', this creates substantive outcomes that are now much closer than over previous decades, although there remain important divergences among all four regimes.

However, although Japan's PL law regime nowadays is quite pro-plaintiff, this has not generated a litigation explosion, nor can one be expected. This stems from the still comparatively attractive alternatives to relief outside tort law, as well as the constraints of Japan's broader civil justice system – especially compared with the US. However, such constraints are often shared especially by continental European legal systems, which continue to influence civil dispute resolution in Japan, and even by other common law countries such as Australia. Access to civil justice in Japan has been widened following the recommendations of the blue-ribbon Judicial Reform Council presented to the Prime Minister in 2001; but litigation can be expected to remain at the low levels found everywhere outside the US. Nonetheless, PL suits filed, won and (especially) settled increased significantly in Japan in the mid-1990s in the wake of PL Law enactment. Another step-up was evident in the early years of the twenty-first century in the shadow of renewed public concern about product safety issues, which also generated widespread recalls of consumer goods around 2000. Considerably more activity can also be uncovered further down the 'dispute resolution pyramid', notably ADR in industry association-based PL Centres established around 1995 and in the government's CLCs, as well as various improvements in product safety measures across most industries (Nottage and Wada, 1998).

The future of PL in Japan, however, depends significantly on the state's involvement in product safety issues. The 'Big Four' PL cases reveal a long tradition of brokering settlements in mass torts, often through the establishment of compensation funds, but in the shadow of potential state liability for negligent oversight of market behaviour. Over the 1970s and 1980s, *ex ante* regulation of product safety also became increasingly controversial. Japan's trading partners complained that this too could amount to disguised barriers to trade, designed to protect domestic industry – not just Japanese consumers. However, Japan's main regulatory regime for securing the safety of general consumer goods (the Safety Law) was quite light-handed. Further, as deregulation accelerated within Japan and at the global level (mainly via the WTO) over the 1990s, product safety has also witnessed a rebalancing away from *ex ante* regulation towards less direct control by means of greater potential for *ex post* compensation claims, namely under the PL Law of 1994.

Nonetheless, even under the WTO regime, Japan is entitled to regulate product safety to protect human health – arguably even on a 'precautionary' basis – provided it attempts a risk assessment in light of accepted international standards. This is increasingly important as advanced industrialized countries are exposed to complex risks such as 'mad cow disease' and 'bird flu'. More generally, the model of 'responsive regulation' increasingly popular in a deregulatory era advocates not only a shift towards softer regulation involving a new partnership with regulated industries, but also stronger back-up powers for the state if industries betray that trust.[15] This helps explain or justify the recent tightening of regulatory requirements (for example regarding recall notifications) in certain product areas. These began with certain consumer electronics, foodstuffs and automobiles, notably after cover-ups involving televisions, Snow Brand milk products and Mitsubishi Motors

Corporation (MMC) around 2000. From 2004 attention was focused on asbestos, buildings that lacked earthquake resistance, second-hand consumer goods, Chinese dumplings, elevators and fan heaters (Nottage, 2006; Nottage and Rheuben, 2008).

Significant 'vertical' (product-specific) re-regulation then generated momentum to revise the 'horizontal' Safety Law applicable to everyday consumer goods not covered by more specific legislation. In 2006, following a revised EU Product Safety Directive but to a somewhat lesser extent, manufacturers and importers faced a new requirement to inform METI about serious product-safety related accidents.[16] Some consumer advocates sought the establishment of a new independent agency to assemble and disseminate such information, but this was only achieved in 2009 with the establishment of the Consumer Affairs Agency (mentioned above).

Consumer contracts generally[17]

Although American commentators are often struck by differences between US and Japanese law, including contract law, there are some very important similarities, especially when both countries are viewed from an Anglo-Commonwealth law perspective. In both the US and Japan, the legal system is set up or operates in fact to allow much more 'substantive reasoning' – open to economic, political or ethical considerations and arguments, even within the judicial process – whereas jurisdictions following the English variant of the common law system instead promote narrower 'formal reasoning' along many dimensions. To address problems of unfairness in contract law, for example, the English tradition still eschews any general requirement that parties to contract act in 'good faith'. In contrast, both Japan (Civil Code Article 1(2)) and the US (via Article 2 of the Uniform Commercial Code or UCC, and the Restatement Second (Contracts) of 1979) have borrowed from German law in this respect, and invoke the good faith principle to maintain balance particularly in long-term Business-to-Business (B2B) relationships such as distributorship contracts (Taylor, 1993).

However, Japanese courts did not prove so vigorous in invoking this principle – or another important 'general clause', Civil Code Article 90 prohibiting contract terms contrary to 'public policy' – in Business-to-Customer (B2C) relationships between firms and individual consumers. Instead, again not unlike the US (where most consumer protection law has developed via statute, albeit often via state law), from the 1960s the Japanese legislature tended to intervene directly and more specifically, siphoning off important categories of unfair consumer contract cases. For example, in the 1990s Kitagawa identified a total of 16 statutes directly controlling aspects of contractual validity, often in transactions on standard forms (Kitagawa, 1999). Each statute's area of coverage was limited, and, even in areas where attempts to expand its scope might have been anticipated, the tendency has been to wait for legislative amendment. To a lesser degree, this pattern held for an emerging tendency to regulate unfairness in contracting through local government ordinances.[18] Combined with some potential for, and actual tendencies towards, formal reasoning even within the case law and commentary involving Article 1(2), and especially Article 90, piecemeal legislative reform – as in such countries as England and New Zealand – injected a somewhat more formal reasoning-based approach to consumer contract law compared with other areas of Japanese law.

However, greater openness to substantive reasoning has re-emerged even in this field over the last decade, thanks to legislative and then judicial innovation in regulating unfair contracts within a more general scheme. Part of the background comprised academic studies of overseas developments, dating back to the early 1980s, such as England's Unfair Contract Terms Act 1977 and early initiatives at the EC level. At that time, general regulation of standard-form contracts was also being investigated by the government's main advisory body, the National Lifestyle Council (*kokumin seikatsu shingikai*). But introduction of general legislation containing new content-oriented standards, drawing on some of those overseas reforms, did not eventuate.

First, Japanese commentators increasingly acknowledged the extent – and sometimes usefulness – of 'administrative guidance' (*gyosei shido*) in regulating various standard forms used in particular industries.[19] In some cases, as in life insurance, the standard form had to be approved by the responsible Ministry, which was therefore in a position to threaten de facto, if not clearly legal, sanctions to control excesses. Such control was heightened by a National Lifestyle Council Committee report in 1984, which identified problems in particular areas after widespread public discussion and research (Kitagawa, 1985). The awareness of such mechanisms, and changes that followed in some of the standard forms reviewed in that report, took some urgency out of the subsequent discussion.

Secondly, the focus of inquiry was broadened, to include discussion not only of particular unfair contract terms, but also of improper behaviour in inducing the contract. This raised more general issues, calling for more consideration of how various private law techniques dealt, or might deal, with this problem. Predictably, it resulted in more general jurisprudential arguments (Hoshino, 1991; Isomura, 1993).

The resultant hiatus left the Japanese law on unfair contracts with substantive roots but with formal counter-tendencies.

As with PL law, momentum re-emerged from the early 1990s. Concern had grown about the inability of administrative guidance adequately to control the broad range of cases involving claims of contractual unfairness, particularly those involving consumers, and there were also growing calls for greater transparency in government more generally. The Economic Planning Agency (EPA), the government entity responsible for coordinating consumer policy at the time, formed a working group that reported in 1994 on the recently enacted EC Directive on Unfair Contract Terms.[20] Following an interim report in January 1998 (Fujioka, 1998), a final report from the relevant National Lifestyle Council committee was published in January 1999, proposing draft legislation. As with UCC Article 2 amendment proposals in the US around that time, the draft attracted considerable opposition, mainly from industry interests. However, the key players involved in the Japanese reform initiative, and the head of the EPA, remained confident that draft legislation would be presented to the Diet in early 2000 (*Nihon Keizai Shimbun*, 10 March 1999). The Consumer Contract Law was duly enacted and came into effect on 1 April 2001.

The Law applies to all contracts between 'businesses' (corporations or other entities dealing with consumers for business purposes) and 'consumers' (individuals, excluding those contracting as or for a business), as respectively defined in Article 2. (To avoid any doubt, Article 12 specifies that this Law does not extend to contracts of employment.) Article 3 requires a business inviting a consumer to conclude a contract to 'make efforts' to provide necessary information about consumers' rights and duties, or other matters as to the contents of the contract, in order to deepen the consumer's understanding, and to try to make the contents clear and fair for consumers. However, this does not create enforceable obligations, unlike the ensuing Parts 2 and 3 of the Law.

The legislation reveals an interesting balance from a comparative perspective, which may be related to the tensions among interest groups in the run-up to enactment. On the one hand, the grounds for impugning the negotiation process and hence cancelling the contract under Part 2 (Articles 4–7) appear quite tightly circumscribed. In contrast, influenced by federal legislation in the US, by the late 1980s Australia and then New Zealand had enacted fair trading legislation that broadly prohibited any 'misleading and deceptive conduct' in trade or commerce. (The EU's recent Unfair Commercial Practices Directive, which member states had to implement by 12 December 2007, also contains a general ban on any unfair or aggressive practice alongside more specific provisions, although – as in Japan – this legislation cannot be invoked against one firm by another).[21] On the other hand, as well as nullifying specified types of contract terms (under Articles 8 and 9), Part 3 of the Law allows – potentially very broadly – for nullification of any term that expands 'one-sidedly', and contrary to the Civil Code's doctrine of good faith, the obligations of consumers compared with the default rules provided by the Code (Article 10).

Specifically, under Part 2, an offer or acceptance made by consumer to a contract can be cancelled if caused by a range of misrepresentations or misapprehensions, specified in Articles 4(1) and (2), arising from the acts or omissions of the business. These mainly relate to 'important matters', defined in Article 4(4) as the quality, use or price, that should usually affect a consumer's decision on whether or not to conclude the contract in question. Article 4(3) similarly allows cancellation when the consumer's offer or acceptance results from being pressured through specified acts by the business. The effect of this 'cancellation' is not specified but is generally interpreted as meaning that no contract is concluded, leading to restitutionary obligations if necessary. However, Article 4(5) preserves the rights of bona fide third parties; and Article 7 limits a cancellation right to within 6 months of when the consumer should have known of it (or, in any event, to within 5 years of conclusion of the contract). Article 5 extends Article 4 coverage to an intermediary entrusted by a business to conclude its contract with a consumer, and the agent of any of these persons.

Article 8 in Part 3, regulating the fairness of contract terms included in a concluded contract, first renders invalid any clauses:

- totally exempting liability for non- or mis-performance by the business;
- partially exempting liability for the same (if intentional or grossly negligent on the part of the business, its representative, or employee); or
- similarly excluding Civil Code liability for damages due to a tort; and
- totally exempting liability for latent defects in goods.

This last mentioned control thus partially turns Civil Code Article 570 defect liability from a default into a mandatory rule. However, contracts can still partially exclude liability, for example, for a consumer's consequential loss arising from the defect, subject to Article 10 of the

Law. Further, Article 8(2) expressly validates clauses restricting liability for defects to repair or replacement of the goods. Next, Article 9 controls clauses specifying in advance an amount payable upon avoidance or rescission (liquidated damages or penalty clauses). Importantly, Article 9(1) invalidates any portion agreed in the clause in question, but exceeding the 'average amount' in damages that the business would suffer from termination in similar consumer contracts, considering the types and timing of the cancellation as may be provided in the clause. Finally, Article 10 provides the catch-all control of unfair contract terms contrary to good faith, outlined above (Nottage).[22]

Consumer groups pressed for more effective enforcement mechanisms in the original Law, but were only able to record some success through an amendment in 2006 that again was influenced by EU law. With effect from June 2007, accredited consumer representative groups can bring injunction proceedings to prevent violations of the Consumer Contracts Law. By mid-2008, six had been accredited by the Japanese government, including the 'Kyoto Consumer Contracts Network' NPO (or NGO). In August the Network filed for an injunction preventing a lessor from enforcing a clause stating that lessees would be unable to obtain any refund of a deposit (*shiki-kin*), usually given only to cover any expenses required to restore the vacated premises to a reasonable state. The lessor provided an undertaking in the Kyoto District Court that it would not enforce this clause against the 12 existent lessees, declaring that it 'didn't intend to go against the trend of respect for consumers' (Kyoto Shimbun, 2008).[23]

Another situation that generated extensive litigation, even by individual claimants, has involved students suing for refunds of fees paid to a university that a student ultimately chose not to enter, after receiving an offer from a better university that had set its own entrance examination and admission procedures (Kozuka, 2009). A series of judgments culminated in a Supreme Court decision (27 November 2006, 60 Minshu 3437) that first drew on a ministerial order on universities to distinguish between the one-off 'entrance fee' and the 'tuition fees'. Referring to the right to education protected under the Constitution (Article 26), the Court held that students were free to choose their university and leave without cause, but such termination of their contract attracted a university's right to compensation – subject to the Consumer Contract Law, specifically Article 9(1). The university, then, was held not to suffer any loss if the student terminated before each academic year started on 1 April, so any tuition fees paid could not be retained by the original university even if the student had agreed that they could be retained; but the university could retain any (much smaller) entrance fee payment.

Because it involved a careful but general balancing of interests, this decision has been seen as evidencing even greater judicial activism than the Supreme Court's judgment (3 April 2007; 61 Minshu 967) in the NOVA language-school litigation, brought under 1999 amendments to the Specified Commercial Transactions Law that allowed termination of specified long-term consumer contracts under certain conditions. (The emergence of mostly pro-plaintiff judgments under the PL Law demonstrates similar levels of judicial activism in favour of consumers.) Arguably, Japanese courts – even the Supreme Court from 1999 – have been even more activist in litigation challenging unsecured consumer credit contracts. In this litigation, not brought under the Consumer Contracts Act, interpretations favouring consumer borrowers appear to go against new legislation in the form of the Moneylenders Control Law (*Kashikingyo Kiseiho*, No. 32 of 1983), as the legislature seemingly intended that lenders should be able to retain 'grey zone' interest – explained next.

Consumer credit[24]

From the 1980s, Japan's overall consumer debt increased to levels comparable to or even higher than other major industrialized economies (Mann, 2006, p. 109). Over the 1990s, the proportion of 'sales credit' (*hanbai shinyo*, associated with purchases of specific goods) grew. There was a corresponding decline in pure 'consumer credit' (*shohisha kinyu*), but the make-up shifted from secured loans (10 trillion yen in 2004) to unsecured loans (*shohisha roon*, 24 trillion yen), especially those provided by non-bank 'consumer credit companies' (*shohisha kinyu gaisha*: 10 trillion yen) as opposed to banks (TAPALS, 2006). Around three out of 14 million borrowers of unsecured loans were considered overindebted in 2006 (Suda, 2006, pp. 180–1). This has underpinned record consumer bankruptcies, debt-related suicides, and increasing concern about aggressive marketing as well as debt enforcement tactics.

Almost all this growth in unsecured lending has occurred through cash advances, rather than credit cards as in countries such as Australia, the UK and especially the US. This difference was due to Japan being a smaller country with a more unified banking system, yet segmented financial markets (with banks focusing on secured or corporate lending); more limited sharing of 'positive information' (consumers' good history regarding credit limits and repayments); and higher telecommunications charges, at least over the 1990s. Further, even after gradual deregulation of banks issuing credit cards as a lending mechanism between 1982 and 2001, they set the default rule as monthly repayment in full (*ikkai barai*). Banks were also cautious about the reputational implications of moving into the unsecured lending market, traditionally characterized by high interest rates and aggressive debt collection practices (Mann, 2002). Consumers probably had similar concerns, although they have slowly become more familiar with consumer credit companies. Greater use of cash for payments may also have contributed to Japan's preference for cash advances.

Such unsecured consumer lending expanded rapidly, however, for rather similar reasons. These included macroeconomic slowdowns; automation and IT (particularly the deployment of automated loan-dispenser machines from 1993); and clever advertising campaigns (promoting a 'safe' image particularly for stressed-out 'salarymen' with regular employment in companies, and then increasingly targeting younger low-income earners). Japan's consumer lenders also developed new business models similar to those found in the US. There are strong parallels both with the 'sweat box' model of credit card companies (aiming to keep borrowers endlessly paying off interest but not the principal: Mann, 2007) and the practices associated with 'payday lending' in the US (Mann and Hawkins, 2007), especially techniques encouraging borrowers to take out further loans with the same or other even less reputable lenders in order to pay off interest on the initial loans. Indeed, among Japan's top lenders, GE Money developed the 'Lake' network from 1994 (but decided to sell it in 2008), and Citigroup took over 'DIC' from 2000.

Japan's expansion of consumer lending occurred in a substantially unregulated and fragmented market. 'Sales credit' was governed largely by the Instalment Sales Law under the jurisdiction of what is now METI, responsible for industrial policy more generally. Other credit was regulated primarily through interest rate and other restrictions under the Interest Rate Restriction Law (IRRL, No. 100 of 1954; but with a precursor dating back to the Meiji Era, Ordinance No. 66 of 1877) and the Capital Funding Law (Law on Investments, Deposit Taking and Other Financial Transactions, No. 195 of 1954: the *Shusshi Ho*). The main regulator has been the Ministry of Finance (MoF), now the Financial Supervisory Agency (FSA), but local governments were also involved in registering consumer credit companies.

Although Japan seems to have deployed most of the techniques for addressing consumer loan problems (Engel and McCoy, 2002, p. 1297), a major focus of legislation and case law has been interest rate control. As specialized private law, the IRRL set a cap of 15–20 per cent (depending on loan amount), but excess interest paid 'voluntarily' by the borrower could not be reclaimed. As criminal law, the *Shusshi Ho* set penalties for interest charged at more than 29.2 per cent (since 2000). This created a 'grey zone' gap between the two legislated rates. In the 1960s, an era of broader consumer activism described in the first part of this chapter, Japan's Supreme Court favoured borrowers by rejecting a literal reading of the IRRL. The Court allowed grey zone interest to be converted into principal repayment, and later allowed recovery of the difference between the excess interest paid and the principal. This prompted the Moneylenders Control Law of 1983, to allow lenders to keep the grey zone interest after all. The Supreme Court upheld this on 22 January 1990 (44 Minshu 332). From the late 1990s, however, it developed both literalist and purposive interpretations of that Law to favour borrowers again. Several judgments held that disclosure and procedural requirements had not been adequately followed. The final nail in the lenders' coffin came on 13 January 2006 (60 Minshu 1). The Court ruled that an acceleration clause in the loan agreement – requiring repayment of the full outstanding amount once the borrower defaulted on some payments – put so much pressure on the borrower that its grey zone interest payments were not 'voluntary'.

Legislation therefore ultimately proved more effective at reining in very high interest rates, as opposed to the other two out of 'three evils' characterizing consumer lending in Japan (*sarakin san-aku*). First, the Moneylenders Control Law had set only vague constraints on excessive lending (and aggressive advertising). Only in 1997 did the three largest non-bank lenders agree not to loan to those who already had loans from three lenders. Secondly, the Law prohibited particularly aggressive debt collection tactics, but enforcement was weak despite even the biggest lenders reportedly abusing borrowers. Dubious practices therefore tended to become a negotiating point for lawyers seeking debt relief for borrowers, on the basis that payments of grey zone interest were not 'voluntary' (Jones, 2007). Lawyers also focused on grey zone interest when negotiating debt relief during or before insolvency proceedings, especially when the Civil Rehabilitation Law (No. 225 of 1999) was amended from 2001 to expand protections for individual debtors in possession (Anderson, 2006). Background private law, namely the Civil Code (No. 89 of 1896) and even the Consumer Contracts Act (outlined above), proved even less useful for distressed borrowers (Kozuka and Nottage, 2009a; Pardieck, 2008).

Another wave of litigation followed the Supreme Court's ruling in January 2006, seeking refunds of grey zone interest paid 'involuntarily'.

By chance, the Moneylenders Control Law was to be reviewed in 2006, so a Study Group (comprising leading scholars and various stakeholder representatives) had already been set up within the FSA the year before. The Group met several times before issuing an 'Interim Report' on 21 April 2006. It suggested abolishing the grey zone, but did not recommend what the single interest rate should be. On 6 July, the ruling LDP and Komeito coalition recommended reducing it to the IRRL's caps of 15–20 per cent, while leaving an exception for small loans. The proposed exception attracted particularly strong political criticism, so it was not included in a legislative package enacted on 20 December 2006 (Law No. 115). The Moneylenders Control Law was renamed the Moneylenders Law, and the following changes were phased in (Pardieck, 2008):

- from 20 January 2007: stricter criminal penalties for unregistered lenders;
- from 19 December 2007: stricter requirements for registration, information-handling, and disclosure; a 'suitability rule' requiring lenders to avoid 'unsuitable solicitation' given the borrower's knowledge, experience, finances and purposes; clearer rights for borrowers to examine their transaction records; restrictions on life insurance contracts over the borrower and certain debt collection practices; and tougher administrative oversight, including establishment of a new industry association;
- by June 2009: expanded minimum capital base for lenders; examinations for compliance officers within them; licensed credit reporting agencies, with new regulations regarding information-sharing among them; and
- by June 2010: further expanded capital base and mandatory qualified compliance officers; mandatory checks on borrowers' ability to repay, a credit bureau's report for individuals, and proof of annual income for loans more than 0.5 million yen (or loans resulting in debts of more than 1 million yen); further suitability rules prohibiting loans exceeding the borrower's ability to repay, or one-third of annual income (absent certain liquid assets, still to be defined by regulations); and abolition of 'voluntary' grey-zone interest, along with amendments to the IRRL regarding certain contract terms.

Although the legislative cap of 20 per cent therefore only came into effect from 2010, lenders were already constrained by the Supreme Court rulings on interest rates.

The sector contracted sharply, with considerable ripple effects on the (increasingly intertwined) mainstream banking system and Japan's macroeconomy, although these developments were then swamped by the effects of the Global Financial Crisis, which also generated some calls to delay full implementation (Bloomberg, 21 January 2010). The number of registered lenders had fallen by two-thirds from March 2006 to September 2009, but the number of illegal lenders does not seem to have grown – the number of complaints to the FSA was similar in 2007 and 2008, at half the 2003 level. The number of borrowers with more than five loans has more than halved from 2005 to 2009, and they are being screened much more carefully. Total outstanding consumer debt has shrunk back from its peak in 2006 to the level it had been around 1999. The government is also promoting alternative financing schemes and debt or budget counselling services, especially at the local level. And case law from the Supreme Court has continued to go in consumers' favour since 2007 (Kozuka, 2010).

The Moneylenders Law reforms also prompted extensive amendments to the Instalment Sales Law in 2008. For example, suppliers of one-off sales credit must be registered (like credit card companies) and must check that the retailer has not engaged in unfair sales techniques. Such suppliers, as well as credit card companies, must not advance credit that will make the consumer excessively indebted, and they must use a credit bureau.

Conclusions

Gaps in substantive consumer rights in Japan have been systematically filled, particularly since the early 1990s, and enforcement has improved, although no country's system is ever perfect and Japanese consumers still face collective active problems and other difficulties in obtaining and implementing consumer rights. Enactment of the PL Law was facilitated by the LDP's brief loss of power during 1993–4, but it would probably have occurred anyway, and courts have generally responded favourably to the subsequent increase in claims – albeit from a low base, as in all countries outside the US. Once back in power, the LDP has continued to seek consumer votes through product-specific re-regulation and amendments to the Safety Law; by enacting the Consumer Contracts Law and other reforms to maintain consumer trust, particularly in services transactions and e-commerce; and with the 2006 package of reforms to consumer credit markets. Prime Minister Yasuo Fukuda also committed the LDP government to the creation of the Consumer

Affairs Agency, with legislation enacted just before it lost the general election of 30 August 2009.

Somewhat more expressly and broadly, in the first major policy speech by the new Prime Minister on behalf of the coalition led by the Democratic Party of Japan, at the 173rd session of the Diet on 26 October 2009, Yukio Hatoyama presented the following proposal (see http://www.kantei.go.jp/foreign/hatoyama/statement/200910/26syosin_e.html, cited in Tani, 2009):

> [A] change to 'an economy for the people'. This means ceasing to gauge the economy through yardsticks that give too much weight to economic rationalism and growth rates. While promoting free competition in economic activity, we must switch to an economy and society which give greater emphasis to the quality of people's lives by preparing adequate safety nets with regard to employment and human resources development, by ensuring food safety and public safety, and by adopting the consumers' perspective.'

When Japan's 'bubble economy' burst in 1990, few would have predicted these outcomes, but they appear less surprising when viewed together and in hindsight. They can be seen as part of a quiet and gradual transformation in Japanese law and society more generally (Kingston, 2004; Nottage *et al.* (eds), 2008). This is driven by less 'patterned' political pluralism and more 'decentralized' production of law, including a somewhat more activist judiciary (Kozuka and Nottage, 2009b; Milhaupt and Pistor, 2008, discussed in Nottage, 2010a).[25] Consumer rights represent another emergent type of rights discourse and praxis in Japan (Feldman, 2000; Scheiber *et al.* (eds), 2007). This remains quite distinct from the ideals (at least) of American liberalism, but some will see that as a positive thing (Tanase, 2010), and there are numerous parallels with developments particularly in Europe.

Notes

1. See http://www.caa.go.jp/en/index.html. (The Japanese-language website explains that the Agency focuses on (i) safety issues in general, (ii) food and agricultural products labelling, (iii) labelling and information disclosure requirements generally, (iv) other consumer contract issues, (v) consumer data management, (vi) planning (policy development, education, international linkages, privacy and whistle-blower protection), and (vii) coordination with other ministries. See also http://www.eastasiaforum.org/2008/10/30/a-new-consumer-agency-for-japan-consumer-redress-contracts-and

product-safety/; and http://blogs.usyd.edu.au/japaneselaw/2009/09/lessons_for_australia.html

2. For more comprehensive outlines of Japanese consumer law, see the succinct materials (in Japanese) via http://www.kokusen.go.jp/category/nyumon.html; Ito *et al.*, 2006; Dernauer, 2008; and Tani, 2009 at http://www.rieti.go.jp/en/special/policy-update/036.html

3. For data on types, volumes and trends in consumer disputing in Japan, see (only in Japanese) the Cabinet Office's 2009 *Shohisha Hakusho [Consumer White Paper]* (especially Part 2.1.3), at http://www5.cao.go.jp/seikatsu/whitepaper/h20/01_honpen/index.html

4. See, for example, Japan's comparative approach to information disclosure and other obligations for consumer transactions under Japanese private and public law: 'The Report on OECD Member Countries' Approaches to Consumer Contracts' (6 July 2007), at http://www.oecd.org/dataoecd/11/28/38991787.pdf, and Kawawa, 2010.

5. Adapted, with permission of the publisher, from Nottage, 2004a, pp. 8–11, 14–15.

6. The name was abbreviated to the Basic Law for Consumers (*Shohisha Kihonho*) when it underwent significant reforms in 2004, envisaging (as in the EU recently) a more empowered – rather than 'protected' – vision of consumers: see Dernauer, 2006. This Law is only available online in Japanese, via http://law.e-gov.go.jp/

7. However, the steady growth of the internet in Japan (Ibusuki and Nottage, 2002) has also given rise to many new types of consumer transactions, complaints and government responses: see Matsumoto, 2002.

8. See further Abe and Nottage, 2006, updated at http://www.asianlii.org/jp/other/JPLRes/2008/1.html (including a succinct outline of legal history, institutions and the profession, and constitutional principles).

9. The Consumer Product Safety Law, PL Law, Consumer Contracts Law (all three discussed further below) and some other legislation cited in this chapter are now translated into English at: http://www.japaneselawtranslation.go.jp.

10. Adapted, with permission of the editor and publisher, from Nottage, 2007, pp. 223, 225–8.

11. These cases involved Morinaga's arsenic-poisoned powdered milk (linked to the manufacturer initially in 1955), Thalidomide drugs resulting in birth defects (1962), chinoform drugs resulting in the 'SMON' nervous system disorder (1970) and Kanemi's PCB-poisoned rice bran oil (1969). For full details see Nottage, 2004a, Chapter 3.

12. Directive 85/374/EEC, partly amended in 1999.

13. *Taishi Kensetsu Kogyo Co., Ltd v. Matsushita Electrical Industrial Co., Ltd*, Osaka District Court, 29 March 1994, 1439 Hanji 29 (translated in Port and McAlinn, 2003, pp. 954–7).

14. See the rough depiction in Nottage, 2005a, and detailed comparisons in Nottage, 2004a, Chapter 3.

15. Ayres and Braithwaite, 1992. On problems like mad cow disease, and regulatory responses at different levels (global, regional and national), see Nottage and Trezise, 2003, and Nottage, 2005b.

16. Directive 2001/95/EC, replacing Directive 92/59/EEC, covers serious product-related injury risks. The revised Japanese law requires disclosure for actual serious accidents, plus risks (even without injuries) as specified in regulations – notably, certain fires and carbon monoxide emissions. It took until 2010 for Australia expected to add a disclosure requirement limited solely to actual accidents: see Nottage, 2010b. Further amendments to Japan's Safety Law, enacted in November 2007 with effect from April 2009, introduced a system for checking the safety of certain consumer durables. For heaters, bathroom dryers and dishwashers, manufacturers must contact purchasers when the appliances approach the end of their usual lifespan. For lower-risk specified products such as fans and TVs, they must indicate the usual lifespan through labelling. See Annex 2 of Tani, 2009.

17. See further Nottage, 2002, Chapter 3, available via http://researcharchive. vuw.ac.nz/handle/10063/778?show=full; and more generally Nottage, 1996.

18. See, for example, the Tokyo City Consumer Lifestyle Ordinance (*Tokyo-to Shohi Seikatsu Jorei*), dating back to 1975 and outlined in: Ito, S., '*Futekisei na Torihiki Koi Kisei ni kansuru To-jorei oyobi Kisei Kaisei no Gaiyo [Overview of the Amendment to the Capital's Ordinance and Regulations relating to the Control of 'Improper Dealings']*' (1995) 1065 Jurisuto 14. See also Note '*Chumoku sareru Shohisha higai boshi oyobi Higai kyusai ni kansuru Chiho jichitai no Shohisha gyosei to Shohi seikatsu jorei no doko [Noticeable Directions in Local Government Consumer Ordinances and Administration relating to Prevention and Compensation of Damage to Consumers]*' (1996) New Business Law (NBL), 5 (586).

19. In general, 'administrative guidance occurs where administrators take action of no coercive legal effect that encourages regulated parties to act in a specific way in order to achieve some administrative aim': Young, 1984, p. 926.

20. See Council Directive 93/13/EEC and Matsumoto, 1994. Foreign observers had also tended to be critical about administrative guidance more generally: see, for example, Dean, 1991.

21. Compare Directive 2005/29/EC (and a succinct explanatory memorandum) available via http://ec.europa.eu/consumers/rights/index_en.htm.

22. See Luke Nottage, 'Japan', in *CCH Doing Business in Asia* (looseleaf, CCH Asia, Singapore, updated in 2005) para JPN ¶30–011. For more detailed analysis see Kano and Nottage, 2008. For further comparative perspectives Nottage and Kano, 2009.

23. See '*Shohisha dantai, hatsu no "shoso"*', Kyoto Shimbun, 22 October 2008, p. 26, and more generally my http://www.eastasiaforum.org/2008/10/30/a-new-consumer-agency-for-japan-consumer-redress-contracts-and-product-safety/

24. Adapted, with permission of the co-author, editors and publisher, from Kozuka and Nottage, 2009b, pp. 200–3.

References

Abe, M. and Nottage, L. (2006), 'Japanese Law', in Smits, J. (ed.), *Encyclopedia of Comparative Law*, Cheltenham: Edward Elgar, p. 357.

Anderson, K. (2006), 'Japanese Insolvency Law after a Decade of Reform', *Canadian Business Law Journal*, 43: 2.

Ayres, I. and Braithwaite, J. (1992), *Responsive Regulation: Transcending the Deregulation Debate*, New York: Oxford University Press.

Bloomberg (2010), 'Japan's Consumer Law to be Enforced Soon', 21 January, available at http://www.bloombergutv.com/news/latest-world-business-news/42940/japan-s-consumer-law-to-be-enforced-soon.html

Broadbent, J. (1998), *Environmental Politics in Japan: Networks of Power and Protest*, Cambridge, UK; New York: Cambridge University Press.

Clammer, J. R. (1997), *Contemporary Urban Japan: A Sociology of Consumption*, Oxford; Malden, MA: Blackwell Publishers.

Dean, M. (1991), 'Administrative Guidance in Japanese Law: A Threat to the Rule of Law', Journal of Business Law, JBL, 398.

Dentsu Institute for Human Studies (2001), 'Value Changes with Globalization – Japan Remains Groping, Asia Takes an Opportunity – the Fifth "Comparative Analysis of Global Values"', Tokyo: Dentsu Institute for Human Studies, p. 40.

Dernauer, M. (2006), *Verbraucherschutz und Vertragsfreiheit im japanischen Recht [Consumer Protection and Freedom of Contract in Japan]*, Tuebingen: Mohr Siebeck.

Eberts, R. E. and Eberts, C. G. (1995), *The Myths of Japanese Quality*, Upper Saddle River, NJ: Prentice Hall.

Engel, K. and McCoy, P. (2002), 'A Tale of Three Markets: The Law and Economics of Predatory Lending', *Texas Law Review*, 80: 1259.

Feldman, E. A. (2000), *The Ritual of Rights in Japan: Law, Society and Health Policy*, Cambridge, UK: Cambridge University Press.

Foote, D. H. (ed.) (2007), *Law in Japan: A Turning Point*, Seattle: University of Washington Press.

Fujioka, B. (1998), '"*Shohisha Keiyakuho (Kasho) no Gutaiteki Naiyo ni tsuite*" no Gaiyo [Overview of the Concrete Contents of the Tentatively-Entitled Consumer Contracts Law]', New Business Law (NBL), 16 (636).

Gresser, J., Koichiro, F. and Akio, M. (1981), *Environmental Law in Japan*, Cambridge, MA: MIT Press.

Haley, J. O. (1978), 'The Myth of the Reluctant Litigant', *Journal of Japanese Studies*, 4: 359.

Hoshino, E. (1991), '*Gendai Keiyaku Ho Ron - Yakkan, Shohisha Keiyaku wo Kien to shite [Contemporary Contract Law Theory – Reconsidered in the Light of Standard Form and Consumer Contracts]*', New Business Law (NBL), 1 (469).

Ibusuki, M. and Nottage, L. (2002), 'IT and Legal Practice and Education in Japan and Australia', *UTS Law Review*, 4: 31.

Isomura, T. (1993), '*Verbraucherschutz und neue Aufgaben des Vertragsrechts in Japan [Consumer Protection and New Tasks for Contract Law in Japan]*', 27 *Kobe University Law Rev* 35.

Ito, S., Chizuko, M., Iwakazu, T. and Suzuki, M. (2006), *Tekisutobukku Shohisha [Consumer Law Textbook]*, Tokyo: Nihon Hyoronsha.

Johnson, C. (1982), MITI and the Japanese Miracle: The Growth of Industrial Policy, 1925–1975, Stanford: Stanford University Press.

Jones, C. (2007), 'Escaping Your Debts in Japan: Hiroyuki Yagi and Masakazu Kaji, Karita Kane Wa Kaesuna [Book Review]', *Journal of Japanese Law*, 12: 259.

Jussaume, R. and Judson, J. H. (1992), 'Public Perceptions About Food Safety in the United States and Japan', *Rural Sociology*, 57(2): 235.

Kadomatsu, N. (1999), 'The New Administrative Information Disclosure Law in Japan', *Zeitschrift fuer Japanisches Recht*, 8: 34.

Kato, M. and Nottage, L. (2008), 'Contract Law', in CCH *Japanese Business Law: Volume 1*, Singapore: CCH Asia.

Kawashima, T. (1963), 'Dispute Resolution in Contemporary Japan', in von Mehren, A. (ed.), *Law in Japan: The Legal Order in a Changing Society*, Harvard: Harvard University Press, p. 41.

Kawawa, N. (2010), 'Japanese Consumer Law and a Duty to Supply Information', *International Journal of Private Law*, 3(1–2): 85.

Kerbo, H. R. and McKinstry, J. A. (1995), *Who Rules Japan? The Inner Circles of Economic and Political Power*, Westport, CT: Praeger.

Kingston, J. (2004), *Japan's Quiet Transformation: Social Change and Civil Society in the Twenty-First Century*, London; New York: Routledge.

Kitagawa, T. and Nottage, L. (2007), 'Globalization of Japanese Corporations and the Development of Corporate Legal Departments: Problems and Prospects', in Alford, W. (ed.), *Raising the Bar*, Cambridge, MA: Harvard East Asian Legal Studies Program (distributed by Harvard University Press), p. 201.

Kitagawa, Z. (1999), 'Contract Law in General', in Z Kitagawa (ed.), *Doing Business in Japan*, New York: Matthew Bender, looseleaf, §1.07[4][b].

Kitagawa, Z. (1985), 'Unfair Contract Terms in Administrative Guidance', *Rechtstheorie*, 16: 181.

Kozuka, S. (2009), 'Judicial Activism of the Supreme Court in Consumer Law: Juridification of Society through Case Law?', *Journal of Japanese Law*, 27: 81.

Kozuka, S. (2010), 'Punishing the Lenders for Whose Sake? Impact of the New Case Law and Follow-ups to the 2006 Reform of Consumer Credit Regulation in Japan', in Backert, W., Block-Lieb, S. and Niemi, J. (eds), *Contemporary Issues in Consumer Insolvency*, Bern: Peter Lang.

Kozuka, S. and Nottage, L. (2009a), 'Re-Regulating Unsecured Consumer Credit in Japan: Over-Indebted Borrowers, the Supreme Court, and New Legislation', in Twigg-Flessner, C., Parry, D. and Nordhausen, A. (eds), *Yearbook of Consumer Law 2009*, Aldershot: Ashgate, p. 197.

Kozuka, S. and Nottage, L. (2009b), 'The Myth of the Careful Consumer: Law, Culture, Economics and Politics in the Rise and Fall of Unsecured Lending in Japan', in Niemi-Kiesilainen, J., Ramsay, I. and Whitford, W. (eds), *Consumer Credit, Debt and Bankruptcy: Comparative and International Perspectives*, Oxford: Hart, p. 199.

Lam, P. E. (1999), *Green Politics in Japan*, London; New York: Routledge.

Low, M., Nakayama, S. and Yoshioka, H. (1999), *Science, Technology and Society in Contemporary Japan*, Cambridge: Cambridge University Press.

McCormack, G. (2001), *The Emptiness of Japanese Affluence*, Armonk, NY: M.E. Sharpe.

McCreery, J. L. (2000), *Japanese Consumer Behaviour: From Worker Bees to Wary Shoppers: An Anthropologist Reads Research by the Hakuhodo Institute of Life and Living*, Richmond, Surrey: Curzon.

Maclachlan, P. (2002), *Consumer Politics in Postwar Japan*, New York: Columbia University Press.

Mann, R. J. (2002), 'Credit Cards and Debit Cards in the United States and Japan', *Vanderbilt Law Review*, 55: 1055.

Mann, R. J. (2006), *Charging Ahead: The Growth and Regulation of Payment Card Markets*, Cambridge: Cambridge University Press.

Mann, R. J. (2007), 'Bankruptcy Reform and The "Sweat Box" Of Credit Card Debt', *University of Illinois Law Review*, p. 375.

Mann, R. J. and Hawkins, J. (2007), 'Just until Payday', *UCLA Law Review*, 54: 855.

Matsumoto, T. (1994), 'EC Directive on Unfair Terms in Consumer Contracts and Japan: Does Japanese Law Meet the Standards Set by the Directive?', *Consumer Law Journal*, 2: 141.

Matsumoto, T. (2002), 'Privatization of Consumer Law: Current Developments and Features of Consumer Law in Japan at the Turn of the Century', *Hitotsubashi Journal of Law and Politics*, 30: 1.

Matsuura, I. (2001), 'Product Liability Law and Japanese-Style Dispute Resolution', *University of British Columbia Law Review*, 35(1): 135.

Milhaupt, C. J. and West, M. D. (2004), *Economic Organizations and Corporate Governance in Japan*, Oxford: Oxford University Press.

Milhaupt, C. J. and Pistor, K. (2008), *Law and Capitalism*, Chicago: University of Chicago Press.

Moehwald, U. (2000), 'Trends in Value Change in Contemporary Japan' in Eades, J.S., Gill, T., and Befu, H. (eds) *Globalization and Social Change in Contemporary Japan*, 55, Melbourne: Trans Pacific Press.

Mosher, M. (1998), 'Machiavellian Politics and Japanese Ideals: The Enigma of Japanese Power Eight Years Later', *Japan Policy Research Institute Paper*, 10.

Noda, Y. and Angelo, A. H. (1976), *Introduction to Japanese Law*, Tokyo; Forest Grove, OR: University of Tokyo Press.

Nottage, L. (2005b), 'Japan', in *CCH Doing Business in Asia* looseleaf, Singapore: CCH Asia, Singapore, para JPN ¶30-011.

Nottage, L. (1996), 'Form and Substance in US, English, New Zealand and Japanese Law: A Framework for Better Comparisons of Developments in the Law of Unfair Contracts', *Victoria University of Wellington Law Review*, 26: 247.

Nottage, L. (2002), *Form, Substance and Neo-Proceduralism in Comparative Contract Law: The Law in Books and the Law in Action in England, New Zealand, Japan and the US*, PhD Thesis, Law Faculty, Wellington: Victoria University of Wellington.

Nottage, L. (2004a), *Product Safety and Liability Law in Japan: From Minamata to Mad Cows*, London: RoutledgeCurzon.

Nottage, L. (2004b), 'Convergence, Divergence, and the Middle Way in Unifying or Harmonising Private Law', *Annual of German and European Law*, 1: 166.

Nottage, L. (2005a), 'Comparing Product Liability and Safety in Japan: From Minamata to Mad Cows to Mitsubishi', in Fairgrieve, D. (ed.), *Product Liability in Comparative Perspective*, Cambridge: Cambridge University Press, p. 334.

Nottage, L. (2005c), 'Redirecting Japan's Multi-Level Governance', in Hopt, K. J., Wymeersch, E., Kanada, H. and Baum, H. (eds), *Corporate Governance in Context: Corporations, State, and Markets in Europe, Japan, and the US*, Oxford: Oxford University Press, p. 571.

Nottage, L. (2006), 'The ABCs of Product Safety Re-Regulation in Japan: Asbestos, Buildings, Consumer Electrical Goods, and Schindler's Lifts', *Griffith Law Review*, 15(2): 242.

Nottage, L. (2007), 'Product Liability and Safety Regulation', in McAlinn, G. (ed.), *Japanese Business Law*, The Hague: Kluwer, p. 221.

Nottage, L. (2008), 'Product Safety Regulation Reform in Australia and Japan: Harmonising Towards European Models?', *Yearbook of Consumer Law*, 2: 429.

Nottage, L. (2009), 'Consumer Law Reform in Australia: Contemporary and Comparative Constructive Criticism', *Queensland University of Technology Law and Justice Journal*, 9(2): 111.

Nottage, L. (2010a), 'Japan' in duPlessis, J, Hargovan, A. and Bagaric M., *Principles of Corporate Governance*, Melbourne: Cambridge University Press.

Nottage, L. (2010b), 'Proposed Australian (and Canadian) Requirements to Disclose Consumer Product Related Accidents: Better Late Than Never?' *Sydney Law School Research Paper*, 10/41: http://ssrn.com/abstract=1600502.

Nottage, L. and Kano, H. (2009), 'Japan', in Kellam, J. (ed.), *Product Liability in the Asia-Pacific*, Sydney: Federation Press, p. 218.

Nottage, L. and Rheuben, J. (2008), 'Chinese Dumplings and Dodgy Foods in Japan: Implications for the Australia-Japan Free Trade Agreement', *Australian Product Liability Reporter*, 19(4): 50.

Nottage, L. and Trezise, M. (2003), 'Mad Cows and Japanese Consumers', *Australian Product Liability Reporter*, 14: 125.

Nottage, L. and Wada, Y. (1998), 'Japan's New Product Liability ADR Centers: Bureaucratic, Industry, or Consumer Informalism?' *Zeitschrift fuer Japansiches Recht*, 6: 40.

Nottage, L., Wolff, L. and Anderson, K. (eds) (2008), *Corporate Governance in the 21st Century: Japan's Gradual Transformation*, Cheltenham: Edward Elgar.

Omura, A. (1998), *Shohishaho [Consumer Law]*, Tokyo: Yuhikaku.

Pardieck, A. (2008), 'Japan and the Moneylenders: Activist Courts and Substantive Justice', *Pacific Rim Law and Policy Journal*, 17(3): 529.

Port, K. L. and McAlinn, G. P. (2003), *Comparative Law: Law and the Legal Process in Japan*, Durham, NC: Carolina Academic Press.

Ramseyer, J. M. and Nakazato, M. (1999), *Japanese Law: An Economic Approach*, Chicago: University of Chicago Press.

Scheiber, H. and Mayali, L. (eds) (2007), *Emerging Concepts of Rights in Japanese Law*, Berkeley: UC Berkeley – Robbins Collection.

Schoppa, L. J. (1997), *Bargaining with Japan: What American Pressure Can and Cannot Do*, New York; Chichester: Columbia University Press.

' "Shohishakeiyakuho" Hoan Teishutsu Miokuri [Presenting a Draft Law on Consumer Contracts Set Back]', *Nihon Keizai Shimbun*, 10 March 1999, p. 7.

Suda, S. (2006), *Karyugui – Shohisha Kinyu No Jittai [The Reality of the Consumer Finance Foodchain]*, Tokyo: Takuma Shinsho.

Tanase, T. (2010), *Law and the Community: A Critical Assessment of American Liberalism and Japanese Modernity*, Cheltenham: Edward Elgar.

Tani, M. (2009), 'Consumer Policy 2009', *RIETI Policy Updates*, 36, http://www.rieti.go.jp/en/special/policy-update/036.html.

TAPALS (ed.) (2006), TAPALS *Hakusho [White Paper]* 2006, Tokyo: TAPALS [Shohisha Kinyu Renrakukai].

Taylor, V. (1993), 'Continuing Transactions and Persistent Myths: Contracts in Contemporary Japan', *Melbourne University Law Review*, 19: 352.

Taylor, V. (1997), 'Consumer Contract Governance in a Deregulating Japan', *VUWLR*, 27: 99.

Upham, F. (1987), *Law and Social Change in Postwar Japan*, Cambridge, MA: Harvard University Press.

Van Wolferen, K. (1989), *The Enigma of Japanese Power: People and Politics in a Stateless Nation*, London: Macmillan.

Vogel, D. (1992), 'Consumer Protection and Protectionism in Japan', *Journal of Japanese Studies*, 18(1): 119.

Vogel, S. K. (1999) 'When Interests Are Not Preferences – The Cautionary Tale of Japanese Consumers', *Comparative Politics*, 31: 187.

Young, M. (1984), 'Judicial Review of Administrative Guidance: Governmentally Encouraged Consensual Dispute Resolution in Japan', *Columbia Law Review*, 84: 924.

Zweigert, K. and Kötz, H. (1998), *Introduction to Comparative Law*, Oxford; New York: Clarendon Press; Oxford University Press.

Part II
Japanese Consumer Groups

4
Elderly Consumers in Japan: The Most Mature 'Silver Market' Worldwide

Emmanuel J. Chéron

This chapter covers the senior consumer market in Japan. Although various terms and definitions have been used to identify the elderly consumer market in Japan, we will focus on Japanese consumers 50 years old and over. The term 'Silver market' is widely used in Japan to refer to elderly consumers in general.

The chapter is organized as follows. First, we present an overview of the current and future demographic situation of this market in Japan. Next, the purchasing power of the silver market will be discussed. Then, we introduce various ways that have been proposed to segment elderly Japanese consumers beyond descriptive variables such as age, gender and income. This will be linked to examples of practical applications developed by Japanese companies for targeting and positioning products and services in the market of elderly consumers. Finally, the chapter will focus in turn on examples of how the traditional controllable marketing decisions of products and services development, pricing policies, distribution channels and communication strategies have been implemented to better solve consumption needs and problems of the silver market in Japan.

Market structure of elderly consumers in Japan

Demography

As shown in Figure 4.1, Japan has the oldest median age in the world, at nearly 43 years. With Germany, Italy and Finland among others, Europe accounts for the other nine countries in the top 10 (*The Economist*, 2007). According to the latest provisional population estimates released by the Statistics Bureau of Japan on 1 April 2010, more than 23 per cent

Figure 4.1   Countries with highest median age
Source: UN Department of Economic and Social Affairs.

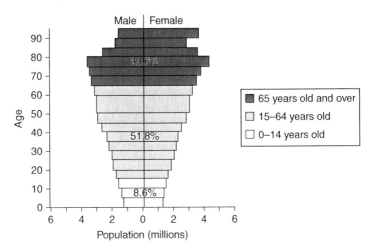

Figure 4.2   Japan's predicted population pyramid in 2050
Source: Statistics Bureau MIC: Ministry of Health, Labour and Welfare, 2010.

of Japan's population is at least 65 years old. The population aged 75 and older, called 'late stage elderly' (*kōki kōreisha*), accounts for 11 per cent. In addition, a low fertility rate means that the total Japanese population is starting to decline.

Demographic trends

As shown in Figure 4.2, the demographic group of 65 years old and above is expected to account for 39 per cent of the population by 2050. In addition compared to other developed countries like France, Switzerland and Sweden (respectively second, third and fourth), Japan has the highest life expectancy at birth, estimated at 79.6 years old for men and 86.4 for women (Statistics Bureau of Japan, 2009). With this even greater longevity, women are expected to form the overwhelming majority of those above the age of 75, as indicated in Figure 4.2.

The number of Japanese people of working age (between 20 and 64) per person aged 65 and above (the dependency ratio) is also expected to decrease from 3.6 in 2000 to 1.2 in 2050.

Geographical distribution of the elderly population of Japan

The population distribution of Japanese 65 years and older, indicates that areas with a high proportion of elderly Japanese are located mostly in rural areas (Statistical Maps of Japan, 2005). The prefectures with 25 per cent of the population 65 years old and over, are Akita and Yamagata, located in the North West of Honshu, and Shimane and Yamaguchi in the West. The prefecture of Kochi, in the South of Shikoku, is also in the same category. Thus, places outside the densely populated urban areas of Kanto, Nagoya and Kansai are at the forefront of dealing with the difficulties of organizing social and economic activities with a very high proportion of elderly people in the population. Those rural places struggle with the challenges of lack of young people and limited financial resources to support essential services, like cleaning up roads after a storm and taking care of the elderly. In some villages of those prefectures, schools have been closed and reopened as nursing homes for the elderly. In addition, lack of manpower resources means that able pensioners have no choice but to do their share of the work to support others and run the place (Dickie, 2009).

However, in order to identify promising potential markets, locations with a high proportion of elderly people must be qualified not only in terms of the absolute number of elderly consumers, but also in terms of available purchasing power. In addition, the elderly consumer groups targeted must show some willingness to buy offered products and services. This requires that products and services should be not only well adapted to the physical limitations of targeted markets, but also designed to be acceptable to older consumers in terms of the lifestyle which they aspire to and expect, and not perceived as being offensive.

Purchasing power

Elderly Japanese are known to be healthy and wealthy. According to the latest estimation of the Bank of Japan in Table 4.1, Japanese above 50 years old account for more than 80 per cent of a total of 1.439 quadrillion yen of financial assets (*The Nikkei Weekly*, 11 January 2010, p. 3). Japanese full-time employees who have been working for a long period with the same employer traditionally receive a large lump sum at retirement. This is intended to help maintain their standard of living, since retirement pay is on average quite low. With this overall very high level of accumulated wealth concentrated among the older generations of Japanese, it is not surprising that they attract the interest of many businesses in such sectors as health, financial, travel and leisure services.

Over the next 3 years, the average purchasing power of a household headed by someone in their sixties is projected to rise by about 580,000 yen (US$ 6,170) while figures for households headed by a thirty-something will fall by some 50,000 yen. According to government data, households headed by people in their sixties have average savings of 22.88 million yen and debt of 2.17 million yen, resulting in net savings of 20.71 million yen. These households also benefit from pension payments that do not decrease with deflation. On the other hand, households headed by someone in his or her thirties have average savings of 6.35 million yen and debt of 8.13 million yen for a net debt burden of 1.78 million yen. In addition, younger people are suffering in an environment of pay cuts. As a result, older people will see their purchasing power increase while younger people will see it going down (*The Nikkei Weekly*, 12 April 2010, p. 5).

Table 4.1 Generational breakdown of Japan's personal financial assets in per cent

Age group	Percentage of total financial assets (%)	Value (trillion yen)*
29 or younger	0.4	5.76
30–39	5.8	83.46
40–49	13.4	192.83
50–59	21.2	305.07
60–69	31.3	450.41
70 and older	27.9	401.48
	100.00	1,439.00

*Based on Bank of Japan's Flow of Funds statistics for July–September 2009 period.
Source: The Nikkei Veritas.

Segmentation and targeting

Because of its size and purchasing power, the market of elderly Japanese has attracted much attention. Many research studies have shown that this market is not homogeneous and needs detailed examination to understand driving needs and motives of various sub-segments. Traditional segmentation systems based on age groups, gender and income are easier to use, but they miss many variables influencing the buying behaviour of elderly people in Japan.

The Hakuhodo (2003) Dankai segmentation system, developed by the Hakuhodo advertising agency, surveyed a sample of 1,233 respondents from 50 to 74 years old. Answers to a series of statements related to perception regarding pleasant and unpleasant life events were used to develop the following five distinct segments in relation to level of health, social communication and financial situation:

- 'Happy' elders (16%) enjoying good health and social communication, and financially well off
- 'Independent' elders (26%) enjoying good health and good social communication with limited financial means
- 'Isolated' elders (24%) in good health but not enjoying good social communication
- 'Cooperative' elders (13%) not in good health but enjoying good social communication emphasizing mutual understanding
- 'Depressed' elders (21%) not enjoying either good health or good human relations

The five segments were then cross-tabulated with questions related to interest in advertising and sources of information on new products, on fashion, on famous brand names, and importance of brand name in buying decisions. Not surprisingly, the 'Happy elders' tended to report a greater interest than any of the other groups in all kinds of sources of information.

The Japanese Values and Lifestyle System (Japan VALS) was developed by Strategic Business Insights (2010) in collaboration with the Research Institute of System Science (RISS) of NTT Data and Communications Corp. The segmentation system relies on openness to innovation and social change in relation to three main lifestyles: tradition, practical achievement and self-expression orientations. According to this system, four main segments and life orientation sub-segments have been identified in relation to how quickly Japanese consumers innovate and adopt new products and services. The main segments, sub-segments and their relative sizes were defined as follows:

- *Integrators*: They combine the two life orientations of practical achievement and self-expression. They are the most informed and affluent; they are trend setters and travel frequently. They have been estimated to account for only 4 per cent of the Japanese population.
- *Innovators* (Subdivided into traditional, practical achievement or self-expression orientations): They account for 19 per cent and are likely to adopt new products and services quickly in relation to their life orientation. For example, traditional innovators will prefer familiar home furnishing and dress and hold conservative social opinions.
- *Adopters* (Subdivided into traditional, practical achievement or self-expression orientations): They account for 31 per cent and will tend to imitate the innovators within their respective life orientation, before adopting new products and services.
- *Followers* or 'me too' segments (Highly pragmatics, low pragmatics and sustainers): They account for 46 per cent of the population. Consumers in this segment are less well-informed, have fewer interests and are not committed to any of the three identified life orientations found for the innovators and adopters. Among the three sub-segments of followers, the sustainers were found to be older, with low education and purchasing power, most averse to innovation and oriented toward the past.

The merit of the Japan VALS segmentation system is to emphasize the importance of the degree of openness to innovation and the importance of targeting the innovators along the appropriate life orientation to drive the strong imitation process existing among Japanese consumers. However, apart from identification of the sustainer segment as older consumers, information about how other elderly Japanese consumers are distributed in this segmentation system is not publicly available.

A recent *Nikkei Marketing Journal* survey of a sample of 2,000 respondents around the age of 50, called 'arafifs', found that 15 per cent were willing to adopt new lifestyles and were ready to spend in spite of educational expenses for their children and their house mortgage. Using questions about interest in staying young and propensity to spend, 15 per cent of the respondents (mostly interested in staying young) were categorized as progressive 'arafifs'. Among 10 million 'arafifs' in Japan, about 15 per cent qualify as progressive. The progressive 'arafifs' enjoyed a net average household income of 9.34 million yen (US$100,000) in 2009. This amounts to 60 per cent more than for the average 'arafos' (those around the age of forty). Compared with 'arafos', the progressive 'arafifs' own twice as many smart phones and are more than twice as interested in buying one as the average 'arafos'. Progressive 'arafifs' use anti-ageing cosmetics twice as much as the average 'arafos' and are three times more interested in using them. However, progressive 'arafos' were found to speak more often with their spouses and to go out together more than the average 'arafifs'. Finally, 69.2 per cent of progressive 'arafifs' said their self-perceived age was at least 5 years younger than their chronological age. This turned out to be 30 per cent more than for the average 'arafos' (*The Nikkei Weekly*, 23 March 2009, p. 20).

As far as Japan is concerned, few studies on perceived age have been published. Among recent studies using self-perceived age (also called cognitive age) in Japan, Van Auken and Barry (2009) collected data among university-educated Japanese seniors. They found that cognitively younger Japanese have better self-perceptions of health, economic comfort, life satisfaction and ageing attitudes, as well as activity participation, compared with cognitively older Japanese. At the same time, however, the cognitively older Japanese in the same sample did not show evidence of a marked decline in health, economic comfort or life satisfaction, even though there was a downward shift in their ability to do things in connection with a declining health level. This may signal an onset of psychological ageing that impacts upon attitudes and activities, and even economic comfort.

In a recent survey of age perception of Japanese elderly (50 years old and over) in Tokyo, respondents were found, on average, to feel 8 years younger than their actual chronological age. In addition, the mean value differences between self-perceived age and chronological age for men and women were not found to be significantly different. The age difference between self-perceived age and chronological age was also found to decrease in relation to lower levels of wealth and health. Further, being in good health appeared to have more impact on the difference than wealth (Chéron and Kohlbacher, 2010). Published studies on self-perceived age in Japan confirm that the concept, developed for Western senior markets, can be extended to the Japanese context as a valid and potentially useful segmentation variable of senior consumers.

These segmentation systems and survey results are showing that the analysis of the silver market in Japan requires much more than variables related to age group, gender and income for a clear understanding of the consumption behaviour of key market sub-segments. In addition to cross-sectional analyses, longitudinal tracking of consumer behaviour over time may also help understand consumption patterns. Looking at cohorts of senior Japanese of similar age groups may reveal underlying consumption motivations. Some companies in Japan have been successful in using nostalgia to target age groups of consumers with products and services that were popular when they were young. The use of celebrities and music that were popular when the targeted consumers were in their twenties is often used in Japan. However, such a 'retro' marketing strategy is difficult to implement, since it also requires updating products and services to find an appropriate compromise between the past and the present level of technology, safety requirements and regulations.

Development of products and services for the silver market

Universal design, barrier-free design in housing, products and services to improve quality of life of elderly people and caregivers

When conducting R&D research on new household appliances, Panasonic places great importance on ease of use for elderly people. Researchers simulate the experience of an elderly user by wearing clothing that limits joint movements, thick gloves and glasses that reduce vision. This has allowed researchers of the Usability Promotion Team to find that ease of use can be hindered, for example, by space between buttons and lack of contrasting colours such as white and yellow (Tomiyama, 2004).

Using this approach, the company was very successful with a washer and dryer series designed with drums tilted 30 degrees. Another example is the complete redesign of the packaging of hearing aid batteries after visiting nursing homes and learning that the task of changing the battery was so much more difficult than expected. By changing the priority in its new products from new functional features to usability following research studies involving elderly people, Panasonic was able to achieve impressive sales results and market share.

Other examples are creative devices designed to help elderly people to take care of themselves and to simplify the work of caregivers. Manufacturers of such products emphasize in their mission the improvement of the quality of life of both elderly people and caregivers. As an example, the company Pigeon has developed an adjustable walker under the brand name of Habinurse, allowing users to select handle position and cart width according to four positions. The cart enables people with weak legs to get around on their own. Aronkasei Co. is another company that has designed a collapsible and easily foldable bath chair to enable older people to take a bath by themselves. Unicharm Corp. and Hitachi Ltd. have jointly developed a system that automatically removes urine from adult nappies. When built-in sensors detect urine on nappies, a pump is activated to remove the fluid. The system can reduce the need for caregivers to change nappies from up to four times a day to only once a day (*The Nikkei Weekly*, 15 June 2009, p. 18). With the growing number of elderly people, home renovation may be undertaken to remove obstacles such as different floor levels and to increase safety by adding handrails to stairs and hang grips in toilets and bathrooms. With more elderly people living alone, new support services are being offered, such as housekeeping conducted on a regular basis and electronic monitoring. These services also help to reduce the anxiety of children who feel unable to take care of their parents. The *Kajitaku* housekeeping service, offered in 23 wards of Tokyo, consists of cleaning the house and checking that everything is fine with seniors living on their own. Tokyo Security Co. offers a Senior Security service allowing subscribers to monitor how their parents living on their own are doing with an in-house sensor system. If there is no response at regular intervals, or if an emergency is detected, the children will be informed and security staff will be sent to the parents' home. When living alone is not possible, rental housing with nursing care from specialized staff is offered by companies such as Message Co. from Okayama (*The Nikkei Weekly*, 14 September 2009, p. 21).

Recent trends in new product development now try to include attractive design in addition to the concepts of usability and barrier-free access. The gradual upgrade of the original model of the *Raku Raku* (*Raku* means easy in Japanese) mobile phone is a striking example. While the first models were emphasizing extreme usability and simplicity to appeal to elderly consumers in Japan, they soon needed to be upgraded to appeal to elderly consumers afraid of being identified as being unable to use more modern fashionable mobile phones with sophisticated features.

An electromechanical device known as the Hybrid Assistive Limb (HAL), looking like a robotic suit, was developed by Cyberdyne Inc. at the University of Tsukuba in the prefecture of Ibaraki. The system allows a patient who has lost muscle power as a result of paralysis to be assisted to move on his or her own when electrical signals from the brain are detected by the system and transmitted to the artificial limbs (*The Nikkei Weekly*, 15 February 2010, p. 25).

A new system to e-mail pictures directly to an electronic frame in the grandparents' home has been developed by mobile phone internet providers such as DoCoMo and Softbank. It is only necessary to plug the frame into a power outlet and place it where it can receive a radio signal. This is very convenient when seniors are not familiar with computers and the Internet. Children of grandparents can send pictures of grandchildren by email, and they will be displayed on the frame at the grandparents' home. A system provided by the Internet provider allows the sender to add or remove pictures, to set up a slide show and to time when the frame is on or off (*The Nikkei Weekly*, 7 September 2009, p. 19). The success of this new service is dependent not only on the cost of the frame but also on the monthly communication fee. A future application that could make the device more useful is the facility to check remotely that grandparents are safe and well. In addition, when text can be displayed on the frame it allows companies to use this two-way communication system to display advertising as well as asking questions and receiving answers from users.

Purchases of reading glasses have increased rapidly among people 45 years old and over. For the large retailer of eyewear, Paris Miki Holdings Inc., sales of reading glasses accounted for more than 50 per cent of sales for the fiscal year ending in 2010.

The domestic market for disposable nappies has shown a reversal, with adult nappies rather than baby nappies now accounting for more than 40 per cent of the market.

To meet the needs of the growing number of elderly consumers at convenience stores, the size of price tags has been increased, shopping baskets made lighter, aisles made larger and shelves made lower. Convenience stores have also developed a special bento lunch box for seniors and increased the shelf space of *wagashi* (a sweet style of Japanese dessert). Prepared food, such as rice ready for the microwave oven, and smaller packages have been designed to meet the need of customers 50 years old and over.

To meet the need for companionship, toy manufacturers have developed talking dolls able to detect voices and to reply with a vocabulary of more than 1,000 words. According to a toy retailer in Tokyo, most buyers are in their fifties and sixties, and they buy the toy to overcome loneliness after their children have left home (*The Nikkei Weekly*, 2 November 2009, p. 25).

In 2009, after 2 years of research on nutrition and ageing, Nichirei Foods introduced a line of low-calorie, low-sodium balanced frozen meals for seniors, the 'Happy Aging' series. The amount of calcium and other nutrients contained in the meals is adapted to the needs of this age group. The target market is over-65 singles and couples, and meals can be easily heated in a microwave oven (Nichirei Press release, accessed 22 May 2010).

Products and services connected to nostalgia

Surveys conducted by the HOPE (Health, Opportunity and Participation for Elders) project of the Hakuhodo advertising agency revealed that for elderly Japanese, both men and women, happiness was most associated with their twenties. In later years, there is a continuous downward trend for men, but there is a resurgence of happiness for women in their fifties (see Figure 4.3). When asked to look back over their lives in decade-long periods, more elderly Japanese men and women said that their twenties were a happy period (76.6 per cent of men and 81.7 per cent of women gave this answer). Elderly Japanese had to face fierce competition, unique to this generation, for university entrance exams in the teenage years. They also grew up during a period glorifying youth culture, symbolized by the Beatles, folk songs and jeans.

Following the 20-year-old decade, there is a steady decline in happiness for men (only 46.4 per cent say they are happy now in their fifties). In contrast, there is an upturn of happiness for women after 50, with 67.8 per cent now saying they are happy. Perhaps, having finished child-rearing and paying off their mortgages, women now find they have the time and money to pursue their interests once again (Hakuhodo, 2006).

A survey conducted by the Cabinet Office (*The Nikkei Weekly*, 2 November 2009) confirmed that Japanese seniors, surrounded by material wealth, are looking for something deeper. The survey found that, while 44 per cent of people in their twenties were interested in material wealth, 66 per cent of those in their sixties were searching for happiness.

At Tokyo Disney Resort, older visitors are increasing in importance. More specifically, women in their fifties, who visited Disney theme parks with their children when they were in their twenties, like to come back to enjoy themselves with a group of friends (*The Nikkei Weekly*, 2 November 2009, p. 25).

Hakuhodo studies revealed that women in their fifties, who had once been proud of being seen as sensible and mature, now expect their friends to see them as looking young and having good taste. As a result, they tend to spend money on courses to educate themselves and to improve

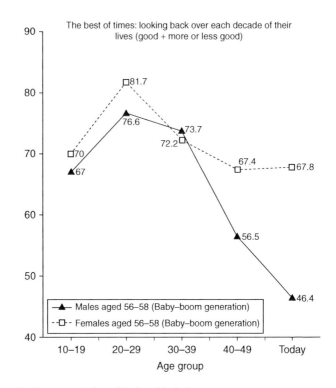

Figure 4.3   Happy periods in life for elderly Japanese

Source: Hakuhodo, 2006. Health, Opportunity and Participation for Elders (HOPE), Survey 2006, Japanese baby-boomers take stock of 60 years of life.

their bodies. Seeing this as an opportunity, karaoke chains and cultural centres started to offer a wide choice of courses in music, dance, language and flower arrangement. They target adult women with classes offered in the afternoon during weekdays. Following this trend, operators of sports clubs have seen the proportion of their customers above 50 years old double over the last 10 years. Curves Japan has been very successful in setting up women-only exercise centres emphasizing light exercise programmes and social communication among female customers.

Taking into account the desire of elderly Japanese women to look young, the cosmetics company Shiseido carried out research on the reasons for old-looking faces, skin colouring and sagging. After finding that the main reason was blood circulation, the company developed a new product line containing emollients to improve blood circulation and restore firmness. The new product line was called Elixir Prior for women over the age of 60. The product line is sold in pink packaging, a popular colour with the older generation. To benefit from nostalgia and the frequent use of celebrities in Japanese advertising, the company selected actress Bibari Maeda, who appeared in commercials for the company in 1966, as a spokeswoman for the product line (*The Nikkei Weekly*, 11 January 2010, p. 21). Another example of the use of nostalgia to target men is the retro design of the SR400 Yamaha motorcycle, looking like the traditional model from the past but with improved fuel injection and exhaust systems to meet new stricter environmental regulations (*The Nikkei Weekly*, 14 December 2009, p. 18).

Financial services, savings and future use for money

Financial services

When retiring, many elderly Japanese collect a large retirement bonus, and are then often re-employed. This money is most often not actively invested, and is therefore attracting the interest of financial companies (*The Nikkei Weekly*, 11 January 2010, p. 5). Some firms, such as Nomura Holdings Inc., have built branches with cafes to attract potential elderly customers. Some online brokers offer a 5 per cent discount to customers above 50 and 10 per cent to customers above 60 years old. Banks have set up clubs targeting customers with assets of 10 million yen or more to offer preferential interest rates and travel information. Financial institutions are also organizing investment seminars to encourage elderly customers to shift from savings to investment.

Savings

Surveys conducted by the Hakuhodo advertising agency about how elderly Japanese planned to invest their retirement benefits revealed that men would consider stocks (70.4 per cent) while women would favour safer term deposits (58.4 per cent). With investment trusts, these forms of investment account for the top three favourite investment vehicles.

There were differences in the investments of choice of men and women. Stocks were the leading choice of men (70.4 per cent), followed by investment trusts (57.0 per cent) and term deposits (45.9 per cent), while for women term deposits were the favourite choice (58.4 per cent), followed by stocks (50.6 per cent) and investment trusts (48.3 per cent). With half of the women expressing an interest in stocks, it appears that elderly Japanese are generally interested in investing their money (Hakuhodo, 2007).

Future use of money

In the same survey respondents were asked how they would use their retirement money. The top main three uses were domestic travel, international travel and personal interests. Both men and women most often allocated money available after retirement to domestic travel, personal interests and international travel. Personal interest in flat-screen TVs, other consumer electronics and home renovation were most often mentioned by both men and women. The genders differed regarding interest in spending on cars (43.5 per cent for men) and entertainment (40.7 per cent for women). The results suggest that elderly Japanese would like to enjoy a new lifestyle with a renovated home equipped with a new flat-screen TV, with electronic appliances and trips out in a new car (Hakuhodo, 2007).

Social life and communication

Surveys conducted by Hakuhodo (2007) among Japanese people aged 50 and over can give very good suggestions regarding types of services likely to be popular among elderly men and women. For example, the top three types of courses that elderly men were already involved in or would like to take up after retirement were cooking (19.9 per cent), languages and gardening (both 19.5 per cent). For women, they were computers (22.5 per cent), sports lessons (21.4 per cent) and languages (20.9 per cent). Men's strong interest in cooking is remarkable, closely followed by interest in languages and gardening. Providers of such services will benefit from the popularity of these trends, likely to be the focus of discussions and joint participation among Japanese retired people.

When asked about their life beyond 60, respondents said they would like to be involved in active social participation (through work and community work). Men wanted to spend 51.1 per cent of their time on such participation and women 41.7 per cent. More specifically, respondents were asked about the percentage of time they would like to spend on work, private life and community work when above 60 years old. The average results showed that, while both men and women definitely want to have their own private time (48.9 per cent of total time for men, 58.4 per cent for women), they also have a strong desire to participate in society through work (34.8 per cent of total time for men, 24.6 per cent for women) and community work (16.3 per cent of total time for men, 17.1 per cent for women). Thus, men look to spending 51.1 per cent of their time participating in society through work and community work, while women look to spending 41.7 per cent of time in this way (Hakuhodo, 2007).

Travel

Retired seniors have more time available to spend on leisure activities such as travel. When they retire, they are likely to be freed from child-raising costs, home loans and household responsibilities. Hence, they are more likely to travel more frequently, stay longer at destinations, travelling during off-peak holiday seasons, as well as travelling for longer distances, than the previous senior cohorts (Funck, 2008).

The current cohort of seniors is in better health, at an increased educational level, and with more travel experience than the previous cohorts of seniors. This allows them to continue travelling internationally or domestically (Funck, 2008). In fact, the increase in the proportion of the 'new senior' cohort is predicted to give rise to the highest growth rate in Japanese outbound tourism, and eventually overtake Japanese in their twenties to forties to be the largest market group in overseas travel by the year 2025 (Mak *et al.*, 2005).

The change in family structure in Japan has also changed seniors' travel consumption behaviours. The rise of the couple-only or single household structure has significantly increased disposable time and income, which could be diverted to leisure activities, including travel (*Statistical Handbook of Japan*, 2010).

Japanese seniors, especially female seniors, are also known to prefer packaged tours, especially special interest tours (Nitta, 2006), including non-inclusive packaged tours (air transportation tickets and accommodation only) (Lim and McAleer, 2005).

Japanese seniors also tend to travel in groups (Funck, 2008). According to a study by Japan's largest travel agency, Japan Travel Bureau (JTB), 50.3 per cent and 57.7 per cent of senior men and women (over 60 years old) respectively used package tours, while 10.1 per cent of men and 6.8 per cent of women (above 60 years old) used group tours.

The increase in elderly people travelling overseas led the travel agency JTB Corp. to open a subsidiary specializing in senior travel. With no time restrictions on seniors, their off-season travel helps to reduce sales fluctuations (*The Nikkei Weekly*, 2 November 2009, p. 25).

Pricing policies for the silver market

Special discounts and promotions are a commonly used marketing strategy by companies targeting seniors in Japan. These are often used to attract senior consumers during off-peak periods and because elderly people may be less easily reached by electronic media. It is, however, not clear whether elderly Japanese have positive or negative attitudes towards senior discounts. Is the acceptance of a discount also acceptance of old age? Is rejection of such promotions a coping strategy to reduce susceptibility to the elderly stereotype, as has been found among the youngest and the oldest subgroups of elderly consumers in Western countries? For elderly people who do not feel old, an offer of a discount may be seen as stigmatizing and therefore rejected.

In spite of uncertainty over the possible reaction of elderly Japanese to special discounts, there are many companies offering such marketing strategies. For example, The Miyuki Restaurant at the Four Seasons Hotel Chinzan-so in Tokyo offers a 21 per cent discount for seniors in an all-you-can-eat dinner (Four Seasons Hotel Chinzan-so). The Fiore Cafe-Restaurant at the Courtyard by Marriott Hotel Ginza (Tobu Hotel) in Tokyo offers a 17 per cent discount (up to 26 per cent on weekdays) to seniors for their buffet.

In connection with the advantage of attracting customers available during off-peak travel periods, many *onsen* (hot springs) resorts and hotels in Japan offer special discounts to seniors. For example, the Nagashima Onsen Resort Hotel in Nagoya offers a special plan for groups including over-60 guests on weekdays all year long (Nagashima Onsen Resort). For 2 weeks before and after the respect-for-the-aged holiday in September 2009, the Solare Hotel chain offered a 60 per cent discount for 60–69-year-olds, a 70 per cent discount for 70–79–year-olds, and so on (free for those at least 100 years old) (Solare Hotels). Oriental Land Co., the operating company of Disneyland and DisneySea in Tokyo, has started selling a special Wednesdays-only pass for the parks for people aged 45 and older, priced at 5,100 yen (*The Nikkei Weekly*, 2 November 2009, p. 25).

In the case of municipal public transport, over-70 seniors can buy a Silver pass for unlimited travel on the bus in Tokyo. In 2010, the price is 20,510 yen for a 1-year pass and 10,255 yen for purchases in the second half of the year. Low-income seniors can obtain the pass for 1,000 yen (Tokyo Bus).

The PC market for senior citizens has been recently targeted with special discount services and computer courses. Bic Camera Inc., a discount retailer of electronic appliances, and its subsidiary Sofmap Co. are offering service packages to consumers over the age of 60. The discount service, offered at less than half price, is called the Raku Raku Anshin Pack and includes delivery, setting up and connection of a personal computer (PC) to the Internet, with unlimited telephone support. Discount service packages for digital cameras and flat panel TVs include connecting printers or recorders for about half the price (*The Nikkei Weekly*, 7 September 2009, p. 20). PC Depot Corporation has also started to offer a senior discount to consumers over 65 years old for PC set-up and technical assistance. PC Depot discovered that elderly consumers who have no one to help them were happy to be offered the service at discount. With low PC sales, the industry felt that there was an untapped market potential among people aged 65 to 69, with computer usage of only 27.3 per cent, and even lower after 70 years old. In contrast, PC usage is much higher, at 86 per cent, among those between 30 and 50 years old. Manufacturers such as Fujitsu have also designed keyboards with different colours for vowels and consonants to help senior users.

Distribution channels for the silver market

Retailing

Sugamo, a shopping neighbourhood in northwestern Tokyo's Toshima ward, is offering a retail laboratory of solutions for shops serving the silver market in Japan. In Sugamo, the main shopping street called Jizo-dori is well known for attracting Japanese senior consumers coming to pray for good health at two popular temples, to shop for food and cloth-ing, and to socialize with their peers in an environment well adapted to their needs.

Sugamo's shopkeepers are pioneers in an increasingly important retailing speciality: selling to seniors. The local McDonald's menu lists French fries simply as 'potato' and Filet-O-Fish as 'fish hamburgers' (Odan, 2008).

Facing strong competition by integrated new formats of specialized retailing companies selling good-quality clothing at discounted prices, department stores are struggling with declining sales. Their high level of service and large choice of traditional products may still appeal to older Japanese consumers, provided the stores are redesigned with eld-erly people in mind. Some department stores have included more sitting areas and trained staff to help elderly people in their shopping activities. The case study of the Keio department store reported by Enomoto (2008) gives a detailed account of how the store was completely redesigned to appeal to the group of senior customers above 50 years old accounting for 70 per cent of sales. An example of redesign for senior customers was to arrange the women's clothing floor by item so that customers can choose clothing according to price, size and colour instead of by brand. In addition, the store layout was redesigned to make it easier to navigate, and an original store brand targeting seniors was developed. For exam-ple, a special shoe section was set up using what older Japanese cus-tomers value most: leisure, health, relaxation and safety. These changes in the department store product selections, with senior customers in mind, led to a significant improvement in sales.

Retailers in Japan need to be aware of the close relationships of elderly consumers with neighbourhood stores and the opportunity for socializing that they offer. Senior consumers have been found to react less to trends and advertising and rely more on word of mouth. When customers rely on word of mouth, top-quality service and communication become especially important. Senior consumers look for suitable merchandise, want to enjoy life and are interested in a more casual, healthy and beauty-conscious lifestyle (Enomoto, 2008).

Direct sales and online shopping

A survey conducted by the *Nikkei Marketing Journal* among 242 direct marketers found that direct sales increased 21.4 per cent in 2007 even though sales via mobile phones dropped by 3 per cent. The increase of direct sales was attributed to an increasing popularity of online shopping among senior consumers. Online shopping with home delivery is quickly catching on among people in their sixties and older, for whom going out shopping every day can be quite demanding. Traditional Japanese grocery shopping is done almost every day on foot or by bicycle, and it can be difficult for elderly people to carry home heavy items such as bags of rice and beverages. In addition to convenience, older Japanese consumers tend to be concerned about healthy lifestyle and food safety. They tend to be interested in direct marketers offering organic food and natural regional products. As an example, Oisix Inc., located in Tokyo, offers organic vegetables and its own brand of natural regional mineral water. During the year 2007, this company attracted 20 per cent of new customers in the age group 60 years old and above. According to direct marketers, once older Japanese consumers are satisfied with their products and services they tend to be more loyal and less likely to switch to other online shopping services than younger customers (*The Nikkei Weekly*, 27 October 2008, p. 37).

Communication and promotional mix for the silver market

Advertising: TV, radio, newspapers, magazines

As shown in Figure 4.4, the higher the age group, the longer the average time spent on watching TV, as either a main activity or a simultaneous activity. The average time of 2.49 hours for both sexes goes up to 3.05, 3.49 and 4.22 respectively for those 55 to 64 years old, 65 to 74 and 75 and above. In addition, average time is higher for men than for women, with 3.09, 4.04 and 4.42 hours respectively (Statistics Bureau of Japan,

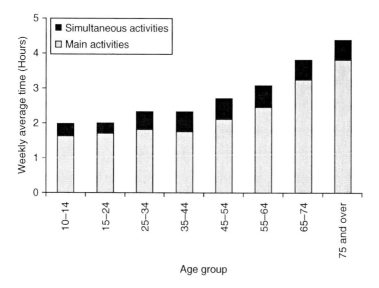

Figure 4.4   Weekly average time watching TV by age group (as a main and simultaneous activity)

Source: Statistics Bureau of Japan, 2007.

2007). Television, which still accounts for 28.5 per cent of advertising expenditures in Japan, (Dentsu, 2008) is thus likely to be an important part of the traditional media mix for companies interested in reaching elderly consumers in Japan.

A large-scale content analysis study on the representation of Japanese older people in television advertising at two points in time (1997 and 2007) looked at the age and gender distribution of people appearing in advertising (Prieler *et al.*, 2008). The only age group showing an increase from 1997 (13.7 per cent) to 2007 (21.4 per cent) was found to be between 50 and 64 years old. In comparison with census data of the Japanese population, all age groups below 50 years old tended to be strongly over-represented in TV ads and those over 65 were under-represented. Only the frequency of those between 50 and 64 was similar to the census. In terms of gender, females outnumbered males up to 34 years old, and males were over-represented for all age groups above 35 years old. As discussed in the section on demographics, with longer longevity, the number of females is dominant in higher age groups in Japan. Thus, the distribution results indicated that older females are strongly under-represented in Japanese TV advertising. Further investigation indicated that among older people shown in TV ads in Japan almost 50 per cent on average were celebrities (either male or female). It was also found that commercials with older people tended to be longer. This can be expected, since, to be more effective, commercials targeting older audiences will work better with slower forms of communication such as information-based commercials or teleshopping demonstrations.

The relative importance of radio in the traditional media mix in Japan is small, around 2.3 per cent (Dentsu, 2008), and has been gradually declining. It can still be a source of commercial information used by elderly people with sufficient hearing capacity. Some commercial radio programs specifically target older consumer groups with nostalgic music from the period when the target group was in its twenties. Establishments, like hotels, *onsen* and karaoke bars, with many elderly customers offer nostalgic music selections, sometimes directly broadcast from commercial radio stations through loudspeakers inside their buildings and even shuttle buses.

Japanese newspapers enjoy the largest circulation in the world. For example, the *Yomiuri Shimbun* sells 10 million copies each morning and another 3.6 million in the evening. The *Asahi Shimbun* sells 8 million copies of its morning edition. According to the *Nihon Shimbun Kyokai* (*NSK*), the combined circulation of morning and evening newspapers fell by only 6.3 per cent between 1999 and 2009. In spite of their apparent strength, newspapers in Japan are gradually losing young readers (only slightly above 50 per cent of those 21 to 30 years old read newspapers, compared with more than 80 per cent of those over 50 and over 60 years old). Newspapers account for 12.4 per cent of the advertising expenditures in Japan (Dentsu, 2008) and they are still an important and credible source of information for elderly Japanese. They should remain part of the media mix targeting elderly Japanese. However they are in danger of serious collapse in future when their elderly readers' eyesight fails (*The Economist*, 2010).

Magazines account for 6.1 per cent of advertising expenditures (Dentsu, 2008). They may be a good source of information for elderly consumers in Japan interested in specific hobbies, leisure activities, travel and fashion. Some magazines have succeeded in serving as a fashion reference for some specific age groups of Japanese consumers. An example is *Hanako*, a magazine targeting Japanese women born between 1959 and 1964. This group of women experienced the height of the Japanese consumption affluence. They were more aware than previous generations of group values, appearance, looks, fashion and new things. The *Hanako* magazine served as a reference to show where to go and what to buy to be fashionable. Because of its past credibility, this magazine still has a following of women now in their fifties and above looking for advice on fashion.

Internet and social networking

The degree of exposure of elderly Japanese to the Internet can be estimated from a large-scale survey on time use and leisure activities conducted by the Statistics Bureau of Japan (2007). The survey explored time spent using the Internet. Figure 4.5 shows how participation in and average use of the Internet varies by sex and age groups. Although use of the Internet tends to decline with age for women, it appears to be stable for men, with a slight increase for the age group between 55 and 64 years old.

The Internet accounts for 10.4 per cent of advertising expenditures in Japan (Dentsu, 2008). The strong success of convenient online grocery shopping appears to have been related to Japanese seniors getting accustomed to using the Internet. After noting the loyalty of senior customers, companies have started to expand their offer of products and services to seniors. With the increasing networking of Japanese seniors, companies have offered package tours in partnership with travel agencies. The experience has shown that there is demand and interest in buying cheap domestic tours to famous hot spring resorts, as well as expensive travel tours overseas, over the Internet (*The Nikkei Weekly*, 27 October 2008, p. 37).

In response to this new trend of senior Japanese joining social communities over the Internet, companies have set up virtual groups of elderly consumers who share their consumption experiences. One of them, dedicated to marketing research among elderly consumers, is Senior Communications Co., Ltd. (2007). The company has set up a website for opinion leaders above 50 years old to join group interviews for product and service development and to answer questions in sur-

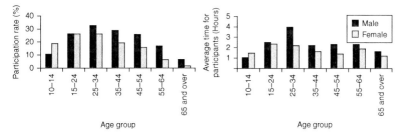

Figure 4.5   Participation rate and average time spent on the Internet by sex and by age group (weekly average)

Source: Statistics Bureau of Japan, 2007.

veys. As a reward, they receive points that can be exchanged for gifts. They also feel that they play a more active role in the market and that they contribute to society, which gives them a sense of achievement. In addition, an interactive Internet community has been set up to understand in depth the needs of mature people and help predict future changes in the Japanese senior market.

With its experience of senior Japanese consumers, Senior Communications describes them as refined consumers who do not usually believe advertisements but tend to listen to what a celebrity or a friend says. Word of mouth is thus a key source of information for older Japanese consumers. Seniors, especially men, show a strong desire to belong to a community or be connected with others when they reach retirement. It seems that the Internet is helping them to be connected. In fact, Japanese seniors have been catching up fast with younger people, becoming more familiar with the Internet and enthusiastic technology adopters (Senior Communications Co., Ltd., 2007).

According to its 'Company Profile' report, Senior Communications Co., Ltd. (2007), the Japanese senior market is characterized by the following seven key concerns and interests:

1. Efficient consumption time: Seniors want to enjoy their time without spending too much and they try not to waste time on routine work at home.
2. Recycling life: They are ready to start something new, such as life-long study and courses on culture. Change perspective from a 'parents' to a 'husband/wife' lifestyle.
3. Real thing: Seniors resent anything fake, and are interested in standards of true value.
4. Community: Seniors want to join groups sharing the same hobbies, and resent meetings organized for elderly people. They tend to show interest in politics, economy and social activities.
5. Peace of mind: Seniors are interested in being in good spirits but concerned about their health status in the future. They worry about their future financial situation. They are interested in simple solutions, such as a one-key condominium home.
6. Human bonding: Older Japanese want to bond with others; they are interested in attending social events to make friends and they enjoy the company of their grandchildren.
7. Inverse life: They wish that they looked from 10 per cent to 20 per cent younger than they are. They feel offended when categorized as 'silver' or 'middle-age/older' people.

In reference to this last point, marketing research conducted in the US has found that older consumers can be sensitive to words and expressions that they consider offensive. For example, the term 'senior consumers' was perceived to be negative and was replaced by 'mature consumers'. Similarly in Japan, the silver market has been found to be sensitive to expressions they perceive as offensive. For example, in April 2008 the government of Japan launched the Late-stage Elderly Health Insurance System to better cover people aged 75 and older. While the system was criticized for various administrative shortcomings, the name was considered offensive. Many felt that 'late-stage elderly' was unacceptable, so the government renamed it 'Long-Life Medical Health Insurance System'. Conducting appropriate pretesting among older consumers could have prevented such mistakes (Pinktentacle, 2008).

Conclusion

According to Hakuhodo's Elder Business Development Division, three things will characterize the age of the elderly in Japan: 1) A population ageing more rapidly than any other anywhere in the world; 2) the emergence of a group of older members of society who really want to enjoy life; and 3) elders generally uneasy about their physical and financial staying power (Hakuhodo, 2010). The current drop in personal consumption has been partly attributed to lower consumer spending by middle-aged and older Japanese. According to the Hakuhodo advertising agency, research studies on issues affecting the lives of Japan's elders contribute to understanding and shaping richer and less uneasy lifestyles, more in touch with the needs of today's older people. Efforts to identify elder lifestyles that reduce uneasiness and renew interest in life can help revive consumption by Japanese elders and thus contribute to improving the Japanese economy.

The silver market in Japan can be seen as bringing huge demographic and financial challenges for the future in terms of health care and social burden, with numerous and difficult government measures needed to find solutions. From a consumer behaviour perspective, the current and future larger size of the silver market means that no private or public organization in Japan can afford to ignore it. This chapter has attempted to shed light on marketing research approaches and practices that can help to better understand the structure of this market. With more relevant information about different segments of the silver market, more successful marketing programmes can be developed to better solve the consumption problems of elderly consumers to the benefit of profit and non-profit organizations serving them.

References

Blazey, M. A. (1987), 'The Differences Between Participants and Non-participants in a Senior Travel Program', *Journal of Travel Research*, 26 (Summer): 7–12.
Chéron, E. and Kohlbacher, F. (2010), 'Understanding Older Consumers through Cognitive Age, Health Condition and Financial Status: Empirical Evidence from Japan', accepted for presentation at the 2010 American Marketing Association Summer Marketing Educators' Conference, Boston, Massachusetts, 13–16 August.
Dentsu, 'Advertising Expenditures by Medium (2006–2008)', available at http://www.dentsu.com/marketing/pdf/expenditures_2008.pdf (accessed 11 May 2010).
Dickie, M., 'Japan's Fiscal Frailty', *Financial Times*, 3 August, available at http://www.ft.com/cms/s/0/c9ca56b0-806d-11de-bf04-00144feabdc0.html?nclick_check=1# (accessed 11 May 2010).
Enomoto, E. (2008), 'Changing Consumer Values and Behavior in Japan: Adaptation of Keio Department Store Shinjuku', chap. 15, pp. 225–55, in Kohlbacher, F. and Herstatt, C. (eds), *The Silver Market Phenomenon. Business Opportunities in an Era of Demographic Change*, Heidelberg: Springer Verlag.
Four Seasons Hotel Chinzanso, available at http://www.fourseasons-tokyo.com/restaurant/plan/plan2/201005_000346.html (accessed 11 May 2010).
Funck, C. (2008), 'Ageing Tourists, Ageing Destinations: Tourism and Demographic Change in Japan', in Coulmas, F., Conrad, H., Schad-Seifert, A. and Vogt, G., *The Demographic Challenge: A Handbook about Japan*, Boston: BRILL, pp. 579–98.
Hakuhodo (2003), *Seikatsu Sōgo Kenkyūjo: Kyodai shijō 'erudā' no tanjō [The Birth of the Colossal 'Elder Market']*, Tokyo: Purejidentosha.
Hakuhodo (2006), Health, Opportunity and Participation for Elders (HOPE), Survey 2006 : 'Japanese Baby-Boomers Take Stock of 60 Years of Life', available at http://www.h-hope.net/english (accessed 11 May 2010).
Hakuhodo (2007), Health, Opportunity and Participation for Elders (HOPE), Report 2007: 'Baby-Boomers Heading into Retirement 3: Spousal Relations', available at http://www.h-hope.net/english (accessed 11 May 2010).
Hakuhodo (2010), Health, Opportunity and Participation for Elders (HOPE), 'Elder Lifestyle', available at http://www.h-hope.net/english/issues/02_life-styles/index.html (accessed 11 May 2010).
JTB (2003), *JTB Report 2003: All About Japanese Overseas Travelers*, Tokyo: JTB.
Kite, M. E., Stockdale, G. D., Whitley, B. E. Jr and Johnson, B. T. (2005) 'Attitudes Toward Younger and Older Adults: An Updated Meta-analytic Review', *Journal of Social Issues*, 61(2): 241–66.
Lim, C. and McAleer, M. (2005), 'Analyzing the Behavioral Trends in Tourist Arrivals from Japan to Australia', *Journal of Travel Research*, 43(4): 414–21.
Mak, J., Carlile, L. and Dai, S. (2005), 'Impact of Population Aging on Japanese International Travel to 2025', *Journal of Travel Research*, 44(2): 151–62.
Nagashima Onsen Resort, available at http://www.nagashima-onsen.co.jp/page.jsp?id=1931 (accessed 22 May 2010).

Nichirei Press, available at http://www.nichirei.co.jp/news/2009/186.html (accessed 22 May 2010).

Nitta, H. (2006), *Capitalizing on Retirement of Japan's First Baby-boomers*, Tokyo: Japan External Trade Organization (JETRO) (Japan Economic Report, 2006).

Odan, Y. (2008), 'Postcard: Tokyo', *Time Magazine*, Thursday 21 February , available at http://www.time.com/time/magazine/article/0,9171,1715074,00.html (accessed 15 May 2010).

Pinktentacle (2008), available at http://www.pinktentacle.com/2008/11/top-60-popular-japanese-words-phrases-of-2008/#9 (accessed 15 May 2010).

Prieler, M., Kohlbacher, F., Shigeru, H. and Akie, A. (2008), *The Representation of Older People in Japanese Television Advertising*, Tokyo: Deutsches Institut für Japanstudien / Stiftung D.G.I.A., p. 44.

Senior Communications Co., Ltd. (2007), 'Corporate Profile', available at http://www.senior-com.co.jp/english/index.html (accessed 23 May 2010).

Solare Hotels, available at http://news.livedoor.com/article/detail/4322955/ (accessed 15 May 2010).

Statistical Maps of Japan (2005), 'Population Census of Japan 2005, Proportion of Aged Population (65 Years and over) by Prefecture and by Shi Ku Machi and Mura', available at http://www.stat.go.jp/english/data/chiri/map/c_koku/index172.htm

Statistics Bureau of Japan (2007), '2006 Survey on Time Use and Leisure Activities', Questionnaire B, available at http://www.stat.go.jp/english/data/shakai/2006/pdf/jikan-a.pdf (accessed 9 May 2010).

Statistics Bureau of Japan (2009), 'Life Expectancy at Birth by Country', available at http://www.stat.go.jp/english/data/handbook/c02cont.htm (accessed 24 September 2010).

Statistics Bureau of Japan (2010), 'Provisional Population Estimates', 1 April, available at http://www.stat.go.jp/english/data/jinsui/tsuki/index.htm (accessed 9 May 2010).

Statistics Bureau of Japan (2010), *Statistical Handbook of Japan*, available at http://www.stat.go.jp/english/data/handbook/pdf/f2_8.pdf (accessed 24 September 2010).

Strategic Business Insights (2010), available at http://www.strategicbusinessinsights.com/vals/jvals.shtml (accessed 14 May 2010).

The Economist (2007), 'Golden Oldies', 18 April, available at http://www.economist.com/research/articlesBySubject/displaystory.cfm?subjectid=7933596&story_id=9032214 (accessed 9 May 2010).

The Economist (2010), 'The Teetering Giants', 4 February.

The Nikkei Weekly (2008), 'Devices Enhance Lives of Elderly', 15 June, p.18.

The Nikkei Weekly (2008), 'Grandma, Grandpa Find New Shopping Center – the Net', 27 October, p. 37.

The Nikkei Weekly (2009), ' "Arafifs" Show Spending Power', 23 March, p. 20.

The Nikkei Weekly (2009), 'Are Grandparents Only Ones Who Will Use Latest Digital Photo Frames?', 7 September, p. 19.

The Nikkei Weekly (2009), 'PC Industry Eyes Seniors for Growth', 7 September , p. 20.

The Nikkei Weekly (2009), 'Adult Children Can Worry Less About Parents', 14 September , p. 21.

The Nikkei Weekly (2009), 'Graying of Japan's Population Puts Older Set in Marketing Driver's Seat', 2 November, p. 25.

The Nikkei Weekly (2009), 'Yamaha Classic Revival', 14 December, p. 18.

The Nikkei Weekly (2010), 'Boomers Wield Financial Clout', 11 January, p. 3.

The Nikkei Weekly (2010), 'Nikkei Marketing Journal Award', 11 January, p. 21.

The Nikkei Weekly (2010), ' "Silver New Deal" Would Do Much to Brighten Japan's Gray Future', 15 February, p. 25.

The Nikkei Weekly (2010), 'Older Generations Carry Consumption', 12 April, p. 5.

Thompson, N. J. and Thompson, K. E. (2009), 'Can Marketing Practice Keep up with Europe's Aging Population?', *European Journal of Marketing*, 43(11): 1281–8.

Tobu Hotel, available at http://www.tobuhotel.co.jp/ginza/restaurants/fiore. html (accessed 14 May 2010).

Tokyo Bus, available at http://www.tokyobus.or.jp/silver/index.html (accessed 14 May 2010).

Tomiyama, A. (2004), 'Matsushita Wins with Smart Design', *The Nikkei Weekly*, September 13, p. 20.

Van Auken, S. and Barry, T. E. (2009), 'Assessing the Nomological Validity of a Cognitive Age Segmentation of Japanese Seniors', *Asia Pacific Journal of Marketing and Logistics*, 21(3): 315–28.

5
The Single Market
Kristie Collins

This chapter will provide an overview of the single Japanese consumer group and highlight particular consumer behaviour characteristics and current trends related to this sector. While the single consumer group has become an increasingly important consumer segment worldwide, population demographic projections indicate that this group will be especially important to Japan's economic future as its population continues to age and the birth rate steadily drops. As this chapter will demonstrate, companies need to better take into account single Japanese consumers of all ages and plan for this consumer segment to grow rapidly in forthcoming years. Particularly as the Japanese economy prepares itself for impending economic recovery and a return to greater prosperity, the key to tapping into business success may lie in the recruitment and retention of the single market.

Single consumers

Singles, as a demographic, are often – erroneously – categorized as a monolithic group with a universal profile. Perceived as simply the converse of the 'married' demographic, the diversity of single experience is habitually overlooked and often presumed to be an unchosen or temporary social status. In fact, singles can be never-married, widowed, or divorced individuals – situations that impact differently upon one's economic and social capital – and they may or may not have children or other dependants in their lives, just as married individuals do. While normative life course patterns have traditionally marked marriage as the transition to 'adult' status in most cultures worldwide, contemporary societies are increasingly being presented with more individualized life choices that allow men and women alternative ways of accessing 'adulthood' through life course paths such as continued education or entry into the workforce. Particularly in the case of single women, access to financial independence through increasing participation in the workforce has called into question the necessity – and desirability – of marriage. And, as recent census figures from the United States indicate, there are actually now more *un*married than married individuals heading households in the US, a trend becoming more prevalent in Japan as well, and thus the importance of the single demographic is coming into focus as a target consumer group worldwide (*Unmarried America*).

Japanese single consumers

The context of Japanese singles and their profile as consumers, however, present various issues that set them apart from singles living elsewhere. For instance, while marriage was a near-universal occurrence in pre-World War II Japan due to the prevalence of arranged marriages, the nation is now one of the latest-marrying populations in the world, and statistics suggest growing numbers of singles in Japan may never marry (as opposed to the large numbers of previously-married singles that make up the single consumer demographic in North America and Europe). Robert D. Retherford, Naohiro Ogawa and Rikiya Matsukura (2001) note the dramatic drop in arranged marriages over the past half-century and its resulting implications for the family and community networks that previously played a part in these arrangements:

> Modernization and the accompanying rise of individualism have eroded the extended family and the local community networks that historically formed the basis for arranged marriage … [B]etween 1955 and 1998 the proportion of marriages that were arranged fell from 63 to 7 per cent … [and the] decline in arranged marriage appears to be closely linked to the end of universal marriage in Japan. (Retherford *et al.*, 2001, p. 86)

The most recent figures available from the Japanese Statistics Bureau support this claim, and provide evidence that numbers of never-married and previously married Japanese men and women are continuing to rise (Ministry of Internal Affairs and Communications). The data from the 2005 census listed the number of single Japanese men over the age of 15 as just short of 20,000,000 (out of 53,000,000 men) and the female statistical counterpart as nearly 24,000,000 (of nearly 57,000,000 women). The survey results also showed an escalation of more than 4 per cent in the ratio of never-married Japanese individuals – male and female – aged 20 to 29, 30 to 39, and 40 to 49, between the 2000 and 2005 census reports, suggesting that marriage rates may still be continuing to drop (see summarized findings at http://www.stat. go.jp/english/data/kokusei/2005/kihon1/00/03.htm [accessed 3 April 2010]).

And yet, while the multigenerational and extended family configurations of the past may be less widespread in contemporary Japan, the arrangement of children living with parents extends far longer into adulthood in Japan than in other late-marrying societies, suggesting that delayed marriage and long-term singleness does not necessarily equate to living alone and taking on the financial responsibilities associated with adult singleness elsewhere. Studies suggest that this is partially due, culturally, to the limited need for independence – from both parents' and children's perspectives – and partly to the considerable social and economic obstacles faced by those who choose to live independently (Raymo and Ono, 2004). According to Mariko Tran, who researches the 'parasite single' phenomenon in Japan,

> Estimates suggest that as many as 60 per cent of single young men and 80 per cent of single young women are living with their parents. International comparisons indicate that these figures show Japan as having the highest ratio in the world of single young adults living at home with their parents. (Tran, 2006, para 5)

'Parasite singles', a term coined by sociologist Masahiro Yamada of Tokyo Gakugei University in 1997, refers to the growing number of single, employed Japanese adults who live in their parents' homes and offer little or no contribution toward household expenses (Tran, 2006, paragraph 1). While Tran gauges the number of parasite singles in Japan to be up to 60 per cent of young men and 80 per cent of young women, other studies have estimated numbers rising as high as 94 per cent for single young women (Retherford *et al.*, 2001). Analysts remain divided, however, on both the economic and social repercussions of the parasite singles trend. Since many of the parasite singles are employed and earning reasonably good salaries, it has been suggested that they fuel the economy through their consumption of high-end goods and services; on the other hand, it is argued that, by living with their parents, they adversely affect the sales of household goods (such as appliances and large furniture items) and hurt the real estate market (Tran, 2006). Furthermore, there are other subcategories of the 'parasite singles' group, including NEET (those Not in Education, Employment or Training) and 'freeter' (a contraction of the English 'free' and German 'arbeiter', or worker, referring to those employed in part-time or non-permanent jobs) singles who also live at home with parents and earn less than USD$1,000 per month, contributing little to the economy in the consumption of goods or services (Tran, 2006; Hashimoto, online report).These concerns will be explored in greater detail later in the chapter.

Another segment of note in the larger Japanese single consumer category is a group referred to as the 'ARAFO' segment (a hybrid of the English words 'around 40'), and, as the term implies, it is made up of single women around the age of 40. Comprising 20–30 per cent of the unmarried, urban Japanese population, ARAFO women are pursued by marketers who recognize them as 'moneyed, mobile, and mainly metropolitan' (*Japan Market Intelligence* report). Having completed their education and/or training at the time the Equal Employment Opportunity Law was enacted in 1986, these single women have earned career advancement opportunities previously unseen by working women in Japan and, as a result, have garnered great earning power and self-knowledge as they approach midlife. Japan Market Intelligence, a market research company that assists international businesses in establishing themselves in Japan, identifies three distinct areas to develop with respect to the ARAFO segment: beauty, health and home (*Japan Market Intelligence* website). As with many single working women residing elsewhere, the 'around 40' women of Japan opt to invest much of their hard-earned money in retail therapy; life choice reassurance in the form of health and beauty products; yoga classes and high-end cooking collections; and real estate and home improvement projects. And, just as the importance of 'the female economy' is gradually being accepted around the world, analysts in Japan anticipate that the role of the ARAFO segment will play a pivotal role in sustaining – and even salvaging – the stalled Japanese economy:

> With the Japanese economy slowing and consumer confidence declining, it is expected that the ARAFO will moderate their lifestyles and more closely manage their spend. However with Japan experiencing net population loss, due to falling birth rates and almost no net immigration, it is likely that the market will increasingly turn

to relatively untouched segments such as single women around 40. (*Japan Market Intelligence*, paragraphs 20–1)

Alongside the mounting numbers of single adults living at home with parents into their twenties and thirties (parasite singles), and growing numbers of successful single women living on their own in their thirties and forties (ARAFO singles), studies also present escalating numbers of single senior citizens in Japan: the 'silver aristocrats'. While figures show that Japanese women will typically outlive their spouses – a common scenario for women in all developed nations – Japanese men also tend to enjoy longer lifespans than do men living in other developed parts of the world, regularly living healthy lives into their late seventies (while Japanese women live on average into their mid-eighties). As the employment structure in Japan is based on a pay scale that incrementally rewards the oldest and longest-serving employees in a company, this aged single demographic is a consumer group with considerable wealth. In fact, some reports suggest that as much as 70 per cent of privately owned assets, including real estate, belong to individuals over the age of 50 (MasterCard Worldwide Insights Report, 2005). And the high ratio of senior citizens in Japan is only going to continue to grow:

> Japan's population is expected to shrink from its present 127 million to about 100 million by 2050...By 2025, over a quarter of Japan's population will be over 65 years old. Japan today has around 20,000 centenarians, a segment that is growing fast, and most of them are women, as they generally outlive men. (MasterCard Worldwide Insights Report, 2005, pp. 1–2)

Thus, in a 2005 report on the Japanese female consumer market, part of a larger review of consumption trends in the Asia/Pacific region, MasterCard International identifies the two key demographics to watch in the coming years: the young singles and the old singles. They note that these dominant segments emerged as a consequence of delayed (or disavowed) marriage for the younger demographic, and increasingly active lifestyles that have positively impacted on (particularly women's) longevity for the older demographic, and attest that both groups will play pivotal roles as consumer segments. The study suggests that the more prominent role, in fact, will likely be played by the 'silver aristocrats', due to their segment's projected growth in forthcoming years, and posit that '*[e]lderly women, as represented by both the empty nesters and old singles segments, will command some US$313 billion of spending power in 2013.*' (emphasis in original). The key, the report concludes, will be in meeting the demand for services for this segment and will hinge on businesses' capacity to innovate.

It is evident that the single Japanese consumer demographic – one that spans both gender and generation – is a key market player. However, the product and service demands of the 'parasite single' are certain to be different from those of the 'ARAFO single', just as they are undoubtedly different between 'parasite single' and 'silver aristocrat single'. In order to establish effective marketing strategies to attract this critical demographic, we turn next to a review of the consumer behaviour of the single Japanese consumer segment.

Single Japanese consumer behaviour

As noted in the previous section, single Japanese consumers are not a monolithic category, and thus, to be more clearly understood, will be examined in this section in the distinct subgroupings of 'parasite single', 'ARAFO single' and 'silver aristocrat single'. While these sub-categorizations do not have set age delineations that define membership, we will propose that 'parasite singles' generally fall into the age range of 22 to 35 years old, the 'ARAFO single' is typically a (female) single between the ages of 36 and 45, and the 'silver aristocrat single' segment is further divided into 'junior seniors' aged 60 to 70 and those in '*old* old age', past the age of 75. These distinct analyses will allow for a more comprehensive overview of consumer behaviour in the single Japanese demographic, and will provide insights into the product and service demands of this fast-growing and increasingly powerful consumer group.

The parasite single segment is the most diverse of the single Japanese consumer subgroups, as it is comprised of *NEET* and *freeter* individuals who earn low salaries and have less disposable income for consumption purposes, and higher-earning parasite singles who – by living at home rent-free with parents – are able to invest the bulk of their salaries in coveted products and services. And yet, even the lower-earning parasite singles are able to spend their small wages on trendy mobile phones, socializing with friends and purchasing fashionable apparel, since they are not responsible for covering their living expenses. Particularly in regard to product and service areas of the luxury market, the (female) parasite single demographic is viewed as a lucrative consumer group. As Tran explains, (female) parasite singles

> ...spend the majority of their income on goods and services, particularly at high-end restaurants and shops and thus are seen as important consumers fueling the consumer market. With 40 per cent of their sales coming from parasite singles, companies doing business in the Japanese luxury market are sure to see parasite singles in a positive light. (Tran, 2006, paragraph 15)

As with many studies of single demographics (both within and outside Japan), much discussion on single Japanese consumers focuses on single *female* consumers. However, it is important to take note that young men also make up a significant part of the parasite single population. Information on their consumer behaviour is sparser than on that of their female counterparts, but it can be presumed that a large proportion of male single parasite consumption is directed towards technology-related purchases, sport and leisure time expenses, and the apparel and amenities necessary for their increasingly 'metrosexual' day-to-day lives. Indeed, contemporary Japanese men have grown steadily more interested in their personal grooming habits, practices previously associated more with women's beauty regimes. Instead, today's hair care and beauty departments in Japanese department stores offer extensive product lines devoted to men's grooming routines, and few male parasite singles would be able to subsist without hair 'product' or 'wax'. All in all, however, research points to female parasite singles as the driving force of the younger single consumer demographic.

Although social pressure to marry and have children continues in Japan (and grows in strength as the population recedes), growing numbers of single women seem resolute in remaining unmarried and enjoying their lives for themselves. Unsatisfied with the traditional configuration of marriage in Japan, which normally requires wives to give up jobs, stay at home, and virtually 'single parent' children while husbands work long hours and contribute little to managing a household, it is perhaps unsurprising that many female parasite singles are happy to maintain their status. This shift in patterns of social development, however, is likely to be less agreeable for single Japanese men, as their salaried work trajectories continue on without the support of a marriage partner taking care of work on the domestic front. However, resistance to moving out of the home of origin is understandable in the Japanese context when one takes into consideration the particularly high cost of setting up house in urban areas where dwellings 'are small, are not furnished with major appliances, and typically require a substantial deposit (*shikikin* and *reikin*), much of which is non-refundable' (Raymo and Ono, 2004, p. 4). Thus, while Western life course development models normally predict sequential moves from home of origin to independent or shared living arrangements (a move that typically leads to a decline in living standards) to a marital home (a move that generally suggests improved living standards), Japanese parasite singles will almost certainly see their standard of living decline in a move out of their parents' home – whether moving towards independent living *or* towards a marital home – and this may instead encourage a longer period of co-residence with parents.

This questioning of traditional gender roles leads naturally to the ARAFO single demographic, which shares many consumption habits and practices with (female) parasite singles. While the younger single Japanese women live at home with parents, however, ARAFO single women more commonly live on their own and set aside a good part of their discretionary income to cover home-related expenditures such as decorative goods, kitchen supplies or furniture items. In fact, ARAFO singles have become such an important consumer segment of the real estate market that it has been reported that some condominium developers designing units exclusively for single women in Tokyo have sold out entire buildings before they were even completed. Just as single women have emerged as an important consumer demographic in the North American real estate market – purchasing in far greater numbers than their single male counterparts – many single Japanese women are also refusing to wait for marriage in order to acquire their own homes. According to Recruit Co. Real Estate Research Institute, 'the average age of single women who buy newly built condominiums is 39.4 years old. And when limited to the 23 wards of Tokyo, single women who purchase condominiums comprise 9.3 per cent of the total which is more than single men.'(*Japan Market Intelligence*, paragraph 18). This profile of single women home owners seems certain to be a sign of things to come: numbers of single Japanese *female* heads of household are predicted to increase, as projections indicate further growth in the single demographic in coming years.

As mentioned in the previous section, as a group, the ARAFO singles are inclined towards spending in the product and service areas of health, beauty and home. As the MasterCard Worldwide Insights report on the female consumer market of Japan notes,

> [Single Japanese women] have cash to spare and they love to pamper themselves – visiting beauty salons, health spas, and follow[ing] the latest fashion trends. Time not spent raising children is [instead] devoted to their careers, and to new hobbies, learning new languages and traditional Japanese crafts. Savings are used to lavishly decorate their homes.

Thus, while middle-aged female singleness has been marginalized in Japan (as it has elsewhere) until quite recently, old labels of 'Christmas cake' and 'New Year's Noodles' – terms referring to perceptions of women's declining social worth after the respective ages of 25 and 31 – and the positioning of singles as 'lacking' in the recent 'loser dog' debate (a popular term coined by author Junko Sakai describing single women in their 1930s in contrast to the 'winner dogs', who are married with children) are being called into question, as the ARAFO single lifestyles are being seen as increasingly enviable by young Japanese women. As economist Eisuke Sakakibara stated in interview with the Washington Post, '[single Japanese women] have discovered they can stay single, spend money more freely, and have fun without having to take on the traditional responsibility of taking care of a man. With those options available, they are asking themselves, "Why get married?"' (Faiola, 2004).

The 'silver aristocrat singles', as noted in the beginning of this section, are more easily understood as two groups within the aged consumer demographic. The 60 to 70-year-old segment is the 'junior senior' group, while the 75 years and over group is referred to as the *'old* old age' demographic. This division is made due to differences in work contexts, as the junior senior singles are typically healthy and are wanting to continue working, while seniors over the age of 75 are likely to be fully retired and may be needing to contend with declining health. The demographic as a whole is perceived as a rather self-indulgent segment of society, in that Japanese traditional cultural values consent to 'maximum freedom and indulgence allowed to babies and the old' (MasterCard Worldwide Insights Report, p. 7). Indulgences include increased investment in adult education and hobby activities, extensive socializing with friends – a pleasure largely denied in the years of work-related responsibilities – and recreational travel to domestic and overseas destinations. Unlike senior citizens in North American and European societies, who tend to retire to small towns or the countryside, trends in Japan show 'silver aristocrats' (both married and single) settling in urban settings. This is good news for businesses that aim to cater to an older consumer demographic, as city dwellers are easier to access than those residing in suburban and rural localities. In fact, it has been noted that:

> [a] whole new service industry has come into existence catering to the special needs of these silver aristocrats: 24-hour convenience stores, department stores that feature more refined products, take away restaurants, health spas, continuing education centers, and amateur associations dedicated to the pursuit of a wide variety of hobbies and interests. (MasterCard Worldwide Insights Report, 2005, p. 7)

Reports suggest that the demand for consumer services is expected to outweigh the demand for consumer goods in the case of the silver aristocrat singles, and, as the Japanese aged segment grows, innovation in this area will be critical for businesses hoping to become or remain competitive. Considering that the average size of inheritance bequeathed by elderly Japanese in the past 15 years was near US$330,000, this consumer group should clearly be a priority in any company's marketing plan.

This section offered an outline of the consumer behaviour profiles of the different subgroups comprising the single Japanese consumer sector. From the consumption of luxury goods and grooming products for younger singles, to investments in home and health for mid-life singles, to the long-delayed gratification of leisure pursuits and socializing for senior singles, it is clear that there remains substantial room for growth in the product and service areas targeting the single Japanese consumer. In the next section, we consider the current trends for single consumers in Japan and attempt to foretell the trends that may emerge in the near future.

Current trends in the single Japanese consumer market

The chapter thus far has provided an overview of the demographic profile and the consumer behaviour of the single Japanese market segment, and it is clear from the statistical data of population growth patterns that the number of single Japanese consumers will continue to grow in the coming years. This certainty positions the single segment as a critical player in the Japanese consumer market, and strongly suggests that companies will benefit by targeting them in marketing plans. To better establish the direction that marketing departments should pursue, we will now take a closer look at current trends in the Japanese consumer market as they pertain to the single consumer demographic. This section looks at three current trends: the shift in consumption patterns of luxury retail, the premium placed on convenience in order to cater to single consumers' busy schedules in Japan, and the projected growth of service needs for the ageing, single Japanese population.

Although Japanese consumers in general – and female Japanese consumers over the age of 30 in particular – are renowned for a propensity towards purchasing luxury goods, recent reports show the rise of individualism and concerns over the current state of the global economy to be significant factors in the ongoing decline in the sales of high-end goods and apparel in Japan. For instance, recent studies are indicating that the acquisition of brand name fashion apparel may no longer hold the same status appeal it once did, and consumers are turning instead towards competitively priced, reliable quality clothing lines such as Japan's own Uniqlo to meet their clothing needs. As a result, while many domestic and international high-end fashion retailers operating in Japan have seen dramatic losses in sales revenue over the past few years, Uniqlo has boasted steadily increasing profits and has seen expansion into foreign markets (Nagata, 2009). Uniqlo attributes this success to the aggressive marketing of strategic sales such as their popular fleece line and their new 'Heat Tech' thermal inner wear, and their ability to tap into the developing desire for quality goods at affordable prices – a trend that is key with the single Japanese consumer demographic.

This budget-conscious strategy is also seen with foreign fashion distributors H&M and Zara (which feature fashionable clothing lines at discounted prices), which are successfully competing with long-standing luxury goods and apparel flagship stores in the trendy fashion districts of Harajuku, Omotesando and Ginza, and seem to be capably wooing shoppers away from their formerly exclusive 'brand badge' consumption habits. In the past, brand items were desired and consumed as a way to attain group acceptance, as Japanese society in general placed value on foreign-made luxury items as 'badges' representing financial success and good taste. However, as McKinsey & Company's May 2009 consumer report on Japan's Luxury Companies indicates, Japanese consumers (and predominantly female consumers, as the largest representative group of consumers of luxury goods in Japan) seem to be no longer bound to such rigid expectations of what apparel and accessories are considered to be 'the' appropriate choices for specific contexts, and are instead developing confidence in their own individual taste to 'mix and match' high-end and discounted items as they see fit (McKinsey & Company Report, 2009). However, it should also be noted that McKinsey's report does not suggest that this marks the end of the luxury market in Japan:

> In any case, we can be relatively certain that the recent structural changes in the market do not represent an end state. As such, luxury players must be forward-thinking and develop the capacities to anticipate and stay abreast of changes in consumer attitudes and behaviors, as well as channel and competitor evolution ... To be clear, despite the recent turmoil ... Japan will remain a large and important luxury-goods market for a long time to come. It will, however, become a more intense battleground in which the ability to build loyalty among existing customers, connect with and capture the next generation of customers, and operate efficiently and profitably will separate winners from losers. (McKinsey & Company Report, 2009, p. 28)

As noted earlier in the chapter, the 'parasite singles', 'ARAFO singles' and 'silver aristocrat' singles (particularly in the case of female members of these categories) have been the chief consumers of luxury goods and apparel in Japan, and have made the nation one of the world's top sources of revenue for luxury brand items. Thus, for luxury retailers looking to expand within, or to enter into, the Japanese market, these findings regarding (single) Japanese consumption trends need to be taken seriously into account. While indications suggest that high-end products may still find a receptive audience in Japan, retailers must be prepared to defend and extend their brands, cater to – and invest in – their loyal customer base, and develop multi-channel strategies to better promote their brands (McKinsey & Company Report, 2009). As the single Japanese demographic emerges as an increasingly key consumer segment, their particular needs and preferences (such as the desire for superior online shopping experiences that cater to busy work schedules) will need to be addressed and incorporated into future marketing plans if retailers hope to attract and retain this affluent consumer group.

Another trend to watch with the single Japanese consumer demographic is their influence in the growing demand for convenience and efficiency in service and retail sectors. While the current global and domestic economic downturn has brought great financial hardship to both retailers and consumers, one market segmentation that has fared well is the convenience retailer segment. According to Japan Inside Market Reports 2009 from the sales and marketing agency G&S, Japanese convenience store sales rose 9 per cent in January 2009, and nearly half of the 10 biggest retail chains listed in Japan were invested in convenience retailing (G&S International Japan Report, 2009). In fact, convenience stores have long been a staple in Japanese day-to-day life, particularly in the provision of pre-made lunches and dinners for salaried workers, but the demand for pre-packaged and prepared foods and drinks is steadily growing alongside the burgeoning single demographic. As contemporary Japan is seen to be moving away from its traditional family configurations – arrangements that typically included stay-at-home mothers who prepared boxed lunches for family members and had homemade meals awaiting them at the end of the day – convenience stores and fast food retailers are observing a surge in demand from customers who do not have the time or desire to prepare meals for themselves. Thus, instead of home-cooked meals being a routine part of daily life, they are increasingly perceived as an extravagance or luxury in Japan. This reimagining of home-cooked cuisine as a 'lost art' may also explain the 'ARAFO single' group's interest in acquiring upscale kitchen supplies and registering for gourmet cooking courses, as they negotiate past expectations of feminine roles in Japan with their new career-oriented lifestyles.

The demand for convenience and efficiency, however, is not limited to the food industry in Japan. As mentioned in the previous section on luxury retail trends, Japanese consumers are steadily becoming more tech-savvy and budget-conscious, and are seeking out easier and more efficient channels through which to make their purchases. And, while Japanese consumer behaviour preferences have traditionally been closely linked to both brand loyalty and risk aversion, current studies indicate that consumers are becoming progressively more interested in the products or services themselves, rather than feeling tied to the 'known' brand names. As online shopping channels and outlet shopping malls expand throughout the country, opportunities to efficiently compare and cull goods and services are enticing consumers to step outside their usual consumption practices – shopping close to home, in familiar stores – to look for 'better deals'. This trend suggests that (single) Japanese consumers are eager to discover discounted goods and services and that they may be willing to shift their consumer habits in order to save both time and money. Companies that are able to provide additional service features such as home delivery and gift-wrapping are also highly valued by single Japanese customers, as these services provide consumers with much appreciated time-saving measures. As Synodinos notes,

> The short amount of free time points to the importance of certain time-saving products and services, and to the value attached to convenience in shopping. Indeed, retailers handle the delivery of certain products (e.g., gifts), thus providing a useful and necessary service for consumers who are short of time. In some instances, a pre-purchase search is difficult because of lack of time. Also, for many products it is important to provide everything needed with one-stop shopping. (Synodinos, 2001, p. 243)

As the single Japanese consumer segment grows, so too will the need to cater to their busy lifestyles. In order to secure and satisfy the single Japanese consumer demographic, companies must anticipate their lifestyle's time constraints and create ways to better meet their particular wants and needs. In recognizing this consumer group's desire to reconcile a long-standing demand for product and service quality with a newly found aspiration for discounted yet trendy goods, emerging companies are faced with a significant challenge in achieving and balancing these objectives. The challenge, however, will need to be met in order to enable a steady foundation in the contemporary Japanese consumer market.

The final emerging consumer trend to be considered in relation to the single Japanese demographic is the anticipated growth in demand for services required to cater to the ageing (single) Japanese society. As mentioned earlier in the chapter, the 'empty nesters' and 'silver aristocrat' singles are believed to be the most affluent segment of the single Japanese demographic, and their numbers are projected to grow significantly in coming years. Companies would be well advised to consider this consumer group in depth, as this demographic is one that is growing and thriving, and is already known to enjoy sizeable discretionary incomes. Services of interest to this consumer segment may include recreational and social services for the younger, single 'junior seniors' aged 60 to 70, who typically enjoy good health for many years, and assisted living services for the '*old* old age' demographic over the age of 75. Whether it is through the offering of specially designed adult education programmes, overseas or domestic travel packages, or the provision of clubs or lessons organized around hobby and leisure pursuits, this consumer demographic is positioned to be the dominant Japanese consumer segment for the foreseeable future, and should be valued as such.

Additionally, for different reasons than for mid-life singles – primarily due to mobility factors, rather than hectic work schedules – home delivery and customer care become key service features with the '*old* old age' singles. Whether in relation to food services, online retail, or any customer service industry, companies need to ensure that they can reach their customers, and not require consumers to travel to them. Fortunately, quick and reliable home delivery is already well established and readily available in Japan, but steps still need to be put in place by new and expanding companies in order to use different channels to effectively promote products and services and to ensure that elderly consumers gain confidence in employing these, perhaps unfamiliar, consumer practices. As mentioned earlier, Japanese consumers are becoming gradually more tech-savvy, but the 'silver aristocrat singles' may be less familiar with online shopping than the younger single consumer segments; thus, companies looking to tap into the elderly single market in Japan need to consider which marketing channels will best reach this demographic.

As a final note on the elderly single consumer segment, companies considering investing in the field of assisted living services for the ageing will find that Japan is taking the lead in this growth industry. While the country has long been perceived to be lagging behind in terms of its provision of assisted living centres and retirement homes (this may, in fact, have been due to the previously common configurations of multigenerational family dwellings, which made such homes less necessary), Japan has been catching up on its eldercare training in various social work and gerontology programmes at university and college levels and has been developing remarkable scientific and technological innovations to (eventually) support the anticipated increase in need for senior citizens' physical and emotional care. As an example, 'service robots' are being designed to provide both physical assistance (for instance, aid with bathing and feeding) and mental support (by engaging the elderly in games and conversation to activate memory skills) and could be made more readily available to the public sector in the next few decades (McNicol, 2008).

Concluding remarks

As demographers point towards a dramatic surge in numbers of single individuals in Japan in the coming years, companies looking to enter into, or expand within, the Japanese market need to evaluate how best to serve this growing demographic. This chapter has provided an overview of three different subgroups within the Japanese single demographic – 'parasite singles', 'ARAFO singles' and 'silver aristocrat singles' – that are expected to play a significant role in Japan's economic recovery and future prosperity, and should therefore be seriously considered in future marketing strategies. In anticipating and addressing the product and service needs of this critical consumer segment, companies will be undertaking the appropriate steps to ensure their own future viability in the Japanese consumer market.

References

Faiola, A. (2004), 'Japanese Women Live, and Like It, On Their Own', *Washington Post*, 31 August , available at http://www.washingtonpost.com/wp-dyn/articles/A47261-2004Aug30.html (accessed 19 December 2009).

G&S International Japan Report (2009), 'Retail and Consumer Goods Japan 2009', presentation transcript available at http://www.slideshare.net/JapanRetailNews/retail-consumer-goods-japan-2009 (accessed 19 December 2009).

Hashimoto, N., 'Expenditure Patterns of One-person Household in Japan, 1989–1999', online report available at http://rcisss.ier.hit-u.ac.jp/Japanese/dlfiles/ronbun/002_Hashimoto_P.pdf (accessed 19 December 2009).

Japan Market Intelligence (2008), Fourth Issue Report, December.

McKinsey & Company Report (2009), 'Luxury Goods in Japan: Momentary Sigh or Long Sayonara?', *Consumer & Shopper Insights*, *Asia*, May, available at http://csia.mckinsey.com/ (accessed 19 December 2009).

McNicol, T. (2008), 'Robots Lend a Hand in Japan', *Robotics Trends*, 22 February , available at http://www.roboticstrends.com/personal_robotics/article/robots_lend_a_hand _in_japan/ (accessed 19 December 2009).

MasterCard Worldwide Insights Report (2005), 'Women Consumer Market in Japan – The Super-aging Society', *Third Quarter*, available at http://www.masterintelligence.com/ViewInsights.jsp?hidReportTypeId=1&hidSectionId=79&hidReport=129&hidReportSection=100&hidViewType=null&hidUserId=null

Ministry of Internal Affairs and Communications, Statistics Bureau, Director-General for Policy Planning (Statistical Standards) and Statistical Research and Training Institute. http://www.stat.go.jp/english/index.htm (accessed 3 April 2010).

Nagata, K. (2009), 'Choice, Chic, Cheap – No One Feels Fleeced', *The Japan Times Online*, 17 November, available at http://search.japantimes.co.jp/cgi-bin/nn20091117i1.html (accessed 19 December 2009).

Raymo, J. M. and Ono, H. (2004), 'Co Residence with Parents, the "Comforts of Home", and the Transition to Marriage among Japanese Women', *CDE Working Paper* No. 2004-16, Center for Demography and Ecology, University of Wisconsin-Madison.

Retherford, R. D., Ogawa, N. and Matsukura, R. (2001), 'Late Marriage and Less Marriage in Japan', *Population and Development Review*, 27(1): 65–102.

Synodinos, N. E. (2001), 'Understanding Japanese Consumers: Some Important Underlying Factors', *Japanese Psychological Research* 43(4): 235–48.

Tran, M. (2006), 'Unable or Unwilling to Leave the Nest? An Analysis and Evaluation of Japanese Parasite Single Theories', *Electronic Journal of Contemporary Japanese Studies*, no. 5, available at http://japanesestudies.org.uk/discussionpapers/2006/Tran.html (accessed 27 September 2009).

Unmarried America, available at http://www.unmarriedamerica.org/ (accessed 27 July 2009).

6
Indulging in Luxury? Japan's 'New Rich' Consumers

Parissa Haghirian

Introduction

Japanese consumers are often said to be very affluent and to have a taste for luxury products. And, indeed, Japanese consumers do have the second-highest purchasing power in the world and, over the postwar decades, have accumulated the highest level of assets among all nations worldwide. The number of households holding financial assets of more than 500 million yen ($5.5 million) was around 52,000 in 2006. The enormous wealth accumulated in Japan over the past decade has led to a particular interest in luxury and Western-brand products. Japan became the first mass luxury market and, until 2008, the Japanese were the most avid buyers of luxury products in the world. With the economic crisis, however, Japanese luxury spending changed: sales have decreased very rapidly and 'fast fashion' companies offering cheaper products are becoming more popular. Nevertheless, the richest of the New Rich have not changed their purchasing behaviour and still enjoy luxury spending. This chapter discusses wealthy consumers in Japan – the so-called 'New Rich' (*nyuu richi*) – and how their wealth was accumulated. The chapter also sets out the major role that luxury products play in Japanese consumption and gives an overview of how Japan's lust for luxury was affected by the economic crisis that began in 2008.

The New Rich

Japanese consumers are famous for being very wealthy and interested in spending large amounts of money on luxury and brand products.

The number of wealthy consumers has resulted in their becoming a focus of attention for Japanese corporations. These 'New Rich' (*nyû richi*, or *fuyûsô*), as they are called in Japan, are widely discussed in the Japanese media. The Japanese term *fuyûsô* can be divided into two parts, *fuyû* and *so*. The general meaning of the word *fuyû* is rich, wealthy and affluent; *so* can mean stratum, layer or streak. The two components combined associate the wealthy with a specific location in the economic hierarchy. A household is considered part of the *fuyûsô* if its financial assets exceed 100 million yen (Miyamoto and Yonemura, 2008). If they exceed 500 million yen, then a member of this household would be considered a HNWI (High Net Worth Individual). Households with financial assets falling in the bracket of 500 million to 100 million yen are considered affluent; between 100 million and 50 million yen, they are considered mass affluent. Households in the bracket of 50 million to 30 million yen are considered the upper mass retail layer, and below 30 million yen they are considered the mass retail layer. In the year 2006, approximately 813,000 households were counted as *fuyûsô*, and approximately 52,000 were considered HNWIs (Table 6.1).

Japan's new upper class is divided into different groups. The first group comprises those whose families have been rich over several generations – the so-called 'long-rich', the *ôrudo richi* or *saisho kara no kanemochi* (Miyamoto and Ogimoto, 2004, p. 20; Usui, 2006, p. 45). Here it is interesting that in Japan there are very few families whose wealth stretches back more than three generations, or was accumulated before World War II. The reasons for this are the high rate of inflation and the high levels of taxation of assets that characterized the period just after the

Table 6.1 Definitions and size of 'New Rich' markets

Net financial assets	Definition	Total wealth	Number of households
More than 500 million yen	HNWIs (High Net Worth Individual)	46 trillion yen	52,000
100 million to 500 million yen	Affluent	167 trillion yen	813,000
50 to 100 million yen	Mass affluent	182 trillion yen	2,804,000
30 to 50 million yen	Upper mass retail	246 trillion yen	7,019,000
Up to 30 million yen	Mass retail	512 trillion yen	38,315,000

Source: Miyamoto and Yonemura, 2008.

war. The fortunes of the long-term rich are primarily composed of assets that were built up by the post-war generation – that is, the grandparents and parents of today's long-term rich.

The second group are the 'grown rich through many years of work', or *kotsukotsu no kanemochi*. Most members of this group have their own companies, but are not listed on the stock exchange. Typical examples are attorneys, accountants or doctors who have developed large fortunes through a generation of successful work.

The third group is the 'suddenly rich', or *no totsuzen kanemochi*. This group comprises those who have become rich through a sudden event such as an inheritance, receipt of pension, or compensation to the IPO by their company or the stock market (Miyamoto *et al.*, 2006, p. 4ff).

Source of wealth

One reason why the Japanese became wealthy is their tendency to save money. A particular feature of Japanese saving behaviour is that the high savings rates have not been hindered by the increasing interest in consumption, even in the post-war years.

> As consumer spending and borrowing soared in the latter half of the 1950s, Japan's saving rate also climbed ever upward, reaching a plateau far above savings rates in the rest of the industrialized world. In 1960 the average Japanese family was saving close to 20 per cent of its disposable income. (Partner, 1999, p. 184)

The national income statistics on the ratio of personal savings to private disposable income in 1976 revealed that, where Japan showed a ratio of 24.9 per cent, the US showed only 7.9 per cent, the UK 11.2 per cent, West Germany 14.5 per cent and France 12.3 per cent (Nakamura, 1995).

But how was it possible to both save and consume (see Chapter 1) at such a high level at the same time? Horioka (2006) lists nine factors which explain Japan's high household savings. The first reason is the high income which was generated during the era of economic growth. He also refers to the low level of assets held by households after World War II as being a spur to people to restore their assets. Consumer credit was not available, which often forced Japanese consumers to save for a long time before a purchase could be made. The Japanese bonus system, in which a large amount of money is received by employees twice a year, also increases the tendency to save money. Another reason that supported this tendency was the low age of the Japanese population during the decades of economic growth, which led to higher rates of saving than in countries where the population is older. Tax breaks for saving and low public pension benefits for the elderly are other factors which explain the high savings rate. Finally, cultural factors, such as a positive attitude towards saving money, also contributed. Partner (1999) points out that the rapid decline in spending on certain essential items, most notably food, as a share of overall expenditures may also be a major influence. Food expenses declined from 40 per cent of the total in 1953 to only 31 per cent in 1960, providing a reserve for other types of consumption and for additional savings. Clothing costs and the tax burden also declined in the middle of the decade. Other important costs, such as housing, remained a very small component of Japanese family budgets (Partner, 1999, p. 185). Since the 1990s the Japanese savings rate has steadily declined. From 11.9 per cent per household in 1995, it fell to only 3.9 per cent in 2003 and declined further to 3.3 per cent in 2007 (*Nippon*, 2010). And at the beginning of the new century the attitudes toward saving changed. Horioka reports that

> The Japanese *were* big savers during parts of the pre-war, wartime, and early post-war periods and throughout the 1955–95 period, yet at some other times they were not and they no longer save at high levels, and household saving rates can be expected to decline even further in the future. The Japanese *did* borrow relatively little at one time, but not any longer. (Horioka, 2006, p. 134)

Luxury consumption in Japan

The rise of the New Rich went hand-in-hand with an increasing interest in luxury consumption. The spread of luxury among the fashionable Tokyoites of the merchant class had already become a matter of discussion during the Tokugawa period: writers reported on 'extravagant women forgetting their proper place' (Francks, 2009, p. 43) and commented that it was not only socially correct but also morally virtuous to dress appropriately according to one's station (Shively, 1991, cited in Francks, 2009, p. 43). Wearing a kimono of good quality and a matching kimono wrap was reputable for women, and the fabric quality and the overall appearance of the kimono were of great importance, reflecting as they did the social class and wealth of the wearer (Carter,

2008). Francks reports that status symbols had played a dominant role for centuries, commenting that:

> Neither the force of the law nor the strictures of moralists could do much to curb the desires of the merchant classes not just for the status symbols – silk clothes, white rice, elegant furnishings – that had once marked out the samurai class, but also for the fashionable goods that identified them as members, ideally leaders, of smart and sophisticated urban society. (Francks, 2009, p. 43)

This custom may have simply been continued into the modern era, substituting the kimono with Western luxury goods and accessories as a way of displaying one's social standing: foreign luxury goods 'may simply be the modern aesthetic mode of signalling social acceptability in Japan' (Carter, 2008).

The first Western luxury goods made their way to Japan in the early 1900s, when Japan started trading with Europe after the long Edo period of isolation. As early as 1920, British Burberry became one of the first luxury brands to set up a shop in Tokyo. World War II, however, had devastating effects on the Japanese economy and as a result luxury brands went into 'hibernation' for several decades (Chadha and Husband, 2008).

During the rapid economic development of the post-war years the interest in consumption grew, as did the interest in purchasing expensive brand and luxury products. During the 1960s and 1970s, the Japanese economy flourished, growing by 3.7 per cent annually, and the post-war generation experienced a dramatic increase in disposable income (Thomas, 2007). This development also gave local designers the opportunity to show off their talents: Kenzo Takada, Kansai Yamamoto, Issey Miyake, Yohji Yamamoto and Rei Kawakubo were among the few who achieved success (Chadha and Husband, 2008). Others were not as fortunate in their entrepreneurial pursuits. The newly formed middle class had strong buying power, and their appetites for luxury were escalating; however, production quality in post-war Japan was quite low, and the majority of Japanese believed that foreign-made goods were superior in quality and durability to domestic productions. The Japanese, therefore, gravitated towards foreign-made products (Atsmon et al., 2009). During the 1980s it was widely perceived that the demand for luxury commodities was growing. In the mid-1980s, well-made, innovative, and fashionable products could be sold at higher prices: high-quality products therefore began to increase their market share at the expense of the middle-class market (JETRO, 1985).

It was in this period that the label 'New Rich' emerged. Fields (1989) comments that the term 'New Rich' suggests a new economic class and that the New Rich are not the same as the Western nouveaux riches. According to his definition, the New Rich are owners of real estate or those who are successfully increasing their wealth via the stock exchange. Notably, they do not shun borrowing – a fact that was seen as a major reason for the rise of the bubble economy at the end of the 1980s (Fields, 1989).

Nevertheless, the distribution of foreign luxury brands in Japan remained very limited, which created a clear imbalance of supply and demand. In order to overcome this problem, entrepreneurial Japanese merchants travelled to Europe, purchased luxury items in bulk, and sold them back in Japan for a profit – at up to triple the price paid. This created a so-called parallel market, which has proved to be very damaging to the brand name (Thomas, 2007). The aggressive shopping patterns displayed by the Japanese merchants and tourists, which left the European stores empty, did not go unnoticed by the luxury brand executives. At first, in order to stimulate sales, European store assistants were trained to speak Japanese; however, as consumption continued to increase rapidly, the luxury companies became alarmed – since they did not have control over their products' distribution overseas – and placed a limit on the number of items that could be purchased by Japanese. Louis Vuitton was among the first brands to react to this phenomenal purchasing behaviour by initiating a research project on the Japanese luxury consumption market with the intention of expanding into Japan. In March 1978, Louis Vuitton was represented in five different department stores in Tokyo – and, later that year, in one in Osaka (Thomas, 2007). The second most popular luxury brand in Japan at the time, Gucci, opened its first Japanese store in 1972 (Chadha and Husband, 2008).

The unique feature of Japanese luxury consumption was that the middle class was the most interested in purchasing luxury goods. This set the Japanese market apart from those in other countries. As Schütte and Ciarliante (1999) comment, 'In Japan, many luxury brands achieved higher market penetration in the middle of the 1990s by gaining acceptance among a clientele in their twenties, which was a new phenomenon. Formerly, consumers this young were considered too young an age group for expensive brand products.' Ownership of luxury goods alone, however, did not put one in the upper-class category, but simply indicated the status and financial capabilities of the owner. Those who were on a budget were willing to sacrifice other purchases, even essentials like food, in order to be able to afford a luxury item. Fashion magazines and department stores aimed their advertising at middle-class consumers (Japan Market Resource Network, 2007).

In the 1980s Japanese consumers were obsessed with luxury products, especially foreign luxury brands from France and Italy. Products were purchased because of their prestige and their value in signalling the aspirations of the owner (Japan Market Resource Network, 2007). At the same time, Japanese consumers changed their attitudes towards brands: Schütte and Ciarlante (1998) reported them to be company-loyal, but not necessarily brand-loyal. The increasing openness of the Japanese consumer emerged as a result of changing lifestyles and the recession of the 1990s. The consumer in this period was highly aware of the price–value relationship, and was no longer willing to pay higher prices for domestic products for the sake of national welfare. This consumer was focused on individualistic satisfaction, and was willing to search for value (Schütte and Ciarlante, 1998).

As a result, the luxury market in Japan boomed in the 1980s, and, despite the economic ups and downs, continued to grow steadily until 2007. At the beginning of this century Japanese consumers had become the world's biggest buyers of luxury goods. In fact, Japan still has the second largest luxury market in the world, following the United States. Sales to the Japanese account for over half of global luxury goods sales: an estimated 20 per cent of all luxury goods are sold in Japan, and another 30 per cent are sold to Japanese travelling abroad. From 2006 to 2008 the sales of luxury goods in Japan remained in the 15–18 per cent range of the total for global sales ($20 billion), not counting sales to the Japanese outside Japan (Atsmon *et al.*, 2009).

Moreover, researchers claim that approximately 40 per cent of Japanese own a Louis Vuitton product (Thomas, 2007). In Tokyo, an often-repeated claim is that 94 per cent of women in their twenties own at least one LV piece, 92 per cent own Gucci, 57 per cent own Prada, and 51 per cent own Chanel (Seeking Alpha, 2008). While these statistics might be thought mythical, it is a fact that a large proportion of the urban population in Japan owns expensive luxury brand items. Louis Vuitton, the most popular brand in Asia, generates 88 per cent of its global sales from Japanese consumers – 38 per cent in Japan and 50 per cent from Japanese tourists (Chadha and Husband, 2008). The ranking of most popular brands in Japan can be found in Table 6.2.

Japanese consumers also continued going overseas to shop for luxury goods. Some of the most famous shopping destinations include Korea and Hawaii. Out of Hawaii's 7 million visitors each year, 1.5 million are Japanese. They stay for a few days and most come just to shop. More than half of Chanel's sales in Hawaii are to the Japanese (Thomas,

Table 6.2   Japanese women's favourite brands

Top ten favourite brands for Japanese women	
1. Louis Vuitton	6. Cartier
2. Coach	7. Dior
3. Hermes	8. Chanel
4. Gucci	9. Prada
5. Burberry	10. Tiffany & Co.

Source: Dominic Carter, September 2008.

2007). Hawaii is not the only Japanese shopping destination. In Korea, in 2008, Japanese travellers charged more to their credit cards than visitors from any other country. The total amount approached $450 million, an 18 per cent increase on the previous year (*Nikkei Marketing Journal*, 2009). Their lavish spending habits made Japanese consumers seem like spendthrifts, willing to pay absurd prices for globally famous brands (McCreery, 2000, p. 7).

Why do Japanese consumers like brand products?

It is not surprising that Japan is called the only luxury mass market: purchasing and adoring luxury products has become such a middle-class phenomenon. Japanese middle-class luxury consumers, however, mostly buy designer bags or fashion items. Only if they are very wealthy would they also spend money on expensive cars and real estate.

Market researchers have tried to find explanations for the great love that Japanese consumers in particular show for luxury and Western brand products. The incredible success and sales figures of luxury brand products in Japan are partly explained by strong collectivism, but are also influenced by different perceptions of luxury among Japanese consumers. Kapferer and Bastien (2009) even see luxury as a means of integration and fitting in: 'The fact that Japanese "office ladies" all carry the same Louis Vuitton handbag does not worry them; on the contrary. In Japan luxury is a luxury of integration: too much rarity would therefore destroy the brand's value' (p. 91). They add: 'In Asian countries, the importance of social integration is such that everyone is ready to pay high prices to buy "instant class"' (p. 91).

In Japan, as in other industrialized countries, luxury items are seen as an easy and modern means to define identity and social status (Chadha and Husband, 2006, p. 3). Another reason for the appetite for luxury is the lower living standards that can be observed in Japan, even today. The post-war era of rapid economic development provided wealth to the mass of the people, but failed to provide a high standard of living. Due to lack of space, the Japanese do not have the same means of displaying their financial capabilities and success as their counterparts in the West. A typical wealthy American, for instance, would build a huge house, buy expensive cars, dig out a pool, spend a fortune on interior decoration, and enjoy himself in that setting. The Japanese do not have that privilege due to land scarcity, jammed traffic, and other limitations. Most Japanese employees, regardless of social status, use public transportation to get to work and are in the public eye for most of the day. The only way the Japanese can make a statement about their status to the public is through the physical symbols on their bodies. Luxury products are perfect agents for that purpose: they are small, expensive, and fit one's physical requirements. This need to show one's social standing to the public explains why the vast majority of Japanese choose to spend money on outrageously priced pieces of clothing, rather than invest in home improvements (Ignatova and Haghirian, 2010). Japanese consumers therefore think that luxury must be expensive; superior quality is of lower relevance. But the most important factor for Japanese consumers when buying luxury products is the prestige they communicate. Furthermore, for the Japanese consumer, luxury products are strongly connected with fashion and art (Kapferer and Bastien, 2009).

Are the Japanese losing their lust for luxury? The economic crisis and its effect

Up until 2008, Japan's New Rich kept spending on luxuries. 'Despite a sluggish economy, tepid retail sales and a weak yen, demand for super-luxury goods and services is up' (ABC News, 2008). But the appeal of luxury and expensive products subsequently changed very quickly. Japan's market for imported luxury goods fell by 10 per cent to $11.9 billion (1.06 trillion yen) from 2007. In 2009–10 it is expected to shrink to 992.7 billion yen, compared with its peak of 1.9 trillion yen in 1996 (*The New York Times*, 2008). Atsmon *et al.* (2009) identify three reasons for the sudden change: the economic crisis in 2008; a 'luxury bubble' between 2004 and 2007; and underlying channel trends and longer-term shifts in consumer attitudes and behaviour that began 6 to 8 years ago.

The economic crisis that hit the world economy in 2008 had the most tremendous effect on the spending of Japanese luxury-lovers. The crisis coincided with the bursting of a 'luxury bubble' which had initially taken off with the enormous interest in foreign luxury brands. This led to a high number of entries into the Japanese market. Successful brands were forced to open up branches within short time intervals. But the appreciation of the Euro (most famous brands have European origins) increased the prices of the goods on offer (Atsmon *et al.*, 2009). Meanwhile, Japanese consumers were being offered an increasing array of luxury products, which might have made them less interesting.

But consumer attitudes have also changed. In 2007, the Japan Market Resource Network had already issued a prognosis of increased confidence and a change in the character of consumer values, such as a new mix of 'high' and 'low' lifestyle, or an increasing acceptance of mixing luxury brands with less prestigious and even lower-quality products. The Japanese consumer seemed to be more confident about purchasing products with lower brand value. Lower-priced items and discount shops became increasingly socially accepted (Japan Market Resource Network, 2007). At the same time, 'fast fashion' – fashion products by cheaper brands – became acceptable substitutes for brand products. McKinsey and Co. principal Brian Salsberg noted that 'for every one luxury [brand] bag, there are 10 Uniqlo, Forever 21, or H&M bags' (McGinn, 2009). Indeed, while the luxury giants are suffocating, the so-called fast fashion retailers have been drawing hundreds of eager shoppers. The Swedish casual-wear chain Hennes & Mauritz (H&M), which entered Japan last year, has opened five shops since September 2008, and opened its first 'concept store' in November 2009. With only two stores open, H&M raked in about $94.4 million in sales in 9 months through to August 2009, which is equivalent to a year's worth of revenue at a regional department store (*Nikkei Weekly*, 2009). US chain Forever 21 debuted at the end of April 2010 in Harajuku, and draws on average 20,000 shoppers a day. Zara, run by Spain's Inditex, already has over 50 outlet shops in Japan and is a year ahead of schedule. The UK's Top Shop is another fast fashion brand that is planning to fully develop its network in the coming year. Larry Myer, the CEO of Forever 21, believes the increase in business has to do with luxury not being 'in vogue' (cocoperez.com, 2009). Harajuku, where many of the so-called fast fashion brands such as H&M, Uniqlo, and Forever 21 are located, reports an increasing number of shoppers. One shop owner is quoted as saying 'the types of people have changed and the foot traffic has increased rapidly' and 'the number of women customers has roughly doubled this year' (*Nikkei Shimbun*, 2009a).

Conclusion – the post-crisis luxury consumer

Up until 2007 the number of wealthy people in Japan continued to grow (Abraham Consulting, 2010) and the Japanese remain wealthy, despite the decline in equity and land prices, and continue to hold conservative investment portfolios (Horioka, 2006, p. 134). Even after the economic crisis a high number of the New Rich seem to have retained their wealth and report only minor losses in income and financial assets. In a *Nikkei Shimbun* survey conducted among 4,000 New Rich individuals, the richest group (owning more than 100 million yen or with a household income of more than 30 million yen per year) reported a loss of 10 per cent or more in their financial assets and 8.2 per cent of the same group reported a loss of 10 per cent or more in their household income. Less wealthy groups with an income of less than 20 million yen per year and assets below 50 million reported an average financial loss of 11.3 per cent (*Nikkei Shimbun*, 2009b).

At the same time, however, Japan's super-rich have not changed their purchasing behaviour. A recent survey of consumers with financial assets of more than 10 million yen ($112,300) reveals that the spending habits of Japan's wealthiest consumers appear relatively unaffected by the economic downturn, and that rich consumers are still looking for exclusive shopping experiences. And the wealthiest Japanese – those owning more than 100 million yen in financial assets or deriving at least 30 million yen in annual household income – are increasingly interested in buying real estate and Western luxury items such as watches and cars (*Nikkei Shimbun*, 2009b). As in Western markets, rich Japanese consumers are also willing to spend a lot of money to minimize their carbon footprints. 'Green luxury' allows these consumers to express their individual identity and it is expected that the Japanese will increasingly demand high-quality products in this category (Japan Market Research Network, 2007). Furthermore, luxury consumers are not only buying luxury products but increasingly looking for luxury experiences. 'One in four women still purchase brand products, but these days really enjoy the experience of a brand, such as its signature café, spa or attending an event, more than just owning the product itself' (JMRN August Consumer Survey, 2007).

The future will show whether Japan can keep its image as the world's only luxury mass market. Luxury products and consumption used to be a particular trait of the Japanese middle class, in which more than 90 per cent of Japanese nationals would count themselves. As the middle class is shrinking (*Nikkei Shimbun*, 2010), and since Japanese middle-class consumer were the main purchasers of Western brand and luxury goods, the luxury market is feeling that change. Japan's high net worth individuals, however, who continue to consume very expensive products, have not changed their behaviour. Luxury in their eyes refers not only to a designer bag, but to luxury experiences, such as travel and dining out, and also to real estate and very expensive luxury goods.

As long as the economy is slowing, it seems that the Japanese luxury market will develop more similarly to its Western counterparts. Middle-class consumers will only buy luxury products on very special occasions, whereas the New Rich have discovered luxury as a new lifestyle. It is not clear how Japanese consumers will react to a recovery of the economic situation, and whether they will return to being the most avid luxury consumers in the world.

References

ABC News Online (2008), 'Japan's New Rich Spend Big on Luxuries', available at http://www.abc.net.au/news/stories/2008/01/07/2133589.htm (accessed 26 March 2010).

Abraham Consulting, Homepage, http://abraham-marketing.com/wealth/out-line/index.html (accessed 14 December 2009).

Atsmon, Y., Salsberg, B. and Yamanashi, H. (2009), 'Luxury Goods in Japan: Momentary Sigh or Long Sayonara? How Luxury Companies Can Succeed in a Changing Market', McKinsey Asia Consumer and Retail (ed.), available at http: www.mckinsey.com/clientservice/retail/pdf/Japan-Luxury-report.pdf (accessed 14 December 2009).

Carter, D. (2008), 'Carter Associates', September, Carter Associates: Marketing Information and Consultancy, available at http://www.carterassociates.net/aboutJapan/view_04_Luxury.html (accessed 29 November 2009).

Chadha, R. and Husband, P. (2008), 'The Cult of the Luxury Brand: Inside Asia's Love Affair with Luxury', London: Nicolas Brealey International.

Cocoperez.com, 'H&M and Forever 21 Take On Japan', available at http://www.cocoperez.com/2009-11-12-hm-and-forever-21-take-on-japan (accessed 12 November 2009).

Fields, G. (1989), 'Gucci on the Ginza: Japan`s New Consumer Generation', Tokyo: Kodansha International.

Francks, P. (2009), *The Japanese Consumer: The Alternative Economic History of Modern Japan*, Cambridge: Cambridge University Press.

Horioka, Ch. Y. (2006), 'Are the Japanese Unique? An Analysis of Consumption and Saving Behavior in Japan', in Garon, S. and Maclachlan, P. (eds), *The Ambivalent Consumer: Questioning Consumption in East Asia and the West*, Ithaca, NY: Cornell Press, pp. 113–36.

Ignatova, E. and Haghirian, P. (2010), *Rise and Fall of the Luxury Market in Japan: A Battle of Socio-economic Forces and Modern Japanese Consumer Tastes*. Case study submitted to the European Case Clearing House.

Japan Market Resource Network (2007), 'Japan's Changing Consumer: Drivers of Change for Luxury Brands', Tokyo: Japan Market Resource Network.

JETRO (1985), *Selling in Japan: The World's Second Largest Market*, Tokyo: Japan External Trade Organization (JETRO).

JMRN (2007), *August 2007 Consumer Survey: Attitudes towards Luxury Brands*, Tokyo: Japan Market Research Network.

Kapferer, J. N. and Bastien, V. (2009), *The Luxury Strategy: Break the Rules of Marketing to Build Luxury Brands*, London: Kogan Page Limited.

McCreery, J. (2000), *Japanese Consumer Behaviour: From Worker Bees to Wary Shoppers* (Consumasian), Honolulu: University of Hawaii Press.

McGinn, D. (2009), 'Japan's Luxury Market Won't Recover Soon', 23 September, available at http://www.newsweek.com (accessed 29 October 2009).

Miyamoto, H. and Ogimoto, Y. (2004), *Aratana fûyûsô*, Nomura Research Institute, available at http://www.nri.co.jp (accessed 20 September 2007).

Miyamoto, H. and Yonemura, T. (2008), 'New Wave of Retail Asset Management Business: From Private Banking to Sales at Bank Branches', Nomura Research Papers, No. 129, available at http://www.nri.co.jp (accessed 20 September 2009).

Miyamoto, H., Mutoh, M. and Ogimoto, Z. (2006), 'Marketing for Newly Wealthy Clients: Targeting the Mass Affluent', Nomura Research Papers, No. 99, available at http://www.nri.co.jp (accessed 20 September 2007).

Nakamura, T. (1995), *The Postwar Japanese Economy: Its Development and Structure, 1937–1994*, Tokyo: University of Tokyo Press.

New York Times, The (2008), 'Versace to Close Its Japanese Stores', New York: The New York Times, 8 October.

Nikkei Marketing Journal (2009), 'Japanese Biggest Visa Card Users in S Korea', 16 October.

Nikkei Shimbun (2009a), 'Bargain Hunt in Harajuku: "Fast Fashion" Chains Offer Stylish Apparel at Affordable Prices', Tokyo: Nikkei Shimbun, 15 June.

Nikkei Shimbun (2009b), 'Rich Classes Still Want to Spend: Despite Economic Downturn, Moneyed Consumers Still Looking for Luxury', Tokyo: Nikkei Shimbunsha, 14 December.

Nikkei Shimbun (2009c), 'Firms Find Way into Deep Pockets', Tokyo: Nikkei Shimbunsha, 14 December.

Nikkei Shimbun (2010), 'Shrinkage of Middle Class Hits Consumption', Tokyo: Nikkei Shimbunsha, 10 May.

Nikkei Weekly (2009), 'Fast-Fashion Chains Thriving', 16 November.

Nippon (2010), *Nippon 2010, Business Facts and Figures*, Tokyo: Libro Kabushiki Gaisha.

Partner, S. (1999), *Assembled in Japan: Electrical Goods and the Making of the Japanese Consumer* (Study of the East Asian Institute, Columbia University), Berkeley: University of California Press.

Schütte, H. and Ciarlante, D. (1998), *Consumer Behavior in Asia*, New York: New York University Press.

Seeking Alpha, available at http://www.seekingalpha.com/dashboard/global_markets?source=headtabs (accessed 15 November 2009).

Shively, D. (1991), 'Popular Culture' in Hall, J. (ed.), *The Cambridge History of Japan IV; Early Modern Japan*, Cambridge: Cambridge University Press, pp. 706–70.

Thomas, D. (2007), *Deluxe: How Luxury Lost Its Luster*, New York: Penguin Group.

Usui, H. (2006), *Nihon no Fuyûsô*, Tokyo: Takashimasha.

7
Male Order: Resonating with Today's Young Male Japanese Consumers

Aaron Toussaint

Introduction

Young Japanese males are often misrepresented, both in their home country and abroad. Very little serious work has been done in the English language to try to understand the effect of recent major changes in the Japanese economy and in Japanese society on young male consumption habits. Instead, reports of 'male bras', sexless couples and weak, hapless 'herbivore' males make headlines in English-language newspapers and magazines as well as Japanese media, giving a distorted picture of this group.

The changes that Japan has undergone in the past two decades are immense. The effect of these changes on the nation's citizenry, including young male consumers, is equally great; however, the result of these changes is not as simple as many people think. The young men of Japan are not one-dimensional stereotypes, but a complex and diverse set of consumers, with different lifestyles and consumption habits. Nevertheless, many of these consumers have certain aspects of consumption in common. These young people share a set of generational life experiences, including the collapse of Japan's economic bubble. These shared experiences and the changes they have wrought on society have resulted in several new consumption trends shared by large numbers of Japanese men.

Due to changing social and economic circumstances – mostly beyond their control – the young men of Japan often behave quite differently from the men of their fathers' and grandfathers' generation. Males are less bound to traditional ideas of masculinity, and therefore exhibit less traditional consumption patterns. As a result, they are becoming less self-conscious as consumers. In short, while they may have anxieties about the future – in fact, many researchers, such as Matsuda (2009) and Ushikubo (2008), assert that young men today are filled with anxiety about the future – their lifestyle choices, and therefore consumption choices, are increasingly sources of security. Young men are buying and consuming what they want, whether it be sweets, cosmetics, skirts, or fruity cocktails, without worrying about whether they are making the correct 'masculine' choice. In the words of Nicole Fall, experienced Asia trend-watcher, young men are increasingly 'more comfortable in their own skin' and their consumption decisions reflect this.

While economic uncertainty may result in less consumption overall by the young men of the 2000s than by the young men of the 1980s, males are still consuming. While the automobile and alcohol industries may be worrying about the future of their respective industries, fashion and male beauty services are two sectors that have seen strong growth in recent years. The preferences of the new Japanese male have created new business opportunities while closing the door on old ones.

Young men used to get married young and start a family, thus curbing the influence they exerted on how the money they earned was spent. But as Japanese men marry later, or not at all, they will naturally have more control over their spending habits, and consequently this group and their unique preferences will become more important. Males develop product preferences in their early adult years, and, as the typical Japanese consumer in 2010 can expect to live into his mid-seventies, correctly identifying the needs and preferences of this group can win loyal consumers for decades. Japanese men are important as consumers in their own right, but may also help to predict the consumption patterns of males around the world. As Japan's population ages and as the country moves further into a post-industrial economy, Japan exhibits many of the problems and phenomena that will appear in other industrial nations later. By looking closely at Japanese men and the causes behind their behaviour, other industrial states can get a glimpse of what their own future may hold.

This chapter will attempt to sketch a picture of the new Japanese male, as well as the myriad factors that contributed to his rise. We will also try and provide some clues about where he may be heading.

The Japanese male in transition

Japan is cited as an extremely masculine country (Hofstede, 2001). Gender roles were clearly defined, and the men who supported Japan

Inc., the office workers or so-called 'salarymen', were known for being womanizing alcoholics. These men bought cars and alcohol to impress the opposite sex as well as to communicate their own success (Ushikubo, 2008, pp. 47, 56–89). The men of the bubble generation in Japan, in particular, were known for their hypermasculinity.

The traditional life-career path of a young Japanese male started with university, followed by graduation and employment. Men would often start their working life single for a few years, and then get married and begin the second job of starting a family. The male would have traditionally been the primary or only breadwinner in the family unit, with the wife spending a considerable amount of time as a homemaker. The male, if he succeeded in gaining employment at a large company, would be virtually guaranteed a stable job with annual rises until retirement age. While he would be the breadwinner, most purchasing decisions and family accounting would be handled by the female, giving him surprisingly little influence in everyday consumption decisions. This was a natural outgrowth of corporate culture in large Japanese firms, because the long hours expected at his company did not leave much time for shopping. His main opportunity for spending came with consumption decisions before marriage. After marriage he can exercise most freedom in purchasing decisions when he is not with his family, for example when out drinking with friends and colleagues. However, in recent years Japanese men have seen their role in society, and therefore their consumption behaviour, change.

Men in Japan are getting married later, and many are choosing not to get married at all. According to statistics from the Ministry of Health, Welfare and Labor, the average age of first marriage for Japanese males was 27.2 in 1960. By the middle of the first decade of the millennium it had increased to 30 years. The percentage of single men in their twenties has also risen over the same time period, from 46.1 to 72.6 per cent. Men in their thirties have seen an even more dramatic increase, with only 21.7 per cent being single in 1960, versus 59.9 per cent in 2005 (a 38.2 per cent increase over 45 years). The decision to marry and mate later gives men more control over their money and purchasing decisions for longer (Ushikubo, 2006).

Many men also found themselves no longer the sole breadwinner in a family (Jyou, 2006). With more women working and female purchasing power rising as a consequence of female independence, women desired different qualities in their mates. As women looked for different qualities in a mate, men were forced to adapt to attract females (the influence of the opposite sex on male spending habits will be discussed later in the chapter); for example, cars, alcohol and designer watches were less important than a stable partner who helped with chores.

Two areas where male consumers have drastically reduced consumption since the 1980s and early 1990s are cars and alcohol. According to a recent survey by Kakaku.com cited in the *Nikkei Restaurant Online*, a food industry trade journal, some 14 per cent of twenty-somethings reported that they did not drink alcohol, while fewer than 10 per cent of 40-year-olds said they abstained and only about 4 per cent of those over the age of 60 reported not drinking. A 2009 book by Hisakazu Matsuda opens the first chapter with the words of a young consumer: 'Buying a car? That's pretty stupid, isn't it?' This assertion is backed by the fact that young people bought around half as many cars in 2007 as they bought in 1980 (Matsuda, p. 17). A similar, though less severe, trend has been witnessed with consumption of other large outlays, such as televisions (.Matsuda, p. 17). It seems clear that today's young men have changed how they spend. We will now sketch a picture of the 'new' Japanese man.

Soushoku danshi and the other 'new males'

The archetype of the new, young Japanese male has come to be called the *soushoku danshi*, or the 'herbivorous man'. This man has been portrayed in Japanese media and popular culture as sensitive, cool to consumption, love, and career advancement. The Japanese media has run several sensational specials on reputable television networks poking fun at the supposedly weak nature of these young Japanese males[1] (Fukasawa, 2009). The foreign media has picked up on this and focused on all the stranger aspects of Japanese men, especially their fashion and lifestyle habits. The result is a stereotype both in Japan and elsewhere of young Japanese men as a monolithic group that is weak, effeminate, and leading the country to ruin. As we shall see in this section, young men are far from a monolithic group. They may share many similar traits, but these traits are often exaggerated to the extreme. Though male bras and boys wearing make-up may attract attention in English media, the reality of Japanese consumers is far more complex.[2]

The woman who coined the term *soshouku danshi*, Fukasawa Maki, has written of her distaste for the sensationalization of young men ('*soshoukudanshi to kekkon, makeinu to nikusyoku jyoushi*' 9 July 2009). Fukasawa, a writer and regular columnist for *Nikkei Business Online*, never expected her term to catch on with the mainstream media, and, in an interview on 9 July 2009, told the *Nikkei Business Online* of her displeasure at the treatment of the new young men. 'These older men, they simply cannot understand young men'; hence the strange treatment in the media. Because of the oddity of the stories, particularly odd topics 'like the men's bra, have spread all over the world, perpetuating a stereotype of Japanese men that seems funny to the West, even though the West's ideas about masculinity are not objectively correct either' (ibid.).

Rather than put all men into a single framework, Ushikubo speaks of the 'diversification'[3] of men (Ushikubo, 2008, p. 25). Ushikubo stresses that not all Japanese men fit into this new mould. The herbivore is but one type of male; there are still Japanese males[4] who behave and consume like their counterparts in the bubble era (like the *Single Princes,* another consumer group term coined by Ushikubo. However, these bubble-era imitations and their voracious consumption habits increasingly seem to be in the minority. Ushikubo also stresses that, far from being the exception to the rule of masculinity, the new men of the Heisei Generation[5] may in fact be leading a revival of traditional Japanese values (Ushikubo, 2008, p. 28).

The new men of Japan, the Heise and late Showa generation, have a confirmed tendency to spend less than the generations of men who preceded them (Matsuda, pp. 16–18, 24–31). As will soon be shown, economic decline and uncertainty have largely made this decision for them. Yet young men in Japan do still have disposable income – remember that the Japanese economy is still larger than every economy outside Asia except the US, and will remain so for a long time. These young men continue to spend, though what they buy, and why, has changed. They are more frugal, likely spurred on by economic uncertainty. In general, they are not voracious consumers and do not seek to accumulate 'unnecessary' items. But a general sense of frugality and a 'cool' attitude to consumption are not the only traits young men share.

Given their ease of access to material goods while growing up, as well as the sheer variety of consumer products in Japan, this new generation also has a short attention span and looks for instant gratification.

They are also, like many young people around the world, eco-conscious (Matsuda, pp. 98–9). The values of frugality and not displaying wealth ostentatiously are values that have been exalted[6] by Japanese society for many centuries. Japan has also had a long tradition of living in harmony with nature; in other words, Japanese consumers have been environmentally friendly since before this became a buzzword.

Today's young man also believes that appearance is important. This manifests itself in a beauty-conscious attitude that makes itself shown in the fashion, health and beauty products, and beauty services sector.

Changing habits of male consumption mean different things for different companies. While the car and beer companies seem to have reason to worry over dropping sales, marketers in other industries are finding reasons to cheer the future. Though many men may no longer see cars as a necessity for life, the men's cosmetics market has seen explosive growth in the past several years, with roughly 47 per cent of men in their twenties saying that they use beauty products; an approximately 20 per cent increase from their fathers' generation (Ushikubo, 2008, p. 125). Other fields traditionally thought of as dominated by females are becoming increasingly invaded by men, including fashion and sweets. Young male consumption today is more focused on immediate needs, and on the consumer himself. Though large luxuries – like BMWs – may be an expense out of reach for most men, in keeping with their emphasis on both appearance and instant gratification young men are more willing to open their wallets for little luxuries that satisfy immediate needs and desires. For many young Japanese men, shopping has become not just a simple act of purchase, but an act of retail therapy (Usihikubo, 2008, pp. 135–8; Fall interview).

The root cause of slower consumption: economic uncertainty

Japanese consumption habits are changing. Several different kinds of new consumer have been identified, giving credence to Megumi Ushikubo's 'diversification' theory. But why is this happening? What is the cause of this diversification? Why has the stereotypical hard-drinking salaryman faded into obscurity? In the next section we will look at macroeconomic data and opinion polls, as well as cultural and workplace changes that are affecting how the Japanese male works, what he earns, how he thinks, and therefore how he spends.

Japan's economic malaise and rise of the Hakken

Japan has never really recovered from the country's 'lost decade'.[7] Although Japan remains the world's second largest economy at the time of writing, it is increasingly difficult to find stable, long-term employment. Japan's youth have been hit with the double blow of a stagnant economy and a rapidly changing work culture, making young men uncertain about their future in addition to being poorly paid.

The economic growth figures for the past several years in Japan are telling. While the Koizumi era produced the longest continuous stretch of economic growth since the end of World War II, it was weak growth (World Bank, WDI, 2010). And, while many of Japan's flagship firms have continued to succeed in the global marketplace, small and medium-sized enterprises have been hit hard. In the face of stiff competition, firms are hiring fewer full-time workers, and instead are relying on more part-time and contract workers. According to the Ministry of Internal Affairs and Communications, Japan has more than two million irregular workers. Although the idea of cradle-to-grave employment in Japan has always been somewhat exaggerated, full-time employees in Japan, or *seishain*, enjoy a high degree of job security. They cannot be fired except for grave transgressions, and, in exchange for sometimes slavishly long hours, were guaranteed annual rises as well as bonuses. This wage system allowed the average businessman to plan his financial life. He knew at what age his salary would be commensurate with buying a house, at what age he could think of buying a new car, and knew that, barring extreme circumstances, he would attain a minimum level of economic security (Jyou, 2006, p. 22). Since the reforms of the Koizumi administration allowed companies greater freedom to hire part-time workers instead of the higher paid *seishain*, the number of part-timers has soared as the number of full-time workers correspondingly fell (see Figure 7.1).

Part-time and contract workers do not have the job or economic security enjoyed by their full-time colleagues. Consequently it is difficult for new hires to make an economic life plan, leading to financial insecu-

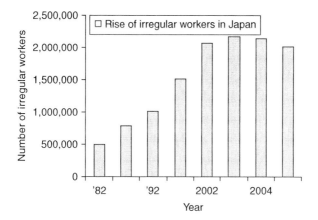

Figure 7.1   Rise of irregular workers in Japan, 1982–2005

Source: Labour Situation in Japan and Analysis, 2006/2007. The Japan Institute for Labour Policy and Training.

rity and a reluctance to spend. Once engaged in temporary or irregular employment, it is much more difficult to attain a *seishain* post. According to labour ministry statistics, fully 75 per cent of irregular workers who transfer to a new job remain in part-time positions (Jyou, p. 136).

Along with the rise of part-time workers, many companies have introduced merit-based pay structures, the idea being that workers should be paid according to work done, not number of years spent at work. This has contributed to the difficulty of financial planning, and hence the difficulty of deciding what to consume. Surprisingly, as companies introduced new merit-based standards for pay rises, wages have actually fallen. This has doubtless had an impact on spending habits, and young men have been hit particularly hard. According to the Japanese tax office, the average yearly salary for men in their twenties is only about $32,000[8] (Ushikubo, 2008, p. 32). This is in comparison to an average salary for all male workers of closer to $53,000 (see Figure 7.2). The percentage of men in their twenties making over $600,000 (the highest tax bracket in Japan) is only 3.5 per cent (Ushikubo, 2008, p. 32). Things look even worse for thirty-something men. As mentioned earlier, thirty-somethings a generation ago would have been married and thinking about starting a family (Ministry of Health, Labour and Welfare Statistics, 2005). During the bubble era and before, Japanese salaries would have been commensurate with marriage and children. However, there is reason to believe that men in this age group have

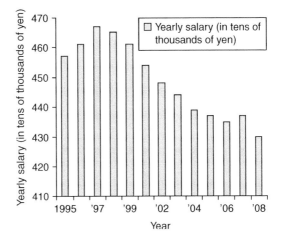

Figure 7.2   Average yearly salary of male office workers (all ages)

Source: National Tax Agency: 'Citizens' Income Status, 2008, Survey Results'. Reprinted at http://nensyu-labo.com/heikin_suii.htm

been hit the hardest by the introduction of new pay standards in Japan. According to NHK and Mitsubishi Research Institute, the average salary for a 35-year-old worker has fallen by nearly two million yen in the past 10 years (2009). In a poll among 35-year-old *seishain,* 42 per cent reported that their salaries had decreased in the past year, and, more worryingly, a full 69 per cent of respondents said they did not believe their pay would rise (ibid). When asked whether things would get better, all things being equal, only 15 per cent responded in the affirmative (ibid.).[9] This consequently makes it more difficult to afford a family.

Twenty and thirty-something men were not the first group affected by the introduction of merit-based pay and corresponding financial difficulties. The first to be affected were older males in their forties and fifties, the generation immediately above this chapter's target demographic (or the *shinjinrui* generation). This group has had a large impact on the thinking and life choices of twenty and thirty-something men. Seeing uncles, older cousins or fathers hit a brick wall in terms of advancement weighed heavily on the young men of today. With the security of constantly rising pay and position gone, yet still being forced to start at the bottom, many young men are questioning the values of the old styles of working. Many say they are seeking security – in the last decade an ever-growing number of young men have said they do not want to be entrepreneurs, but want to work for big companies, and also do not want merit-based pay scales (Ushikubo, pp. 35, 162). Yet many quit within the first 3 years of starting a new job[10] (Jyou, 2006, p. 27). Many have also seen their parents hit the brick wall, and are reluctant to even begin full-time work, gravitating instead to part-time work or other alternative employment. This has sparked serious concern in Japan; young men are not economically secure, and, given the current economic conditions, their situation is unlikely ever to resemble the heady days of the bubble economy, making a return to the spending patterns of their fathers unlikely.[11] Matsuda (pp. 17, 18) asserts that, even if young men do attain the affluence of their parents, their consumption expenditures may not rise accordingly. New male modes of consumption are therefore unlikely to change to resemble those of the bubble or post-war generation in the near future.

Changing values and the influence of mating

Japanese society is rapidly changing, along with the Japanese economy. As well as the environment in which today's men were raised, the changing nature of women may also affect male consumption habits.

Today's young men have no firm recollection of the bubble economy, and this has shaped the way they look at life and work (Ushikubo,
2008, pp. 20–3). While their parents grew up surrounded by a hyper-
consumerist culture, obsessed with catching up, today's young people
grew up in an environment of affluence (Ushikubo, p. 28). While the
parents of today's twenty and thirty-something males grew up listening
to the immediate post-war generation talk about rebuilding Japan and
seeing their fathers work long hours to re-create the country, our target
of today's 20 and 30-year-olds grew up when Japan had already come of
age as a modern industrial power. Though the fathers of today's young
men were famous for working long hours, the underlying motivations
were different from those of the immediate post-war generation. The
men of the bubble were not working out of desperation to escape poverty, like their parents in the post-war period, but to finance an affluent
lifestyle. Today's young men, having grown up in an environment of
affluence, are less inclined to work themselves to death to attain a style
of living they have been accustomed to since birth.

Growing up surrounded by affluence, many of today's young Japanese
men place less emphasis on defining status by purchases. As seen earlier, sales of alcohol and cars, to name just two items men typically consume, have been steadily decreasing recently. Beer and cars can both be
seen as status items, as only a few decades ago neither of these could be
obtained by all consumers. Though it is difficult to fathom today, being
able to drink beer (or whisky) was a luxury to the post-war generation.
Hoppy, a beer-taste drink added to Japanese liquor, was the closest that
many consumers got to beer in the post-war years. The feeling of luxury
and attainment brought on by drinking beer was communicated to the
children of the post-war generation, today's 40 and 50-year-olds. An
interesting parallel can be seen with North Korea. The state recently
launched television commercials for beer showing men in suits – a rare
sight in the hermit kingdom – drinking beer with attractive waitresses.
It was the first commercial for a product broadcast on North Korean
state TV ('North Korea's First Beer Commercial', accessed 6 July 2009)
and the commercial clearly seeks to create an image of abundance.
Today beer is no longer a luxury item, but is an almost necessary item
for men in company life. It has been tainted by the uncool image of
50-year-old businessmen, and has lost its appeal factor to younger consumers, becoming another social straightjacket.

Another factor that may be influencing men to spend less is the
women they spend money on. As the nature of romance changes, so
must the nature of how men woo. While women in the bubble era may

have demanded to be wined and dined, then taken home in a fancy car, today's women are less impressed by a man with high economic status than by a man who will stick with them and be a partner in raising a family and keeping a home. As women become less dependent on men for economic support, they want friends and partners, not providers, as mates. In Japan the traditional criteria for selecting a good mate were referred to as the '3 *kou*'. These three criteria (tall, good school, good salary), were all written with the Chinese character for tall or high, pronounced '*kou*'. As women have become financially independent, salary has become less of a requirement in a mate. Similarly, as Japanese employment patterns have changed, school history has also become less important. Studies have also shown that women prefer mates who have less high-flying jobs (and hence lower salaries) as it means they are more likely to be around to help with the work of raising a family and caring for offspring (BBC, 9 February 2007, 'Why Women Fall for Mr. Average').

As a replacement for the 3 *kou*, Megumi Ushikubo proposes the '3 lows': low-key, low-risk, and low-dependency (Ushikubo, 2008, pp. 24–7). According to Ushikubo, women today want a man who is less flashy. They aren't seeking fancy gifts like their counterparts a generation ago. They would rather have a man who is straightforward and honest, who doesn't worry so much about impressing them. They also want a man with less risk. A man with an extremely high income is an easy target for mate-poaching.[12] Women are seeking more equality in a relationship. A man with a lower-paying job cannot claim to be providing for a woman and therefore cannot claim that she is dependent on him. Furthermore, a man with a lower-paying job is likely to be around more, and complain less about helping with childcare and housework.

Women seem to have changed the conditions they are looking for in selecting a partner. Beyond this, many people in Japan are getting married later or not at all. Starting families later, or deciding not to have a family, naturally influences consumption decisions. In some cases, having no children leaves a man with more money to spend in ways that he sees fit. This is often by buying model railroads and Gundam figurines. But in many other cases a single man simply consumes less than he would have done after producing a few offspring. This choice to have a family later or not at all is not a consumption decision *per se*, but a life choice that has profound implications for consumption throughout a male's lifetime.

Changing economic conditions, as well as the changing rules of mating, play a part in the development of the new male, his outlook on life, and therefore his outlook on consumption. But what about male role models? The influence of fathers (or father figures) growing up shapes ideas of masculinity. Boys see their fathers and often take the first cues of masculinity from this arguably most important male role model. Why aren't more men following the examples their fathers set as they enter adulthood? Part of the answer, as discussed above, lies in the changing economic realities that made many young men question the way their fathers worked, along with what their fathers purchased. Another part of the answer may be that, while young boys were growing up, fathers were less of a presence in their lives than mothers. With long hours at the office and a traditionally less involved male attitude toward parenting, female influence may have been more prevalent in everyday life (Fall interview). Feminine role models, as well as a home primarily kept by females, produce a more feminine environment. This is not to say that men became more feminine, but rather that a lack of ever-present male role models simply did not impart a strong impression of what a 'masculine' role should ideally involve (Fall interview).

Changing consumption patterns

Before continuing, we will take a short look at some of the more interesting and important consumer groups that have been identified in the Japanese media. Here are some of the newer and more important consumer groups identified among young men in Japan. This simplified representation (Table 7.1) aims to show that young males are a diverse group, and a consumer segment that is far from static.

It was mentioned earlier in the chapter that men are buying fewer cars and less alcohol. Due to changing economic conditions, men are less willing and less able to spend on conspicuous consumption. We will now look at some areas where male purchasing behaviour is remarkably different from that of previous generations, as well as providing some examples of how old products have retooled for success with young men.

The male sweet tooth

Today it is not hard to find chocolate products that are geared to appeal to men. Japanese office workers, both during the bubble and before, seemed to regard chocolate as somehow un-masculine (Ushikubo, 2008, pp. 135–8). There is some scientific evidence to suggest that men prefer salty snacks, and women prefer sweet. This stereotype, coupled with a somewhat sexist working environment, may have helped to create a bias against sweets in the mind of the Japanese male. However,

Table 7.1   *Tayouka*-Diversification: taxonomy of different consumer groups and attributes

	Age range	Defining characteristics	Press
Soushoku Danshi (草食)	Most in teens or twenties, some thirty-somethings exhibit similar characteristics.	Named by writer Maki Fukasawa. Less hypermasculine than earlier generations of men. Not as focused on sex or career advancement.	Ushikubo (2008), Fukasawa in *Nikkei online*
Soushoku Danshi (装飾)	Typically teens or twenty-somethings.	Characters mean 'decorated'. Men concerned with fashion. Often blurring gender boundaries.	Recent development
Dokushin Oji (独身王子)	Have reached mid-career level pay, typically late thirties or forties. Some younger.	'Single Princes'. Term coined by writer Megumi Ushikubo. Have disposable income and no family, are able to exert maximum control over purchasing decisions. Many consume as if the bubble economy had never ended.	Ushikubo (2006)

more and more companies are trying to persuade men to come back and rediscover their sweet tooth. As mentioned earlier, one of the hallmarks of this new Japanese man is his readiness to indulge in little luxuries as a sort of retail therapy. Ushikubo's book (2008), widely credited for introducing the concept of the herbivorous man to the wider public, opens with these words: 'There are some around you too. A convenience store, 9 p.m.; the happy looking man buying a treat filled to the brim with whipped cream' (Ushikubo, 2008, p. 4). To Ushikubo, sweets are central to the new Japanese male. On 25 November 2009, in a profile on NPR dealing with the new Japanese man, Yasuhito Sekine and his online dessert club is cited as an archetype for his generation (Louisa Lim, 2009).

Men's fashion

Just like their predecessors at the office, young men want to look good because it makes them feel confident and successful. Certainly there are new ideas about what is fashionable and what is masculine, but the basic idea behind the willingness of men to spend on looks is the same. The major change is in the external trappings, while the underlying motivation for clothing – helping young men feel sexier, suaver or more confident, whatever the occasion – has not changed.

A recent fashion trend picked up by the Japanese language *Nikkei Marketing Journal (MJ)*,[13] men's leggings or 'meggings', helps to paint a picture of the current state of men's fashion. The article starts out with the tag line 'a formerly women's fashion item, leggings have now become firmly established, underwear makers are working hard to get them into men's departments for the fall season' (*Nikkei MJ,* 16 September 2009, p. 16). Of course, Japanese men are not cross-dressing *en masse*, but they are wearing more fashion items that were once the preserve of women. Fashionsnap.com, a Tokyo-based street fashion website, regularly features males wearing clothing designed for females. This is not limited to meggings, but also skirts (worn over pants). The demand for the latter has become large enough that a web store retailing skirts for men has sprung up, allowing male consumers a place to shop for skirts where they can easily find their size, and not have to ask potentially embarrassing questions of apparel store staff. According to Tokyo trend agency Five by Fifty, many male styles today are the result of a revival of traditional styles, as well as the product of female influence. Many men in their twenties and thirties today were raised primarily by mothers, with fathers away working long hours. The skirts and jewellery of today's men can be seen as revivals, modern-day equivalents of the flowing kimonos and elegant swords worn by male samurai.

Perhaps we should speak less of men dressing more like women and more of a blurring of the gender lines that divide apparel. This is not unique to Japan. *The New York Times* recently profiled young urbanities in the US buying and wearing clothes designed for the opposite sex. A walk through a shopping street in a fashionable section of Tokyo will quickly provide examples of the new battle lines of gender and fashion. Young couples in Japan are dressing more and more alike, with skinny jeans, loose tops and scarves being in vogue for both sexes.

It has been shown that the economic climate for young men in Japan today is a difficult one. Many researchers, including Matsuda (2009) and Ushikubo (2008), assert that young men are in general nervous about their future. With falling incomes, they are no longer able to buy designer watches and suits like their bubble counterparts. However, with luxury brands being out of reach and more local brands springing up, fashion has become freer. With more freedom in fashion, and less expensive 'fast fashion' becoming more widespread, men are able to take more control over their appearance, providing a sense of self-esteem as well as an area of life where men do not have to feel anxious (Fall interview).

The new Japanese male's desire to purchase can be seen as a form of retail therapy. When feeling upset they turn less to wives or families as confidants, and instead turn to shopping to lift their moods (Ushikubo, 2008, pp. 135–7; Fall interview). As men get married later and go out less with work colleagues, retail therapy – shopping to improve one's mood – has taken over as a stress relief outlet for many young men. While these men are not wealthy, they have no qualms about spending the disposable income they do have on little luxuries for themselves.

Men's beauty products

As part of its consumer research, Shiseido, a famous manufacturer of health and beauty products, asked young men in their twenties to spend a day without styling their hair. Many of them were unable to do it (Ushikubo, 2008, pp. 120–1). In another 2007 study, when asked what expenses they would cut back on, young men (those in their twenties and thirties) answered that the first priority was cutting back on eating out (Ushikubo, pp. 106–8). This is not terribly surprising, as eating out is a luxury item, and a typical casualty of hard economic times. However one category where men were extremely reluctant to cut back

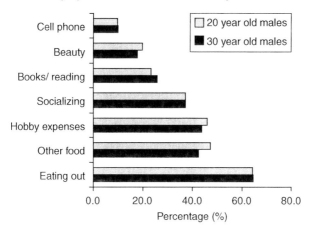

Figure 7.3 How men choose to save money: when money is tight, food and socialization expenses are the first to go (Ushikubo, 2008, p. 107)

Source: 'Kongetsu kitsui na to Omottara, Dono Shouhi ga Hazuru' [In a tight month, what expenses do you cut?] (At Home Group.'Ki ni Naru Hitorigurashi no Seikatsu Jyouhou. 2007.' [Interesting Information Pertaining to those Living Alone]).

was food and beauty spending (Ushikubo, pp. 106–8.; see Figure 7.3). This further illustrates a new emphasis on male consumers spending on their appearance, a luxury for themselves.

The market for men's beauty products and services has expanded dramatically in the past several years. This phenomenon is also not unique to Japan. In his book, Turngate asserts that the market for men's grooming products rose by nearly a third in the 5 years between 2001 to 2006 (Turngate, 2008, p. 13). Turngate asserts that male grooming has not had the success predicted since the inception of the category in the late 1980s, but that 'Nonetheless the market is growing' (Turngate, 2008, p. 13). In 2010 the worldwide men's beauty market is expected to reach approximately 40 per cent of its female counterpart. Turngate seems to suggest that these predictions are a bit over-optimistic, but here in Japan the male market is about one-sixth the size of the women's cosmetics market (Turngate, p. 13; Ushikubo, p. 125). While men across the world may not be living up to the expectations of the beauty industry, the new Japanese man is doing his part (see Figure 7.4).

What is more important that the general growth of the male beauty industry in Japan is the specific products and services that are seeing sales numbers rise. Male aesthetic salons have seen much higher growth than the aesthetic industry[14] as a whole over the past several years. While the industry as a whole is expected to grow between 1 and 2 per

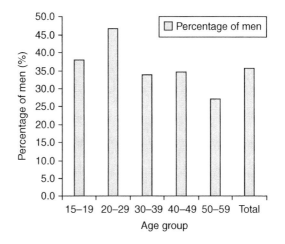

Figure 7.4   Male cosmetic consumers in Japan by age group
Source: Intage, Men's Beauty Market Trends, 2007.

cent a year, the male aesthetic industry is supposed to see YoY growth ranging between 7 and 10 per cent (Delta I.D. research, 2008).

Men are increasingly paying attention to their skin, again hoping to look young and attractive, and as a result feel successful and confident (Turngate, pp. 11–37; Ushikubo, 2006, pp. 138–43; Ushikubo, 2008, pp. 123–4). Self-tanners and skin whiteners, long popular with female consumers, are now starting to see a rise in male users. Again, this trend is perhaps not unique to Japan. The emphasis here is on the formerly feminine beauty products that are now being actively marketed to men (Turngate, pp. 23–4). This is happening in tandem with the blurring gender lines of fashion mentioned earlier. In Japan and other Asian countries, which are perhaps seeing a faster blurring of gender lines than Western societies, the men's cosmetics market lacks as many growth constraints as in certain Western markets (Turngate, pp. 26–8). This changed outlook regarding beauty and personal care is creating new markets in Japan.

Beer rebrands

Beer and whisky have suffered over the past few years. According to *Media* magazine, beer sales in Japan have fallen almost 11 per cent from their 1994 peak (Smith, 4 June 2009). While Japanese brewers keep bringing out new product lines, especially in the *happoshu* and third beer categories,[15] market share for the entire beer and near beer market keeps falling.

One of the main reasons for the decline in beer sales is a lack of beer drinkers among young men. In consumer interviews conducted for her book (2007), Ushikubo found out that many young men don't drink alcohol at all, let alone beer (Ushikubo, 2008, pp. 112–14). According to a survey citied in the *Nikkei Business Press Online*, the number of people in their twenties who do not drink is roughly 14 per cent, while the number of thirty-somethings who do not drink alcohol is only around 10 per cent. Looking to still older generations, only 4.3 per cent of those over 60 years of age do not drink (Kakaku.com Research, 2009; see Figure 7.5).

While beer may be the most obvious sector hurting in Japan's alcoholic beverage market, it is not the only struggling category. whisky, traditionally seen as a high-class, masculine drink, has fared even worse in recent years, with nearly 70 per cent of twenty-somethings saying they either did not drink, or did not much care for the beverage. According to the same survey cited by the *Nikkei* online article, there is also a growing preference among young people for sweeter drinks, such as cocktails, chuhai,[16] and plum wine (*Nikkei Restaurant Online*, 21 August 2009).

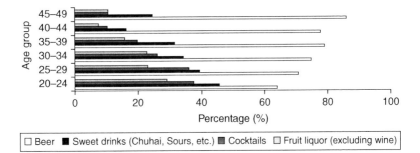

Figure 7.5 'What Do You Enjoy Drinking?' (both at home and drinking out) by age group

Source: Media Shakers, 2009, 'M1F1 Topic Vol. 22 July 2009', http://www.m1f1.jp/m1f1/files/topic_090728.pdf

Although the surveys cited here seem to indicate a growing preference for other types of alcohol over traditional standby 'masculine' drinks, beer still remains an important part of Japan's alcohol market, and many young males still consume it. However, beer sales of all types have been shrinking since 1994, and, given the age breakdown of beer consumers, it is impossible to ignore the connection between falling beer sales and younger consumers moving away from the beverage.

One product in the beer category that has gained the attention of the twenty-something market has been Sparkling Hop, a third-genre beer from Kirin that is fruity-tasting and lightly carbonated. While older hard-core beer drinkers shun this fruity beer-taste drink, young people have tried it in large numbers (Ushikubo, 2008, pp. 110–11). The beer appeals to young people in two ways. First, it is fruity, and matches their tastes more closely. Second, it is very different from other beers on the market. Many of those who try this new Sparkling Hop brand may not become regular consumers, but Kirin has played on the short attention span and curiosity of younger consumers, who will try anything once, if only for the experience (Ushikubo, pp. 110–11). When products are formulated with young males in mind, they can still succeed, even if they are in markets traditionally seen as being in decline.

Another area in which young men have been lured back to alcohol is the highball craze. In the case of Japan, 'highball' has a slightly different meaning, typically being a cocktail made with (Suntory Kakubin) whisky, soda water, a twist of lemon, and often some sweetener. Though many young men do not like the taste of whisky, Suntory's market researchers found that highball culture had a certain retro appeal to young men. The beverage is cheaper than draft beer, helping it to gain additional support from cost-conscious consumers. Through its consumer research, Suntory found out that a traditional highball mixture contained too much alcohol and was therefore too strong for most young men. By adding less whisky and more soda and sweetener to the mix, Suntory, the largest whisky maker in Japan, has presided over an impressive reversal of whisky's image (at least in highball form). According to the Diamond Online, the number of stores retailing highballs with Suntory's Kakubin Whisky has increased from around 15,000 *izakayas* and bars to more than 60,000 establishments at the end of 2009. The company also planned a 15 per cent production increase for Kakubin Whisky, the first production increase in 11 years (*Kansai Sankei Shinbun*, 22 September 2009).[17]

However, it should be mentioned that many young consumers who like whisky highballs do not like drinking whisky *per se*; their aversion to the taste of the liquor is proof of that. The consumption ritual behind the drink, as well as the link to more stable times (and of course cost performance), are all likely more important factors in the cocktail's success than the whisky itself.

The success of Kirin's Sparkling Hop and Suntory's Highball revival show that there is hope for alcohol sales to increase among young men. Many young men can be convinced to alter consumption habits if the product or service offered can be tailored to resonate with their goals and their life image. Kirin saw that the sparkling soft drinks market had seen impressive growth over the past few years and decided to offer an extra-carbonated beer to consumers. This trend of extra carbonation in canned alcohol has since been picked up by both Suntory and Asahi, two of Kirin's rivals. Suntory meanwhile discovered that, though young people may not like the taste of whisky, when it was mixed with a higher proportion of soda than normal, and a twist of lemon and some sweeteners added, the company could sell whisky cocktails cheaply, both raising sales and appealing to cost-conscious and trend-conscious consumers.

Cars

During the bubble era, a car was considered a must-have item. Over the past several years, Japan has seen car sales dip by approximately 1.5 per cent from 1980 to 2007 (Matsuda, pp. 16–17). For young people (aged 20–29) the decline has been much more severe – about 50 per cent (Matsuda, pp. 16–17). But here too there is a bright spot – the performance of hybrid and environmentally friendly cars. While more and more men are saying they do not want to buy a car – 45 per cent, according to a 2007 survey conducted by the *Nikkei* – many will still have to buy one at some point (Ushikubo, 2008, pp. 94–6). When young men are buying a new car, there is a growing trend towards more practical, eco-friendly vehicles (Ushikubo, 2008, pp. 98–9).

Young men are not regarded as voracious consumers, but when they do consume they tend to do so with a conscience. These men attempt to consume less, and state that they do consume; they do so with an emphasis on cost-performance calculations, as well as an eye to the environment. A car that uses less petrol or an appliance that uses less energy can help save the consumer money in the long run. This is an important consideration when thinking of the economic status of many young men today.

Conclusion: today's young male consumer

Throughout this chapter, we have looked at some ways in which young men are changing consumption habits. Young males today buy fewer cars and drink less alcohol than their peers 20 years ago. As beer and car sales drop, and these industries see their consumer base age, marketers are bound to worry. Though young men may not treat themselves to fancy cars or a pint after work, young men today are spending more on other luxuries for themselves. Fashion is becoming an increasingly important source of self-esteem for many men as more traditional career-based achievement paths are closed to them. Men feel freer to spend on fashion that would have been taboo to their parents, and do not think twice about investing more money in their appearance, whether it be through visiting aesthetic salons or buying more beauty products. While men may no longer consume cars and alcohol as they once did, they are voracious consumers of products in other categories. Consumption habits change, and, though some industries may suffer because of this, others will prosper, and still others will be created.

This chapter has attempted to show that many factors have led to a change in male consumption habits. The changing face of the Japanese labour market has introduced more uncertainty into the life of Japanese employees, and in many cases has also resulted in decreased pay and less affluent living conditions. This, coupled with an increase in female workers and female salaries, has had a profound effect on society. As men get married later or shun matrimony altogether, consumption patterns naturally change. A family will consume differently from, and likely more than, a single male. However, those men who do desire to get married must adapt to the changes prospective female partners have undergone. As female incomes grow and women become more independent, they look for different qualities in a mate, and for a male to be successful in finding a mate he needs to adapt; for example, high income is now less important to females than a man with low risk who will spend time helping to raise the family. Living up to the new woman has certainly had an effect on male consumption and lifestyle habits.

We have also seen how the new Japanese male is not one single monolithic consumer group. In fact, there are many kinds of new Japanese men, though they are creatures of their age. They share many of the same experiences and have been affected by many of the same changes. As a result they share many common characteristics, namely eco-consciousness, emphasis on convenience and speed, and worries about the future; have high personal care standards; and view both their work lives and their love lives in a different way than Japanese men of a generation ago. However, this is not to say, as many Western and Japanese commentators have said, that Japanese men are becoming more feminine or weaker. They are simply not caught up in previous traditional notions of masculinity. The Japanese male is changing, and some men may be choosing a lifestyle that is closer to a traditional feminine role; however, the life choices of a few Japanese men should not be projected onto an entire generation. Trends have inertia. In other words, when a trend moves too far in one direction it inevitably begins to swing back. As young Japanese males move further away from traditional ideas of masculinity, more men will begin to rediscover and retool traditional ideas of masculinity. These neo-traditional ideas of masculinity will not be identical to those of their fathers, but will certainly contain an echo of them. Young men are interesting in their own right both as consumers and as barometers of future consumption behaviour of young men in other industrialized countries in transition. But this group also serves as a reminder that Japan is not static and Japanese consumers will continue to change with the evolution of new consumer groups.

Matsuda asserts that there is a very real danger of young people not consuming enough (Matsuda, 16–17). However companies should focus on the positive, and begin retooling for the next wave of consumers. The new Japanese male may consume less than his father, but he will consume as his income and life needs dictate. Businesses and researchers must attempt to leave their preconceived notions of male consumption behind and work to understand this new group of consumers. Companies cannot succeed by selling the same products in the same way to a new generation of males. If marketers can uncover the themes that resonate with young men and create products and messages that reflect these themes, they can be successful. This chapter has given several examples of products that changed their message or formula to resonate with a new group of consumers, who then rewarded them with purchase. With today's young Japanese male expected to live well into his seventies, it should be mentioned once again that males form product preferences in their twenties and early thirties. By reaching out to young men today, companies can gain loyal consumers for decades.

Notes

1. For a thorough summary see Fukasawa Maki's article *'sousyokudanshi to kekkon, makeinu to nikusyoku jyoushi'* on 9 July 2009.
2. See *Japan Times* article on 10 May 2009, 'Office Workers Out in Front in Demand for Men's Bras', and *New York Times* article on 19 November 2007, 'In Japan it's the Men who Want to be Skinny and Cute.'
3. Using the term *'tayouka'* （多様化）.
4. Fukasawa identifies 23 different kinds of Heise men alone.
5. In the Japanese calendar, Heisei refers to the reign of the current emperor, starting in 1989. The Heise generation is thus the Japanese who have been born since 1989.
6. Though certainly not always practised. While social constraints demanded 'modesty', this was largely determined by one's social status and the situation.
7. Japan's 'Lost Decade' refers to the period between 1991 and 2000 after the Japanese 'Bubble Economy' crashed. Slow reforms and debt-burdened banks led to a decade of nearly zero economic growth before slow economic growth began again under the Koizumi administration.
8. With an exchange rate of approximately 100 yen = US$1, not adjusted for purchasing power parity.
9. A summary can be found on NHK's *'Asu no Nihon'* website (in Japanese). http://www.nhk.or.jp/asupro/koyou/koyou_01.html
10. In Japan it is often said that it takes 3 years to learn a job; therefore quitting by the second year doesn't even count as having gained experience.
11. Many of the figures given here have been taken from Shigeyuki Jyou, *Wakamono ha Naze 3 nende Yamerunoka? [Why do young people quit after 3 years?]* This book and its author are controversial in Japan, but the book gives an excellent overview of the changing work patterns in Japan and how this is affecting young men and their company lives. For those seeking to better understand the problems facing younger workers and their motivations, this book would be a helpful read.
12. For a more detailed discussion of mate-poaching see Robin Baker (1996), *Sperm Wars*, New York: Thunder's Mouth Press
13. The *Nikkei Marketing Journal (MJ)* or *Nikkei Ryutsuu Shinbun* is a thrice-weekly paper put out by the Nikkei Newspaper company, publishers of the world's

largest circulating business daily, that specializes in advertising and marketing trends.
14. Aesthetic salons provide a variety of services, from tanning to hair removal
and other grooming services.
15. In Japan, grain is heavily taxed. To lower tax rates and therefore prices,
many 'beers' in Japan feature little or no malt. Depending on the malt content, beer can be *happoshu*, containing less than two-thirds, and third beer,
which need not contain any malt.
16. *Chuhai* is a (typically sweet) cocktail that blends Japanese liquor with fruit
flavouring.
17. Japanese title: 'ウイスキー20年ぶり売り上げ増 飲食店が支えたハイボール効果'

References

Baker, R. (1996), *Sperm Wars*, New York: Thunder's Mouth Press.
Bulik, B. S. (2008), 'How the Male of the Species Shops', *Advertising Age*,
79(8): 12.
Fields, G. (1989), 'The Shinjinrui: A Species with No Hang-Ups', in *The Japanese
Market Culture*, Tokyo: The Japan Times Ltd.
Fukasawa, M. (2007), *Heisei Danshi Zukan [A Guide to the Heise Boys]*, Tokyo:
Nikkei Business Press.
Hofstede, G. (2001), *Culture's Consequences: Comparing Values, Behaviors,
Organizations and Institutions Across Nations*, Teller Oaks, CA: Sage.
Japan Times (2009), 'Office Workers Out in Front in Demand for Men's Bras' (10
May).
Jyou, S. (2006), *Naze Wakamono ha 3nende Yameru noka? Nenkoujyoretsu ga Ubau
Nihon no Mirai [Why do Young People Quit in 3 Years? The Lifetime Employment
System Stealing Japan's Future]*, Tokyo: Kobunsya.
Matsuda, H. (2009), *Iyashohi Sedai no Kenkyu: Keizai wo Yurugasu 'Hoshigaranai'
Wakamonotachi [Cool Consumption Generational Research: The Young People
whose Lack of Consumption Desire is Shaking the Economy]*, Tokyo: Touyou Keizai
Shinpousya.
Nikkei MJ (2009), 'Meginzu' Gaichu Kappo' [Meggings – Male Leggings – Striding
Down the Street], (16 September), p. 16.
Nikkei MJ (2009), 'Murasaki Iro no Happoushu' [Purple Near-Beer] (2 November),
p. 7.
Smith, G., 'Innovation Backfires for Japanese Beer Giants', *Media*, *Sector Insight*
(4 June), p. 21.
The New York Times (2007), 'In Japan It's the Men Who Want to be Skinny and
Cute' (19 November).
Turngate, M. (2008), *Branded Male: Marketing to Men*, London and Philadelphia:
Kogan Page.
Ushikubo, M. (2006), *Dokushin Ouji ni Kike! [Listen to the Single Princes!]*, Tokyo:
Nikkei Shimbun Publishing Company.
Ushikubo, M. (2008), *Shoushokukei Danshi 'Ojyouman' ga Nippon wo Kaeru
[Herbivorous Men, The Princesses Who Will Change Japan]*, Tokyo, Japan:
Kodansha Plus Alpha.

'35sai' wo Sukue: Naze 10nennmae no 35sai yori no Nenshu ga 200manen mo Hikui no ka? [Save the '35-year-olds': Why are Salaries 2,000,000 yen Lower than 35-year-olds 10 Years ago?] (2009), Tokyo: NHK and Mitsubishi Research Institute.

Online sources

Aditi, N., 'North Korea's First Beer Commercial', Foreign Policy.com, available at http://blog.foreignpolicy.com/posts/2009/07/06/north_koreas_latest_launch_beer_ads (accessed 6 July 2009).

Asahi Brewery Press Release, 'Aiming for a Whisky Revival' (17 August 2009), available at http://www.asahibeer.co.jp/news/2009/0817_2.html

At Home Group (2007), 'Kongetsu kitsui na to Omottara, Dono Shouhi ga Hazuru' [In a Tight Month, What Expenses Do You Cut?], 'Ki ni Naru Hitorigurashi no Seikatsu Jyouhou' [Interesting Information Pertaining to Those Living Alone], available at http://www.athome.co.jp/oyakudachi/research/

Delta I.D. Research (2008), '2008 Aesthetic Salon Industry Composition Research', available at http://www.deltas.jp/view/20080204/

Diamond Online (2010), 'Uisuki 20 Nennburi Uriagezou, Insyokuten ga Sasaetai Haibouru Kouka' [First Increase in Whisky Sales in 20 Years, the Result of Bars and Restaurants Supporting Highballs] (22 January 2010), available at http://zasshi.news.yahoo.co.jp/article?a=20100122-00000000-diamond-bus_all

Fashionsnap.com, available at http://www.fashionsnap.com/streetsnap/2010/winter/8091/; http://www.fashionsnap.com/streetsnap/2010/winter/8153/

Fukasawa, M. (2006), 'Daigokai, Soushoku Danshi' [Number 5, Herbivorous Men], *Nikkei Business Online*, U35 Danshi Marketing (13 October) (accessed 16 November 2008).

Fukasawa, M. (2009), 'Soushoku Danshi to Konnkatsu, Makeinu to Nikushoku Jyoushi' [Herbivorous Men and Marriage, The Women Who Lose and the 'Carnivores'], *Nikkei Business Online* (9 July), http://www.nikkei.co.jp (accessed 11 June 2009).

Intage (2007), 'Men's Beauty Market Trends' (13 August), available at http://www.intage.co.jp/news/2007/6/

Japan Center for Labor Policy and Training (2006), 'Labor Situation in Japan and Analysis: General Overview 2006/2007', available at http://www.jil.go.jp/english/index.html

Kakaku.com Research (2009), 'Biiru, Happoshu, Dai-san Biiru, Kono Natsu Nomitai no ha?' [Beer, Low-malt Beer, Third-category Beer, What Do You Want to Drink This Summer?], *Kekka* Report no. 032 (16 July), available at http://kakaku.com/research/backnumber032.html

Kirin Company News (2007), 'Kirin Sparkling Hop wo Shinhatsubai' [Sales to start of Kirin Sparkling Hop] (21 August), available at http://www.kirin.co.jp/company/news/2007/0821_01.html

Lim, Louisa (2009), 'In Japan, "Herbivore" Boys Subvert Ideas of Manhood', *NPR* (25 November), available at http://www.npr.org/templates/story/story.php?storyId=120696816 (accessed 15 December 2009).

Media Shakers (2009), 'Wakamono no "Biiru Hanare" no Kenshou' [Young People Moving Away from Beer Investigation], *M1F1* Topic Vol. 22 (July), available at http://www.m1f1.jp/m1f1/files/topic_090728.pdf

Ministry of Health, Labor and Welfare (2005), 'Nenreibetsu Mikonritsu no Suii' [Transition of Single Population Ratio, by Sex], available at http://wwwhakusyo. mhlw.go.jp/wpdocs/hpax200601/b0003.html

National Institute of Population and Social Security Research (Kokuritsu Shakai Hoshou.Jinkou Mondai Kenkyusho) (2006), 'Bankonka no Shinkou: Heikin Shokon Nenrei no Suii' [To a Later-Marrying Society: Age of First Marriage in Transition], available at http://www.ipss.go.jp

National Tax Agency (2008), 'Citizens' Income Status, 2008, Survey Results', reprinted at http://nensyu-labo.com/heikin_suii.htm

Nikkei Resturant Online (2009), 'Wakamono no "Sakebanare" ga Kencyo! Gaishoku yori mo Iede Osake Nomu Hito ga Zouka!' [Young People Moving Away from Alcohol! More People Drinking at Home!], (21 August), available at http://nr.nikkeibp.co.jp/topics/20090821/ (accessed 9 December 2009).

Ushikubo, M. and Fukasawa, Maki (2009), 'Kuruma wo Kawanai Soushoku Danshiha, "Mikou Shouhi" Shinai' [Herbivores Who Don't Buy Cars Shun Conspicuous Consumption], *Nikkei Business Online* (12 March), www.nikkei.co.jp (accessed 5 July 2009).

World Bank (2010), 'World Development Indicators', available at http://data.worldbank.org/data-catalog/world-development-indicators?cid=GPD_WDI.

Interviews

Fall, N. (2010), personal interview, 19 May.

8
Otaku Consumers

Patrick W. Galbraith

'They [*otaku*] despise physical contact and love media, technical communication, and the realm of reproduction and simulation in general. They are enthusiastic collectors and manipulators of useless artifacts and information. They are underground, but they are not opposed to the system. They change, manipulate, and subvert ready-made products, but at the same time they are the apotheosis of consumerism and an ideal workforce for contemporary Japanese capitalism. They are the children of the media.' (Volker Grassmuck, 1990)

Introduction

Perhaps no consumer group has captured the popular imagination as much as *otaku*. The word '*otaku*' is often followed by descriptions of young Japanese men hunched in front of computer or TV screens alone in darkened rooms (Gibson, 1996; Grassmuck, 1990; Greenfeld, 1993). This image of *otaku* is insufficient to grasp the vibrant culture that has emerged around Japanese media and technology. There are male and female *otaku* across a wide age demographic in Japan and around the world. They are not a handful of outcasts, but a major market, estimated at US$1.87 billion in Japan in 2007.[1] *Otaku* are enthusiastic consumers of manga, anime and computer/console games, and technologies to view and engage these media. Hobbies extend into related merchandise and personalities. They are notable for the intensity and longevity of their interests, which often includes some level of creative engagement. More than just a consumer or fan culture, however, *otaku* represent a mode of existence in information-consumer society.

146

Otaku tend to consume information, or treat consumption as a source of information. They are oriented towards information-rich hobbies. For example, manga (still images), anime (moving images) and games (interactive images) each provide fans with a web of technical details. Okada Toshio defines *otaku* as people who have developed an 'advanced visual sense' (*shinka shita shikaku*) through sustained interaction with media and technology (Okada, 1996, p.10). They have a different way of seeing things. That is, they visualize and analyse objects of interest, and consumption becomes a form of knowledge production. Further, manga, anime and videogames are organized into a 'media mix', where characters and stories appear across platforms to create networked, synergetic meaning. Mizuko Ito argues that this model extends the influence of media and makes it an 'intimate presence' in everyday life (Ito, 2008, p. 13).[2] Media mixes practically require fan engagement: '"Reception" is not only active and negotiated but is a *productive* act of creating a shared imagination and participating in a social world' (Ito, 2008, p. 5). Personal and creative engagements with commercial material result in 'peer-to-peer ecologies of cultural production and exchange (of information, objects, and money)' (Ito, 2008, p. 8).

Otaku are thus prone to 'hypersociality' or 'social exchange augmented by the social mobilization of elements of the collective imagination' (Ito, 2008, p. 8). Nakajima Azusa describes *otaku* as 'hermit crabs' that build up and ferry around 'shells of self' in hobbies, and, referring to one another as *otaku* experts of certain hobby areas, mutually endorse affiliation (Nakajima, 1995, pp. 44, 49). She ties the *otaku* search for self to the loss of paternal or national authority in their lives. As Azuma Hiroki states, '*Otaku* shut themselves into the hobby community not because they deny sociality but rather because, as social values and standards are already dysfunctional, they felt a pressing need to construct alternative values' (Azuma, 2009, p. 27). To understand *otaku* it is first necessary to understand the social context of their activities.

Otaku occupy an ambiguous position in Japan. Lawrence Eng posits that *otaku* are 'reluctant insiders' in capitalist consumer society (Eng, 2006, p. 24). They are middle-class and have access to resources, and yet are disenfranchised. *Otaku* engage in alternative consumption and unintended appropriation of media and technology to gain power and status in *otaku* knowledge communities (Eng, 2006, p. 34). This does not necessarily translate into mainstream social or economic capital. *Otaku* are early adapters, and their movement on the margins can link to underground economy. Consumption and production in *otaku* communities may be independent of corporations, or not directly beneficial to them. However, Eng points out that *otaku* are 'a voice of reasoned restraint', and pair information-sharing activities and derivative creation with support for companies and 'a strong ethic in favor of intellectual property' (Eng, 2006, p. 216). Matt Hills notes that cult fans in general tend towards 'anti-commercial ideologies and commodity-completist practices' (Hills, 2002, p. 28), but *otaku* display significantly less ambivalence towards mass culture.

The issue, then, is the place of *otaku* in the consumer market. For Kitabayashi Ken, *otaku* are the 'driving force for bringing about industrial innovation' (Kitabayashi, 2004, p. 1). *Otaku* pursue ideals, and consume to be closer to them (Kitabayashi, 2004, p. 4). As these ideals cannot be realized, *otaku* cannot be satisfied and endlessly consume. They pour nearly all their disposable income into the pursuit, but in their fervour eventually lose focus and move on to new goals or into other fields. On the other hand, Eng points out that *otaku* are deliberate in consumption, often researching products and knowing more than even the creators (Eng, 2006, p. 154). *Otaku* consumption is somewhere between losing control and exercising control, and oscillates between these extremes. Due to the segmented and specialized nature of hobbies, *otaku* seek out communities to share information. They study to become experts, and by extension may produce derivative and original contents. Production, like consumption, is to materialize the ideal. Kitabayashi suggests that companies can observe and absorb *otaku* creativity before releasing products to general consumers (Kitabayashi, 2004, p. 7). Thus *otaku* do not merely represent an attractive test market, but also a source of consumptive and productive energy. This positive evaluation of *otaku* comes after decades of struggling with this culture in Japan. This paper will outline the history and sociocultural context of *otaku* in order to better understand their behaviours.

Post-war foundation

Rather than beginning with possible pre-modern precedents for *otaku*-ism in Japan (Murakami, 2005; Okada, 1996), it is more effective to place *otaku* in the context of mass media and material culture after World War II. After the war, a devastated Japan needed cheap entertainment, and manga was ideally suited. Frederik L. Schodt notes that authors of manga as well as 'red comics' (*akahon manga*) produced outside the industry centre in Tokyo, were often young newcomers frustrated in other fields (Schodt, 1983, p. 62). For example, Tezuka Osamu was originally interested in film, but settled on manga, which he innovated with superb storytelling, cinematic style and experimental techniques. '[C]omics came to be regarded as a creative medium accessible to anyone – unlike novels or film which required education, connections, and money' (Schodt, 1983, p. 66). The rapid rise of manga as pulp entertainment with lower barriers for participation and (relatively) greater creative control invited an array of talented creators. Because manga evolved to cover a wide range of topics, the readership was vast and diverse, and supported a vast and diverse market. Affordability, accessibility and appealing presentation and content were elements that contributed to the establishment of manga as mass culture.

The same can be said for anime. The household appliance boom from the late 1950s into the 1960s saw a rapid rise in television ownership: in 1958, 7.8 per cent of households had a television, but by 1966 this number had reached 95 per cent.[3] This set up the distribution network for television anime, which began in 1963 with Tezuka's *Mighty Atom* (known overseas as *Astro Boy*), revolutionary for its format of 25-minute, serialized episodes. This was an experiment that few expected to succeed, but Tezuka cut costs by limiting motion (eight frames per second, as opposed to the average 18 frames per second in Disney animation) and using a bank of stock images. Tezuka priced his works far lower than they were worth (approximately 500,000 yen per episode), which made it a cost-effective choice for broadcasters, but also established a precedent that keeps animators and studios desperately poor.[4] Anime was produced as mass entertainment for kids and a form of creative expression. Ōtsuka Eiji argues that Japanese anime is a hybrid of animation and other imported media, for example Russian avant-garde cinema.[5] This contributed to creators approaching the medium in a different way, and adopting topics and techniques rarely seen outside Japan. Animation was not seen as categorically different from narrative cinema (Ortega-Brena, 2009, p. 23). As Hills summates, media with 'double-coding' is more likely to support both child and adult engagements, and be retained as important 'transitional objects' throughout life (Hills, 2002, p. 109). Anime and manga are precisely such media, widely available and supported by both children and adults.

Popular rebellion

The accessibility of such popular media opened it up as a contested terrain. In the shadow of mass-market manga for children, more adult works were produced, bound in hard covers and available at 'rental libraries' (*kashihonya*). The 1950s saw the advent of *gekiga*, a genre of sexual, violent and morally complex comics that became extremely popular in the 1960s as a forum for anti-establishment commentary.

Images of war and undertones of pathos were also present in less explicit manga and anime for children. Susan J. Napier points out that fantasy is a way to work through trauma, and connects the prevalence of dystopia and destruction in Japanese fiction with the devastation of World War II (Napier, 2005, pp. 165–6). Pop-artist Murakami Takashi further argues that discussion of the war and atomic bombings was suppressed in the post-war era, and the collective memory or imagination of these events seeped into popular entertainment (Murakami, 2005, pp. 122–4). Okada adds that the most famous anime creators in Japan tend to have been students or young adults at the time of the demonstrations against the Japan–US Security Treaty, including Miyazaki Hayao and Oshii Mamoru (Galbraith, 2009, p. 174). Their works are characterized by acute social awareness and commentary.

Naturalization and trivialization

Japan recognized early on the subversive potential of popular media (especially newspapers and political satire in comics), and struggled to control it. In the late 1920s, police empowered by the Peace Preservation Law arrested editors and shut down publishers thought to undermine authority. Schodt points out that this resulted in self-censorship and a move towards safer genres such as manga for children and 'erotic grotesque nonsense' for adults (Schodt, 1983, p. 51). Similarly, red comics emerged in Osaka as an alternative to expensive conservative manga published in Tokyo (Schodt, 1983, p. 62), but successful artists such as Tezuka were brought to Tokyo and under the control of publishers. *Gekiga* and rental libraries appeared, but were squeezed out by cheaper and more widely circulated manga. In 1959, Kōdansha began its *Shōnen Magazine*, the first weekly publication devoted entirely to manga. With a higher page count and distribution frequency, artists had more work to do and less time to do it in; editors became important in managing productivity. By the mid-1960s, major book publishers in Tokyo controlled the manga industry, which was tied to TV and merchandising, and formulas for commercially successful stories were favoured over experimental or controversial ones.

Information-consumer society

The 1970s was a turning point in Japan so drastic that Yoshimi Shunya argues it was the beginning of 'post-postwar society' (Yoshimi, 2009). The tumultuous years of economic recovery and social upheaval were over, and consumerism was rising (Murakami, 2005, pp. 119, 192). Vigorous mass marketing assisted this process. Tokyo was one of the most capital-saturated urban centres in the world, and an unprecedented amount of this capital was invested in advertising, packaging, design and image production (Yoshimi, 2009, p. 56; see also Kitada, 2002). This was an environment in which everything was commoditized and mediatized (Yoshimi, 2009, iv–v). Here begins what Ōsawa Masachi calls 'the age of fiction' (*kyokō no jidai*) (Ōsawa, 1996). Grand ideals and narratives of society and progress collapsed and became fiction. Ōsawa notes that people compulsively consume items that connect them to larger networks of information and meaning (Ōsawa, 2008, pp. 94–5). People became 'information maniacs' (*infomaniakku*) generating and gathering information in consumption (White, 1993, p. 14, see also Ōhira, 1990 and Ōtsuka, 1989b).

Manga and anime were part of this information-consumer society. Consumption accelerated, and became embedded in media mix market strategies (led by Kadokawa). Even as cinema became more conservative and less appealing, animation was invigorated by young creative talents and their ideas (Napier, 2005, pp. 16–17). Increasingly sophisticated anime such as *Space Battleship Yamato* (1974–5) and *Mobile Suit Gundam* (1979–80) proved information-rich, and speciality anime magazines such as *Animage* (from 1978) appeared. This shaped a form of knowledge production among consumers, who would come to be called *otaku*. The burgeoning adult audience became the target for expensive merchandise. This saved *Gundam*, a commercial failure taken off the air that became a phenomenon with *otaku* support for scaled models of the giant robots appearing in the series. *Super Dimensional Fortress Macross* (1982) was conceptualized by *otaku* to visualize mechanical designs and sell toys to other *otaku* (Lamarre, 2009, p. 202). *Macross* marks the first time the word *otaku* was used in the mass media, likely the vernacular of the creators slipping into character dialogue (Macias and Machiyama, 2004, p. 14). In the 1980s, young Japanese were surrounded by a wealth of anime, manga, videogames and character merchandise (Okada, 2008, pp. 78–9), and this is the background for the emergence of *otaku* culture.

Otaku consuming girls

The young girl, or '*shōjo*', became a dominant image in the media, representing consumptive pleasure suspended from productive functions (Ōtsuka, 1989a, p. 20). Ōtsuka argues that the *shōjo* became a symbol for Japanese society itself:

> 'The Japanese are no longer producers. Our existence consists solely on the distribution and consumption of "things" brought to us from

elsewhere, "things" with which we play.…These "things" are continually converted into signs without substance, signs such as information, stocks, or land. What name are we to give this life of ours today? The name is *shōjo*'. (Ōtsuka, 1989a, p. 18; quoted in Treat, 1993, p. 353).

It is possible to understand *otaku* culture as '*shōjo*' culture. This is not to imply that *otaku* are literally *shōjo*, but rather that they are 'pure consumers' (*junsui na shōhisha*). *Otaku* are also not unproductive. Rather, like *shōjo*, their labour and creativity are unrecognized and undervalued. It is not fully articulated, or is outside the institutions of work and home. *Otaku* engage hobbies, or play with 'things', to produce information for personal pleasure.

Otaku emerged from an environment of urban middle-class affluence. The model of 'Japan, Inc.' corporate culture was men working in the company and women supporting them from the home (Allison, 2006, pp. 68–71). Women also supported children in their schooling, and coddled them at home. Okada points out that children were given a generous allowance, which they could use between home and school without adult supervision (Galbraith, 2009, p. 174). Children had a certain amount of freedom outside the home, and indulgence inside the home. Kotani Mari suggests that those who stayed home with their mothers and enjoyed TV and toys are precisely those 'homebodies' who came to be known as *otaku* (Kotani, 2003, pp. 119–20). By Kotani's estimation, *otaku* had no male role models in absent fathers, and so took after their mothers, up to and including referring to others using the indirect, polite, second-person pronoun '*otaku*' (literally 'your home'). Volker Grassmuck adds that deepening social apathy[6] encouraged young Japanese to go into 'hiding behind piles of toys, comics, and play machines' (Grassmuck, 1990, p. 5). The education system taught them to take in the world as fragmentary data, and disconnected knowledge production readily applied to hobbies. Information became a fetish, valued regardless of its actual use (Grassmuck, 1990, p. 6). Young Japanese retreated into private spaces of consumptive pleasure disconnected from broader social and political concerns.

Already associated with the consumer (*shōjo*) and home (mother), *otaku* found themselves increasingly out of step with ideals of masculinity. They turned to products of popular culture to negotiate a problematic gender position. Honda Tōru argues that women became more choosy about partners in the 1970s and 1980s, and there emerged a system of 'love capitalism' (*renai shihon shugi*) in which only wealthy men were in demand (Honda, 2005, p. 66). Men marginalized by this system, especially those spending money on hobbies and without the skills to strategize social relations, turned to the fictional women of manga, anime and videogames (Honda, 2005, pp. 59, 81, 151).[7] One conspicuous character type was the young and innocent *shōjo*. Desire for the *shōjo*, for the young girl who exists only as fantasy, was called *lolicon*.[8] Itō Kimio discusses this as a move towards a 'culture of distance', or the tendency to avoid direct physical engagement and instead visualize and control fantasy objects (Itō, 1992, pp. 93–5). For Itō, the roles of women changed rapidly in the 1970s and 1980s, while the roles of men remained static. This complicated interactions, beyond the ability of some to handle. Sharon Kinsella suggests that the *shōjo* is the form that most captures the tensions and concerns of male viewers, who both abuse and identify with her to navigate an ambiguous gender position (Kinsella, 2006, p. 83). The *shōjo* is a performance scripted by and for men, and she became central for *otaku* as they transitioned from the 'male' position of producer to the 'female' position of consumer.

A new way of viewing

Access to new technology aided and accelerated the growth of *otaku* culture in the 1980s. The VCR provided an apparatus to view media with special attention to details (Okada, 1996). TV programs could be recorded and replayed, and elements of production could be visualized and analysed. The VCR also facilitated material acquisition and storage of videotapes, usually in one's home or room, reinforcing the retreat into private spaces of consumption. Facing a declining television anime market, a shrinking population of children and an increasingly savvy *otaku* audience, creators started making higher-quality, more experimental and adult (sexual and violent) works to be released direct to video. These works targeted niche audiences, namely *otaku*. Those with the means could purchase extravagant machines to play videotapes, Betamax cassettes and Laser Discs. Most *otaku* organized into 'circles', inspired by and often connected to organized after-school activities (*bukatsudō*), to share resources and knowledge.

One of the clearest windows onto the activity of *otaku* circles is *dōjinshi*, or materials published outside official channels. These were first produced by female[9] coteries, but advances in copying technology in the 1970s lowered costs and simplified production, and smaller groups and men began to participate. Like early manga and red comics, *dōjinshi* are cheap, and have low barriers to participation. For this reason their subversive potential is high, though more devoted to pleasure than politics. In the 1980s, *dōjinshi* shifted to 'parody' of mainstream commercial properties, placing characters from anime and manga in unintended relationships or situations. For the most part, *dōjinshi* are not about social struggle and success (coded as masculine), but rather romantic relationships in private, domestic settings (coded as feminine) (Harrell, 2007, p. 10).[10]

Dōjinshi demonstrate how *otaku* break images and patterns down into operable data, which they consume and master to fuel creation. Azuma calls this 'database consumption', noting how characters and narratives from manga, anime and videogames are broken down into constituent parts, plugged into a database of acquired knowledge and remixed (Azuma, 2009, pp. 54, 84). The characters are a crucial source of pleasure. Thomas Lamarre refers to characters as 'soulful bodies' with spiritual, emotional and psychological qualities inscribed on the surface (Lamarre, 2009, p. 312). Affective elements are isolated and remixed. Exploring potential movements of soulful bodies, especially movements of affect, is the primary concern of *dōjinshi* – and of mass-produced manga, anime and videogames as *otaku* become producers and dominant consumers. *Dōjinshi* are tolerated because the producers tend to be the most enthusiastic consumers of the original works, and are creatively engaging (not copying) them (Kitabayashi, 2004, p. 6).[11] *Dōjinshi* events such as Comiket, a biannual market that draws over half a million buyers and sellers over the course of 3 days, further provide companies with free market research. The ideas and talents developed here permeate into the mainstream market.

Otaku as deviant

In the late 1980s and 1990s, the *otaku* image came to the fore of social anxiety about the direction of Japan's information-consumer society. This was emblazoned by Itō Seikō's *No Life King* (1988), a novel about youth that could no longer tell the difference between the real and virtual. In 1989, the media went into a frenzy over the arrest of infamous paedophile and cannibal Miyazaki Tsutomu. Around 6,000 videotapes were found in his room, including some examples of *lolicon*, and it was discovered that he was involved with *dōjinshi*. The media picked up on the buzzword '*otaku*' to decry his deviance. While Miyazaki may have been an *otaku* (he was not aware of the word; Ōsawa, 2008, p. 87), he was certainly a sociopath, which became the stereotype of all *otaku*. Kinsella writes:

> '*Otaku* were portrayed as a section of youth embodying the logical extremes of individualistic, particularistic and infantile social behaviour. In their often macabre descriptions of *otaku* lifestyle and subculture, social scientists conveyed, perhaps, their deeper anxieties about the general characteristics of Japanese society in the 1990s' (Kinsella, 1998, p. 294).

On the other hand, the treatment of *otaku* as a coherent culture, and their own reactions against '*otaku* bashing' in the media, contributed to a growing community consciousness.[12]

Otaku as normal

Japanese society, and assumptions about *otaku*, underwent radical changes after the economy crashed in the 1990s. Neoliberal deregulation transformed labour into 'flexible' or 'irregular' forms, which destabilized income and the family unit based on it (Allison, 2006, pp. 74–6). It became increasingly difficult to adopt stable roles and responsibilities, the institutional markers of adult members of society. This encouraged the naturalization of *otaku*, but the process was slowed due to lingering associations with Miyazaki Tsutomu, and later the apocalyptic cult Aum Shinrikyō. It took a mass media success story to change the image of *otaku*. In the late 1990s, the media franchise *Neon Genesis Evangelion* became a social and economic phenomenon, christening a new generation of *otaku* consumers. The series coincided with a boom in toy figures, the maturation of the media-mix model and the rise of the Internet, which accelerated the spread of information and community consciousness (Kitabayashi, 2004, p. 5). At the end of the 1990s, criticisms of *otaku* were weakening with changing social realities, enthusiastic consumption was embraced as a bright spot in the recessionary economy, and fans were connecting through shared experience of media and technology.

The once private world of *otaku* began to manifest in public. Not only did attendance at *dōjinshi* events like Comiket skyrocket, but Akihabara transformed into an '*otaku* city'. Akihabara is an area of Tokyo known historically as the leading market for electronics. As stores in the suburbs and at commuter stations began dealing in home appliances and electronics, Akihabara shifted to personal computers. In 1976, NEC launched its low-cost TK-80 microcomputer assembly kit, and opened a Bit-INN Service Centre in Akihabara. The area became a haunt for computer specialists and hobbyists – young male *otaku* (Morikawa, 2008). During the recession in the 1990s, many stores closed in Akihabara and land prices plummeted, making room for more niche offerings.[13] In 1997, figure-maker Kaiyōdō moved its showroom from Shibuya to Akihabara. The rising tide of post-*Evangelion otaku* descended on Akihabara to buy anime and figures; more stores opened in the area to tap the market. Morikawa Kaichirō points out that the city became an externalization of an *otaku*'s bedroom, complete with images of sexy anime girls posted up on building walls (Morikawa, 2008, p. 3). In the absence of normalizing forces such as work, family or the opposite sex, an entire neighbourhood was transformed into *otaku* space or pure consumer space.

This did not occur in a power vacuum (Morikawa, 2008), but rather as part of the revaluation of *otaku* consumers. As the population and profile of *otaku* increased, their consumption practices drew attention (Kitabayashi, 2004). Companies began to target the *otaku* test market in Akihabara (Fujita and Hill, 2005, p. 29). According to a 2003 report by the Japanese government, 742 software developers, Internet ventures and data-processing companies are located within one kilometre of the Akihabara train station. The Tokyo Metropolitan Government invested 100 billion yen in IT development projects next to the station (Fujita and Hill, 2005, p. 30). Akihabara is important not only for IT, but also for its dense population of manga, anime and videogame fans. Digital/creative contents were valued at some 11 trillion yen a year in 2000 (Fujita and Hill, 2005, p. 59), and Akihabara was the symbolic centre. Anime provided impetus to government and industry promotion (Choo, 2009), especially after the sweeping global success of the *Pokemon* media mix at the turn of the new millennium. According to a government report in 2004, over 60 per cent of the animation shown in the world is Japanese, and exports grew by some 300 per cent between 1992 and 2004, compared with an average growth rate of 20 per cent. The understanding was that *otaku* are the ones spurring innovation:

'Japan's success in the world animation, comics and games software markets derives from fierce firm competition inside of Japan for the attention of a large, demanding and diverse range of consumers....Animators test their products in Tokyo first before marketing them in Japan and overseas. And animators look to Tokyo's participatory antenna districts for new product ideas and strategies' (Fujita and Hill, 2005, p. 57).

In 2004, The Ministry of International Trade and Industry ratified The Contents Industry Act.[14] That same year, Morikawa organized 'OTAKU: persona = space = city' at the ninth International Architecture Exhibit of the Venice Biennale. Under the auspices of the Japan Foundation, he turned the Japan Pavilion into a miniature Akihabara. In 2005, Fuji TV aired *Train Man*, a romance starring an *otaku* and a career woman, much of it filmed in Akihabara. Alisa Freedman argues that *Train Man* can be read as the recoding of dysfunctional *otaku* masculinity into model consumer masculinity (Freedman, 2009). Honda argues that it was a didactic message for *otaku*, an attempt to rehabilitate them into 'love capitalism' (Honda, 2005). In any case, as more and more tourists poured into Akihabara from across Japan and around the world, *otaku* made an awkward transition from subculture to pop-culture (Galbraith, 2010).

Conclusion

Otaku are the most enthusiastic members of information-consumer society. They are 'information elites' who approach the alienating deluge of information

'by engaging it and *creating* meaning, context, and value. ... *Otaku* have an impressive amount of media literacy that allows them to excel in activities that require memorization of data, processing of symbolic/abstract codes, and understanding the linkages of meaning that exist between them. ... This type of knowledge allows them to be innovative – to create new information, new combinations of existing elements' (Eng, 2006, pp. 75, 110).

Otaku appropriate media and technology to generate information and gain status in knowledge communities. *Otaku* are 'hyper-consumers', often better informed about products than creators (Eng, 2006, p. 56). They are extremely involved and invested consumers, demanding a say in what is produced and the freedom to personalize and remix it (Eng, 2006, p. 155). This does not necessarily translate into profit for companies. Further, Kitabayashi cautions that *otaku* innovations are not always marketable products (Kitabayashi, 2004, p. 7). Lamarre also points out that the '*otaku* movement' is difficult to mobilize to productive ends

(Lamarre, 2006). *Otaku* consume and produce in the service of ideals rather than industry. Their endless pursuit, however, inspires other consumers and producers. The challenge is to present ideals that captivate *otaku* and to direct their creative energy towards productive ends.

Notes

1. 186.68 billion yen, according to an industry survey by Media Create. The Nomura Research Institute estimates that there are 2.85 million *otaku* in Japan (Kitabayashi, 2004). There are five subgroups: closeted *otaku* (25 per cent), traditional *otaku* (23 per cent), information-sensitive 'multi-*otaku*' (22 per cent), sociable *otaku* (18 per cent) and fangirls (12 per cent).
2. Page numbers refer to online version: http://www.itofisher.com/mito/ito.imagination.pdf
3. According to the Akihabara city website: http://www.akiba.or.jp/history/. The imperial marriage in 1959, the Apollo Space Programme from 1961 and the Tokyo Olympics in 1964 made TV a must.
4. He also established the so-called 'production committee system' by which corporate sponsors fund an anime project and receive a portion of the profits; this lowered costs for studios, but contributed to the disempowerment of animators.
5. Personal interview, 2 October 2009.
6. Japan's first world's fair, Expo 1970 in Osaka, was about 'Progress and Harmony for Mankind', but was marred by news of war and environmental disaster (Murakami, 2005, pp. 192–3). The Japanese Red Army Incident of 1972 signalled the final desperate struggles of the left, this time as terrorism. Soon after, the Oil Shocks of 1973 and 1974 slowed economic growth.
7. For example, Lum, the main character from Takahashi Rumiko's *Urusei Yatsura* (1981–6), is frequently cited as the most important sex symbol for Japanese boys coming of age in the 1980s. See interviews with Bome and Ichikawa Kōichi (Galbraith, 2009, pp. 46–8, 74–7).
8. Lolita Complex. Derived from Vladimir Nabokov's 1955 novel *Lolita*. Wada Shinji used the word *lolicon* in his manga *Stumbling Upon a Cabbage Field* in 1974. In 1979, Azuma Hideo penned *Cybele*, an erotic (though humorous) *lolicon* work. That same year was Miyazaki Hayao's *Lupin III: The Castle of Cagliostro*, and princess Clarisse was appropriated as a *lolicon* idol (Macias and Machiyama, 2004, p. 48). *Otaku* started scouring shows for little girls, searching for virtual idols. Companies targeted them to increase sales. *Magical Princess Minky Momo* (1982), for example, is a show for girls, but features sexy characters designed for adult men; these 'big friends' (*ōkii otomodachi*) support the work by buying merchandise. Enix produced a game called *Lolita Syndrome* in 1983, and Japan's first pornographic anime was *Lolita Anime* in 1984.
9. For attendance records, see 'What is the Comic Market?' http://www.comiket.co.jp/index_e.html
10. Page numbers refer to online version: vcas.wlu.edu/VRAS/2007/Harrell.pdf
11. Unofficial distribution of Japanese anime in the United States, at least in its early stages, followed a similar pattern (Eng, 2006, p. 97).

12. There also emerged public *otaku* personalities and spokesmen, the most important being Okada Toshio. Okada was a founding member of animation studio production house Gainax and produced *Otaku no Video* in 1991, a mock documentary about the rise of *otaku* culture in the 1980s. Between 1992 and 1997, he gave a series of lectures at the prestigious University of Tokyo, where he presented the idea of 'otakuology' (*otakugaku*). In 1996, he published *Introduction to Otakuology*.
13. Messe Sanoh was a leader, selling 'dating simulator' games for the PC from 1987, *dōjin* games from 1992 and *dōjinshi* from 1994. Toranoana opened a store devoted to *dōjinshi* in 1994.
14. In 2002, journalist Douglas McGray wrote 'Japan's Gross National Cool' for *Foreign Policy* magazine, suggesting that Japan's real power came from the popularity of its pop-culture. The article was translated into Japanese the following year and became a hot topic among politicians such as Kondo Seiji and Asō Tarō.

References

Allison, A. (2006), *Millenial Monsters: Japanese Toys and the Global Imagination*, Berkeley: University of California Press.

Azuma, H. (2009), *Otaku: Japan's Database Animals*, Abel, J. E. and Shion, K. (trans.), Minneapolis: University of Minnesota Press.

Choo, K. (2009), 'The Making of Cool Japan: Japanese Policy Towards the Anime Industry', PhD dissertation submitted to the University of Tokyo.

Eng, L. (2006), '*Otaku* Engagements: Subcultural Appropriation of Science and Technology', PhD dissertation submitted to Rensselaer Polytechnic Institute.

Freedman, A. (2009), 'Train Man and the Gender Politics of Japanese "*Otaku*" Culture', *Intersections: Gender and Sexuality in Asia and the Pacific*, 20: 5.

Fujita, K. and Hill, R. C. (2005), 'Innovative Tokyo', World Bank Policy Research Working Paper, available at http://papers.ssrn.com/sol3/papers.cfm?abstract_id=660088

Galbraith, P. W. (2009), *The Otaku Encyclopedia: An Insider's Guide to the Subculture of Cool Japan*, Tokyo: Kodansha International.

Galbraith, P. W. (2010), 'Akihabara: Conditioning a Public *Otaku* Image', in *Mechademia 5*, Lunning, F. (ed.), Minneapolis: University of Minnesota Press.

Gibson, W. (1996), *Idoru*, New York: Penguin Books.

Grassmuck, V. (1990), ' "I'm Alone, But not Lonely": Japanese *Otaku*-kids Colonize the Realm of Information and Media: A Tale of Sex and Crime from a Faraway Place', available at http://www.cjas.org/~leng/otaku-e.htm

Greenfeld, K. T. (1993), 'The Incredibly Strange Mutant Creatures Who Rule the Universe of Alienated Japanese Zombie Computer Nerds (*Otaku* to You)', *Wired*, Issue 1.01, March/April.

Harrell, M. (2007), 'Slightly Out of Character: *Shōnen* Epics, *Dōjinshi* and Japanese Concepts of Masculinity', *Virginia Review of Asian Studies*, 10, Fall.

Hills, M. (2002), *Fan Cultures*, London: Routledge.

Honda, T. (2005), *Moeru otoko [The Budding Man]*, Tokyo: Chikuma Shobō.

Itō, K. (1992), 'Cultural Change and Gender Identity Trends in the 1970s and 1980s', *International Journal of Japanese Sociology*, 1(1): 79–98.

Ito, M. (2008), 'Mobilizing the Imagination in Everyday Play: The Case of Japanese Media Mixes', in Drotner, K. and Livingstone, S. (eds), *International Handbook of Children, Media and Culture*, London: Sage Publications.

Kinsella, S. (1998), 'Japanese Subculture in the 1990s: *Otaku* and the Amateur Manga Movement', *Journal of Japanese Studies*, 24: 2.

Kinsella, S. (2006), 'Minstrelized Girls: Male Performers of Japan's Lolita Complex', *Japan Forum*, 18: 1.

Kitabayashi, K. (2004), 'The *Otaku* Group from a Business Perspective: Revaluation of Enthusiastic Consumers', Tokyo: Nomura Research Institute, available at http://www.nri.co.jp/english/opinion/papers/2004/pdf/np200484.pdf

Kitada, A. (2002), *Kōkoku toshi Tōkyō: Sono tanjō to shi [Advertisement City Tokyo: The Birth and Death]*, Tokyo: Kōsaidō Shuppan.

Kotani, M. (2003), 'Otakuiin wa otakuia no yume o mita wa' [Ota-Queen Had a Dream about the Ota-Queer], in Azuma, H. (ed.), *Mōjō genron F-kai*, Tokyo: Seidōsha.

LaMarre, T. (2006), 'Otaku Movement', in Yoda, T. and Harootunian, H. (eds), *Japan After Japan: Social And Cultural Life from the Recessionary 1990s to the Present*, Durham: Duke University Press.

LaMarre, T. (2009), *The Anime Machine: A Media Theory of Animation*, Minneapolis: University of Minnesota Press.

Macias, P. and Machiyama, T. (2004), *Cruising the Anime City: An Otaku Guide to Neo Tokyo*, Berkeley: Stone Bridge Press.

Morikawa, K. (2008), *Shuto no tanjō: Moeru toshi Akihabara [Learning from Akihabara: The Birth of a Personapolis]*, Tokyo: Gentōsha.

Murakami, T. (ed.) (2005), *Little Boy: The Arts of Japan's Exploding Subculture*, New Haven: Yale University Press.

Nakajima, A. (1995), *Kommyunikeshon fuzen shōkōgun [Communication Deficiency Syndrome]*, Tokyo: Chikuma Bunko.

Napier, S. J. (2005), *Anime: From Akira to Howl's Moving Castle*, New York: Palgrave Macmillan.

Ōhira, K. (1990), *Yutakasa no seishin byōri [The Spiritual Pathology of Affluence]*, Tokyo: Iwanami Shinsho.

Okada, T. (1996), *Otakugaku nyūmon [Introduction to Otakuology]*, Tokyo: Ota Shuppan.

Okada, T. (2008), *Otaku wa sudeni shindeiru [You're Already Dead]*, Tokyo: Shinchosha.

Ortega-Brena, M. (2009), 'Peek-a-boo, I See You: Watching Japanese Hard-core Animation', *Sexuality and Culture,* 13(1).

Ōsawa, M. (1996), *Kyokō no jidai no hate [The End of the Fictional Age]*, Tokyo: Chikuma Shinsho.

Ōsawa, M. (2008), *Fukanōsei no jidai [The Age of Impossibility]*, Tokyo: Iwanami Shinsho.

Ōtsuka, E. (1989a), *Shōjo minzokugaku [Young Girl Folklore Studies]*, Tokyo: Kōbunsha.

Ōtsuka, E. (1989b), *Monogatari shōhiron [A Theory of Narrative Consumption]*, Tokyo: Shinyōsha.

Schodt, F. L. (1983), *Manga! Manga! The World of Japanese Comics*, Tokyo: Kodansha International.

Treat, J. W. (1993), 'Yoshimoto Banana Writes Home: *Shōjo* Culture and the Nostalgic Subject', *Journal of Japanese Studies*, 19: 2.

White, M. (1993), *The Material Child: Coming of Age in Japan and America*, New York: Free Press.

Yoshimi, S. (2009), *Posuto sengo shakai [Post-Postwar Society]*, Tokyo: Iwanami Shinsho.

Part III

Consumer Trends in Japan

9
Beyond Sushi and Tempura: An Overview of the Japanese Food Market

Stephanie Assmann

The current state of the Japanese food market in the light of consumer trends

Offering fresh vegetables, fruits and daily food items such as milk and eggs, Fujitake Fresh Shop in Sendai, a city of approximately one million inhabitants in Northern Japan, caters to customers living in the immediate neighbourhood. Housewives especially visit the store on a regular basis to shop for daily small amounts of fresh food, which also provides them with an opportunity for a chat with the owners of the store, a married couple in their fifties. In contrast, located a few miles away in a busy commuting area surrounded by a co-op store,[1] a video rental shop and a number of restaurants and fast food eateries, the large-scale supermarket *Seiyu* – which is part of the US retail giant Wal-Mart – offers quite a different view. Vegetables and fruits are followed by pre-packaged fish and meat, a tofu corner, and a large section with dairy products, rice and noodles, including Italian pasta. At the other end of the supermarket, pre-sliced breads are available, followed by beverages, including a fine selection of imported wines and an assortment of ready-made meals. Seiyu is open 24 hours all year round, and its retail prices are slightly lower than those at Fujitake. For example, one litre of low-fat milk costs 163 yen ($1.79) at Fujitake, whereas Seiyu offers one litre of low-fat milk at 158 yen ($1.74) along with a weekly low-price offer of fresh milk at 99 yen ($1.09). Selling one litre of low-fat milk at 209 yen ($2.3), the convenience store Lawson is a third and more expensive food retailer within walking distance of Fujitake. Also open 24 hours all year round, Lawson offers ready-made meals, *bentō* (lunchboxes), frozen foods, fast food items, beverages and practical household items. Recently, the assortment has been augmented by a variety of fresh vegetables and fruits, and frequent deliveries during the day ensure the freshness of the food. Despite higher retail prices, the store is always filled with customers, younger people in particular, who purchase smaller quantities of food for immediate consumption. Another example of a food retailer is the local department store Fujisaki, in downtown Sendai, which operates an exclusive food market as a shop-in-the-shop system in the basement of the store. Founded in 1819, Fujisaki is the local department store and operates affiliations in various prefectures of the Tohoku Region such as Akita, Morioka, Yamagata and Fukushima. Fujisaki is more than a shopping outlet. The department store also serves as a popular meeting point and is used for socializing in the in-store coffee shops or in frequent exhibitions taking place in the department store. A walk through the food market located in the basement of Fujisaki leads to an adaptation of a French bakery that sells Japanese interpretations of French and German breads, pastries with sweet fillings, curry breads, and slices of pizza and quiche. Further exploration of the food market reveals elaborate gift boxes in different sizes filled either with cakes or with Japanese rice specialties (*senbei*), followed by a bakery selling refined cakes such as strawberry cakes or cream tarts. A delicatessen market at the end of the food market offers a selection of regional food items such as a variety of *sake* (Japanese rice wine) from the Tohoku region in Northern Japan next to a selection of European wines, several kinds of Sendai *miso* (bean paste) characteristic of the region that are available next to a fine selection of French and German cheeses and hams.

The food retailers described above offer contrasting examples of the fragmented structure of the food retail sector in Japan, which is characterized by a coexistence of small family enterprises such as Fujitake Fresh Shop, supermarkets, department stores, convenience stores, discount stores, drugstores and a number of food speciality stores. The description of food retailers also highlights differences in food consumer behaviour. Small stores such as Fujitake represent typical mom-and-pop shops that are still popular with quality-conscious homemakers, who tend to shop for smaller amounts of fresh food on a daily basis instead of purchasing larger quantities once a week, whereas larger food retailers cater to increasing demands for convenience, ready-made meals and a diversity of domestic and international food products.

The aim of this chapter is to illuminate the changes and the current state of the Japanese food market through identifying recent trends in food consumer behaviour and developments on the food retail market that correspond with transformations in food consumer behaviour. The first part of this chapter will examine trends in food consumer behaviour, particularly in the light of demographic developments and lifestyle changes such as a diversification of eating habits. Taking these changes of food consumer behaviour into account, the second part of this chapter provides an overview of major food retailers and key market players in the Japanese food market, such as department stores, supermarkets, drugstores, food speciality stores, and the ubiquitous convenience stores. Despite the existence of diverse food retailers, expenses on food consumption are currently declining in Japan. Data compiled by the Bank of Japan show a decline in per capita food consumption from 310,470 yen ($3,004) in 2006 to 307,713 yen in 2007 ($2,978) (BMI, 2009, p. 19). Also, the number of food retailers in Japan is declining. As data on food consumption compiled by the Japanese government show, the number of food retailers in Japan has been falling, from a total of 1,300,057 retail outlets in 2002 to 1,238,049 retail outlets in 2004 (*Shokuseikatsu Dēta Sōgō Tōkei Nenpō*, 2009, p. 25). A closer look at individual company data of retail forms such as department stores (see below) reveals that a number of food retailers have been struggling for a longer period of time with gradual declines in sales. However, newer retail forms, such as the convenience stores and supermarkets that were established during the 1960s and 1970s, have become an integral part of the food retail market in Japan and are even showing signs of expansion. Furthermore, food retailers have responded to falling sales with the introduction of low-price systems, own-label systems and an expansion of retail outlets overseas.

The impact of demographic changes and lifestyle changes on food consumer behaviour

An analysis of the Japanese food retail market needs to be seen in the light of demographic changes and the changing lifestyles of Japanese consumers. Demographic changes include the birth of fewer children. The Japanese are increasingly delaying marriage and parenthood. In 2006, the average age for first-time marriage was 30.0 years for men and 28.2 years for women (Cabinet Office, Government of Japan, 2009). In a country where single-parent families remain a rarity, the average age for a woman to have her first baby was 29.2 years in 2006. As a result, Japan's total fertility rate has been declining since the 1970s. After reaching a first-time record low of 1.57 in 1989, the total fertility rate further declined to 1.32 in 2006 and currently resides at an average of 1.26 (Cabinet Office, Government of Japan, 2007). However, despite the delay of marriage and parenthood, conventional patterns of family life persist once people eventually do get married. Women account for 41 per cent of the workforce in Japan, but – as legal expert Shibata has pointed out in his study on equal employment opportunities for both genders – approximately 70 per cent of all women in full-time employment withdraw from the workforce upon the birth of their first child in order to dedicate time to family responsibilities (Shibata, 2007, p. 34). As a result, despite a high participation in the workforce, employment patterns of women are still characterized by full-time employment from early until late twenties, followed by a period of family responsibilities, before women re-enter the workforce, mostly as part-timers.

These demographic transformations have had an impact on food consumer behaviour. The rising labour participation of women and the delay in marriage and parenthood have created a demand for more convenience in the form of ready-made meals, snacks and frozen foods. This trend toward a higher demand for convenience is reflected in the existence of food retailers that cater to different needs of consumers, with 24-hour convenience stores being the most rapidly expanding retail form despite higher retail prices and recent declines in sales. Other retail outlets that cater to new customer demands for speciality foods, health and diet food products as well as food gifts include supermarkets, department stores, drugstores and food speciality stores. Once the knot has been tied, Japanese families follow a more conventional pattern of family life, with the wife and mother either being at home or being occupied in part-time employment. Hence, the need for supermarkets and small family enterprise food retailers that sell fresh foods on a daily basis is likely to continue to coexist with the need for convenience of full-time working consumers. With regards to demographic changes[2] the ageing of society is also likely to create a greater demand for convenience and shopping possibilities for less mobile persons. Home delivery services have been offered by consumer cooperatives (co-ops) that were founded in the 1950s in Japan on a communal basis to consumers living in particular vicinities, but such services have also been taken up by other food retailers, such as department stores, that increasingly use modern communication technology such as the Internet in their distribution of food products. Using innovative distribution channels that enable consumers to do their grocery shopping from home will play a significant role in the food consumer behaviour of ageing citizens. The convenience of home deliveries will not merely be a luxury but will become a necessity for older consumers.

Changes of eating habits

Demographic changes and associated lifestyle changes are significant aspects of food consumer behaviour. Among these lifestyle changes are the transformations of eating habits in Japan that have taken place over the past century. As Katja Schmidtpott shows in her work on milk consumption in Japan, nutrition in Japan in the 1920s mainly consisted of three major staple foods: rice (415 g), fruits and vegetables, especially vegetables (374 g) and potatoes, in particular sweet potatoes (213 g) (Schmidtpott, 2000, p. 122). Over the hundred years since then, a comprehensive diversification of eating habits has taken place, including a shift from a decrease in rice consumption to an increased consumption of meat, eggs, milk, and wheat products, in particular bread and noodles (Schmidtpott, 2000, p. 126). Culinary influences from abroad have had some impact on the nutritional shifts that have been adapted and integrated into Japanese food culture. For example, a major change in nutritional habits occurred at the end of World War II, when the US food aid programme coordinated the provision of school lunches (*kyūshoku*) for Japanese school children of all ages during the occupation period (1945–52); these consisted of powdered milk and bread, and replaced rice as a major component of school lunches. These school lunches shaped the eating habits of an entire generation, who grew up accustomed to milk and wheat products and incorporated these food products into their adult eating habits (Cwiertka, 2006, pp. 157–9; Schmidtpott, 2000, pp. 124–5). Age plays an important role in the acceptance of diversified food practices. For example, the younger generation of Japanese are likely to embrace a Western-style breakfast consisting of toast, coffee, eggs and sausages instead of a traditional Japanese breakfast consisting of a *miso* (soy bean paste) soup, rice, fish and pickles, whose preparation is more time-consuming.

A tangible change, along with the diversification of eating habits, is the decreased consumption of rice – traditionally Japan's major staple food. Since the 1960s, the consumption of rice has been gradually declining from a share of 48.3 per cent in the daily diet of a Japanese adult in 1960 to 30.1 per cent in 1980. In 2004, rice amounted to only 23.4 per cent of the daily diet of a Japanese adult. In the same time period, the intake of meat increased from a mere 3.7 per cent in 1960 to 12 per cent in 1980, and is currently at 15.4 per cent of the share of a person's daily diet. Likewise, the consumption of oil and fat rose from 4.6 per cent in 1960 to 14.2 per cent in 2004 (MAFF, 2008; Suematsu, 2008, pp. 44–6). The increasing acceptance of milk and wheat products is reflected in the variety of food retailers, such as supermarkets and convenience stores, that offer a selection of breads and milk products such as cheese and yoghurt. A further shift of nutritional habits occurred with the arrival of fast food chains such as McDonald's in 1971 and the establishment of Japanese interpretations of fast food restaurants. The restaurant chain Mos Burger – established in 1972 – is a prominent example of a Japanese fast food eatery that offers teriyaki chicken burgers and burgers served on rice instead of a bun. The arrival of the American coffee house chain Starbucks in 1996 marked further acceptance of American fast food culture. Fast food has become an integral part of the food market in Japan, and is not only sold by fast food eateries such as McDonald's but is also available to take away from convenience stores and some supermarkets.

Food nostalgia: resurgence of native and regional foods

Despite the widespread acceptance of fast foods and processed foods, the attention paid to fresh foods is closely related to a particular alertness to food safety, which has become a sensitive issue in Japan, in particular since the occurrence of food scandals such as the Morinaga milk incident in 1955,[3] and has been further challenged in the past decade as a number of food scandals have been revealed. Food safety scandals occur in different variations and include the use of expired and/ or tainted ingredients, the use of illegal or contaminated additives and pesticides, the mislabelling of food ingredients, and the falsification of production dates and expiry dates. In 2000, the company Snow Brand Milk Products sold contaminated milk products, which led to food poisoning cases involving 14,000 people. In June 2007, the president of a Hokkaido based meat-processing company, ironically named Meat Hope, had to confess that he had mislabelled croquettes (*koroke*) made of minced beef, pork, and chicken as 100 per cent ground beef croquettes for a period of several years before this was discovered. In the same year, the confectioner Fujiya had to halt its production after admitting the repeated use of expired ingredients and the mislabelling of use-by dates on its products (BMI, 2009, p. 28). Also in 2007, an investigation of the Mie prefectural government revealed that the confectioner Akafuku, based in Mie prefecture, had falsified production dates of its popular bean-jam sweets (*Japan Times Online*, 2 March 2007 and 21 October

2007). In 2008, this series of food-related incidents culminated in the discovery of imported Chinese dumplings that were contaminated with pesticides, which led to food poisoning involving at least 10 people in Hyogo and Chiba prefectures (MHLW, 2008; Yoshida, 2008).

These incidents have recently triggered an interest in supposedly safer native foods. Interestingly, despite the fact that a number of food scandals have involved products manufactured and distributed by Japanese food companies as opposed to only imported food products, Japanese consumers tend to equate food safety with the consumption of domestic products (*kokusan*). Food scandals such as the scandal of tainted dumplings imported from a Chinese manufacturer in 2008 have shaken the trust of Japanese consumers in imported food products. As a telephone survey conducted by Kyodo News on 9 and 10 February 2008 revealed, 76 per cent of the respondents intended to avoid Chinese food products after this food scandal (*Japan Times Online*, 11 February 2008). Distrust in imported food products has also become apparent in the Japanese government's recent decision in June 2009 to suspend imports of frozen beef from the United States of America after two packages of the imported beef had shown the presence of spinal column material, which has been banned due to the fear of the outbreak of mad cow disease (BMI, 2009, p. 24). Protectionist measures such as import bans on American beef are augmented by a call for a return to supposedly safer domestic food products, as a recent special edition dedicated to the consumption of local and reasonably priced food products in the magazine *Takarajima* documents (Takarajima-sha, 2008). Partially in response to food-related incidents, governmental initiatives such as Food Action Nippon are beginning to market regional agricultural products such as vegetables, fruits and cattle that are cultivated in specific regions of the country (Assmann, 2009).

One reason for the emphasis on domestic and local food products lies in the fact that these products are associated with high traceability and transparency of distribution channels and origins. This trend is being reflected in the diversification of choices now being offered by convenience stores and supermarkets, including organic food products[4] and fresh local foods such as vegetables and fruits cultivated in different regions in Japan (for instance, apples from Aomori prefecture or leek onions from Miyagi prefecture in Northern Japan).[5] Further, some food enterprises have responded to the anticipated need for food safety of Japanese consumers. For example, the Japanese fast food chain Mos Burger – a Japanese interpretation of a fast food chain – began to use organically grown vegetables and inform their customers about the origin of their vegetable supplies long before the outbreak of the recent series of food scandals in order to enhance the transparency of origins of the food products they used. As early as 1997, Mos Burger started cooperating with 2,000 farmers, using their agricultural products for their fast food menus under the motto 'fresh vegetables of Mos' (mosu no nama yasai) and 'vegetables that reveal the faces of producers' (seisansha no kao ga mieru yasai) (Mos Burger Japan, 2008).

The second reason for the preference of domestically grown produce is the enactment of food laws that place an emphasis on food quality checks, such as the Food Safety Basic Law (*Shokuhin anzen kijun-hō*) and the Food Sanitation Law (*Shokuhin eisei-hō*), which aims to ensure food hygiene and investigations of food products. Apart from food scandals in Japan, a further reason for the recent embrace of domestic and regional foods is the concern about the country's food self-sufficiency, which has been politicized in the media (Takarajima-sha, 2008). The reasons for the gradual decline of the food self-sufficiency rate lie in a complicated relationship between the diversification of food practices, which has necessitated imports of food items not available in Japan, and a decline of farming.[6] According to data released by the Ministry of Agriculture, Forestry and Fisheries (MAFF) for the year 2003, Japan currently has the lowest food self-sufficiency rate among the major industrialized countries, at roughly 40 per cent, and remains highly dependent on food imports from China, the United States of America, Australia and Canada.[7] By comparison, the United States of America had a food self-sufficiency rate of 128 per cent in 2003, while Australia's self-sufficiency rate was 237 per cent in the same year.[8] The calorie-based food self-sufficiency rate gradually declined from 78 per cent in 1961 to 50 per cent in 1987 and reached a record low of 37 per cent in 1993 (MAFF, 2008). Even though Japan can be considered a global food paradise, especially in metropolitan areas, it is intriguing that the country is struggling with long-term food security and food safety issues.

The first part of this chapter has provided an overview of recent trends in food consumer behaviour, including the impact of demographic changes and an embrace of native and regional food products. The second part of this chapter seeks to illuminate how food retailers cater to the diverse demands of consumers. Food retailers of the high-end market, such as department stores and food speciality stores, promote exclusive food products, luxury foods, imported food products and food gifts that play a significant role in a gift-giving-oriented society such as Japan, whereas newer retail forms such as supermarkets and convenience stores market food products needed in daily life.

Drug stores cater to the needs of health-oriented and diet food products, which is significant in a society conscious of body weight and
lifestyle-related diseases. Starting with convenience stores, the second
part of this chapter will introduce prevalent food retailers, their key
market players, marketing concepts and diversification strategies in cor-
respondence with consumer demands.

Convenience stores

As a new way of catering to the needs of consumers for convenience,
convenience stores (*konbiniensu sutoa* or *konbini*) entered the Japanese
food market in the 1960s. Interestingly, convenience stores as distributors of processed and pre-packaged food products, and in that sense
supposedly the enemy of local food producers, have started to take up
recent demands for fresh food, organic food products and local foods as
new business concepts. An example for a fresh food-oriented convenience store is the retailer Lawson, which has – in addition to its standard
convenience store operations – expanded in the discount food sector
and the fresh food sector. The company launched a discount convenience store concept under the name Lawson Store 100 in the year 2000
and has recently opened fresh food and health food-oriented convenience stores under the name Natural Lawson (BMI, 2009, p. 67). This
diversification of business concepts allows convenience stores to coun-
terbalance the fierce competition in the food retail market and to target
new consumer groups in an unfavourable economic climate.

Convenience stores are self-service mini-supermarkets with a sales
area between 30 m^2 and 250 m^2 and opening hours of more than 14
hours per day (*Shokuseikatsu Dēta Sōgō Tōkei Nenpō*, 2009, p. 25). Most
convenience stores are open 24 hours a day, 7 days a week. A characteristic of convenience stores is their location in the centre of cities,
at train stations and in the suburbs, which makes them a ubiquitous
sight throughout the country. As the earlier description in the introduction documented, convenience stores sell processed foods and
drinks, including alcoholic beverages, fast food items and fresh foods.
Recently, convenience store retailers such as the enterprise Lawson have
diversified their offering by including fresh foods such as vegetables,
eggs and seasonal fruits. In addition to food items, convenience stores
offer a number of services such as banking, postal and copy services.
Convenience stores represent the most rapidly expanding food retailer
in Japan. In 2004, the number of convenience stores increased from
41,770 outlets to 42,738 outlets operated throughout the country,

with yearly sales rising from 671.36 billion yen to 692.22 billion yen (*Shokuseikatsu Dēta Sōgō Tōkei Nenpō*, 2009, p. 25).

The four big convenience store retailers that dominate the Japanese food retail market are Seven Eleven, Lawson, Family Mart and Circle K Sunkus. In 2009, Seven & I Holdings occupied 34 per cent of the convenience retail market share in Japan, followed by Lawson Inc., which operates approximately 9,625 convenience stores throughout Japan with additional operations of 294 outlets in Shanghai and occupies a retail market share of 19.7 per cent (BMI, 2009, p. 58; Lawson website, 2010). Family Mart follows with a market share of 15.1 per cent and Circle K Sunkus with 11.1 per cent (BMI, 2009, p. 58). The American business concept of convenience stores proved to be very successful in Japan. After acquiring a licence from the US retailer Southland, Seven Eleven Japan opened its first outlet in Japan in 1973 (Meyer-Ohle, 1994, p. 178). In 2003, the number of Seven Eleven stores in Japan had topped 10,000 outlets; in 2004 the first Seven Eleven store opened in Beijing (Ito-Yokado Website). The retail group Seven & I Holdings currently operates an estimated 11,750 convenience stores in Japan with an additional overseas network of 6,000 stores in the United States of America and operations in Hawaii and Beijing (BMI, 2009, p. 66).

What are the reasons for consumers preferring convenience stores despite their higher retail prices? First, locality and convenience play an important role. According to a survey conducted by Marketing Communications Opi-net Community in July and August 2006 among 4,336 people about the use of convenience stores, almost 70 per cent of the respondents replied that they favoured convenience stores since these were close to either their home or workplace, whereas 56.5 per cent of the respondents used convenience stores because they were able to use them day and night. The possibility of conducting financial transactions and using postal delivery services seemed attractive to 44.3 per cent of the interviewees (*Shokuseikatsu Dēta Sōgō Tōkei Nenpō*, 2009, p. 136). A closer look at the food items sold at convenience stores reveals that ready-made meals, snacks and soft drinks are among the most popular. Despite the decline of rice consumption mentioned earlier, interestingly, convenience stores offer a popular fast food made of rice. According to the survey cited above, the most popular food item, purchased by 47.6 per cent of the respondents, were *o-nigiri* – rice balls pressed into a triangular form wrapped in seaweed with different fillings (*Shokuseikatsu Dēta Sōgō Tōkei Nenpō*, 2009, p. 137).[9]

The supermarket

Like convenience stores, supermarkets (*sūpā*) are a newer retail form, established in the 1960s and 1970s. Supermarkets are also large-scale retail outlets that tend to be concentrated in suburbs and are easily accessible for daily shopping needs. Unlike food markets at department stores, which offer exclusive and expensive food specialities, supermarkets sell basic food items needed for daily life. There is a difference between general supermarkets (*sōgō sūpā*), medium-size supermarkets (*chūgata sūpā*) and food supermarkets (*shokuryōhin sūpā*), whose range consists of more than 70 per cent of food items. In 2004, the number of food supermarkets amounted to 18,485 stores in Japan (*Shokuseikatsu Dēta Sōgō Tōkei Nenpō, 2009*, p. 25). Supermarkets play an essential role in food distribution in Japan with regards to choice and location. However, despite their vital role as a key player in the food market, supermarkets have also suffered declines in sales. According to data from the Japan Chain Stores Association, supermarket sales have declined by 3.4 per cent to 1.08 trillion yen in August 2009 (BMI, 2009, p. 51).

The two key players in the supermarket sector are the Japanese companies Aeon Co. Ltd. and Seven & I Holdings. Seven & I Holdings is the leading player, with sales figures of 5,649.9 billion yen (US$ 60.8 billion) (BMI, 2009, p. 66). The retailer operates the supermarket chain Ito-Yokado and a network of 11,750 convenience stores in addition to an extensive network of 6,000 convenience stores in the United States and Beijing (BMI, 2009, p. 66). The retail giant Aeon was founded in 1969 and operates 900 retail outlets in Japan with sales figures of 5,230.8 billion yen (US$56.3 billion) as of February 2009. Aeon operates different food retailers, among them the supermarket chain Aeon and the supermarket chain Saty, as well as 2,000 convenience stores such as the convenience store chain Ministop and 2,500 drug stores such as the drug store chain CFS (Aeon website, 2010; BMI, 2009, p. 68). However, this retailer is best known for its general merchandise supermarket chain Jusco, which operates 292 retail outlets in Japan and has also developed a presence overseas in China, Malaysia and Thailand.

Drug stores

A retail form that does not primarily focus on food items, but has included food items in its range, is drug stores. The key market player among drug stores is Matsumoto Kiyoshi, which operates a network of 653 stores in Japan and occupies a market share of 14 per cent (Matsumoto Kiyoshi website, 2010). The products offered at drug stores consist mainly of prescription-free medication, household items and beauty products, but drug stores also offer a variety of food products, especially a number of vitamin drinks, sports drinks, and health-related and diet food products (*kenkō shokuhin*). Some food products are not actually foods but vitamin, calcium and iron supplements. Interestingly, despite the slight decline in the number of drugstore outlets from 14,664 outlets in 2002 to 13,095 drug stores in 2004, sales figures increased from 249.5 billion yen to 258.7 billion yen in the same time period (*Shokuseikatsu Dēta Sōgō Tōkei Nenpō*, 2009, p. 25).

The department store

As opposed to convenience stores that operate on small sales areas, department stores (*hyakkaten* or *depāto*) are large-scale retail outlets whose sales areas extend above 1,500 m², and between 3,000 m² and 6,000 m² for large-scale department stores (*ōgata hyakkaten*) (*Shokuseikatsu Dēta Sōgō Tōkei Nenpō*, 2009, p. 25; see also Meyer-Ohle, 1994, p. 175). As self-service retail outlets, between 10 and 70 per cent of their range of merchandise consists of clothes, household items, furniture and food items. Food items are an integral part of department store sales. According to data from the Japan Department Stores Association, the sales of food items (*shokuryōhin*) amounted to 26.1 per cent of department store sales in 2008 (JDSA, 2009/2010). In addition, department stores operate restaurants, beer gardens and coffee shops that account for 2.7 per cent of department store sales (JDSA, 2009/2010). Including sales of food items and catering services, food sales account for almost a third of department store sales. Department stores – as the example of Fujisaki in Sendai demonstrates – represent an exclusive retail form in Japan. In the course of several economic downturns such as the collapse of the 'bubble economy' in Japan and the outbreak of the current global economic crisis in 2008, this retail form has experienced difficult times since the beginning of the 1990s. Recently established shopping malls that concentrate in the suburbs of cosmopolitan areas and are popular with younger consumers pose further challenges to department stores. For example, in Sendai, two major shopping malls that are located on the outskirts of the city compete with conventional food retailers. The number of department stores in Japan has been gradually falling since the early 1990s. In 1991, 455 department stores operated in Japan, whereas the number of department stores in 2002 amounted to only 362, and further fell to 308 retail outlets in 2004 (*Shokuseikatsu Dēta Sōgō Tōkei Nenpō*, 2009, p. 25; see also Meyer-Ohle, 1994, p. 175). Likewise, according to recent data from the Japan Department Stores Association (JDSA), sales figures of department stores have gradually declined from 8.99 trillion yen (US$ 99.12 billion) in 1999 to 7.38 trillion yen (US$ 81.45 billion) in 2008 (JDSA Website, 2009/2010). Key market players in the department store sector are Mitsukoshi Isetan Holdings, with sales figures in March 2009 of 1.426 billion yen and a sales share of 17.2 per cent in the department store market segment. The well-known Japanese department store group Mitsukoshi was founded in 1673, and currently operates 13 department stores within Japan as well as 22 department stores overseas in major cosmopolitan locations such as Paris, London, Taiwan and Shanghai. Despite the recent economic malaise and the growing popularity of suburban shopping malls, Japanese consumers display a high sense of loyalty to retailers that have a long history, such as Mitsukoshi, which represents high-quality products that have transformed the department store into a nationally and globally marketed brand. The retailer has included innovative distribution channels in addition to standard in-store retail operations, such as online shopping, home delivery and mail order services, including the online distribution of food items through these channels (Mitsukoshi website, 2010). Mitsukoshi Isetan Holdings are followed by Japan Front Retailing (JFR), which operates the department store chains Daimaru and Matsuzakaya. Japan Front Retailing occupies a sales share of 13.2 per cent, with sales figures of 1.09 billion yen as of 2008. Daimaru and Matsuzakaya department stores concentrate primarily in the major population clusters of the country, in the Kantō Region around Tokyo, the Kansai Region around Kyoto, Osaka and Kobe, in Nagoya and to a lesser extent in Kyushu. Daimaru and Matsuzakaya operate their own supermarkets in the basements of their retail outlets. Third in line are Seven & I Holdings, which operate the department store chain Seibu – which merged with the department store chain Sogo in 2009 – with 15 retail outlets in the country.[10] Seven & I Holdings occupy a sales share of 12 per cent with sales figures of 993 million yen, closely followed by the department store Takashimaya, which occupies a share of 11.8 per cent with sales figures of 976,117 million yen.[11] Takashimaya is another department store with a long history; it was established in 1919 and operates 20 retail outlets in Japan as well as three department stores overseas.

The proximity of department stores to the centre of major cities and train stations contributes to the continued importance of department stores as an accessible retail outlet for commuters who shop for food items or a *bentō* on their way home. As the example of the local department store Fujisaki demonstrated, department stores are more than mere retail outlets. Department stores are used as meeting points and for socializing, which is of particular importance since cultural events such as exhibitions are held in department stores. As opposed to supermarkets selling food items for daily needs, exclusive food markets in department stores operate food markets mostly located in the basements of department stores as a shop-in-the-shop system, with a variety of food speciality stores such as bakeries, confectioners, regional delicatessen markets, supermarkets and imported food stores. It is important to note that food markets usually do not offer restaurant services, which are usually located on the top floors of department stores, are dedicated to eating out and consist of a variety of Japanese, Korean, Italian, Thai and French restaurants. However, food sold at food markets is not meant to be consumed on the spot. Freshly made delicatessen and *bentō* are part of the standard assortment of food markets in department stores, as are elaborate gift boxes containing, for example, Japanese sweets (*wagashi*) and Western sweets (*yōgashi*), rice snacks (*senbei*), or coffee and tea specialities. Department stores continue to play an essential role in the Japanese food market, in particular with regard to the distribution of exclusive food items and the custom of gift-giving, which is deeply embedded in Japanese culture. Foods as gifts play a vital role in Japan as a souvenir (*omiyage*) brought back home by travellers. In addition, the mutual exchange of gifts, including food items, is of particular importance during the two main gift-giving seasons in Japan in the summer (*ochūgen*) and at the end of the year in December (*seibo*). These gift-giving seasons are tied to the bonus seasons in June and December, when private companies and public employers pay their employees a bonus that amounts to double or sometimes even triple the regular monthly salary and is an integral part of the salary package. Department stores use these bonus seasons to advertise gifts and further encourage the purchase of point cards whose use results in slightly cheaper purchases when sufficient points are accumulated. The custom of mutual gift-giving among colleagues and acquaintances is essential in Japan, since it reflects mutual dependency and obligation and the integration of individuals into hierarchical networks. When selecting a gift for someone, it is vital to choose a present for a superior that reflects the hierarchical status of the gift-giver as well as the receiver. As cultural anthropologist Millie Creighton describes, 'Gift giving acknowledges the embeddedness of individuals in groups, the importance of social hierarchy, and the centrality of giri (duty and obligation)' (Creighton, 1992: 45).

Food speciality stores

Another food retailer at the high-end market is food speciality stores that market exclusive domestic food products and imported foods. In 2004, 190,788 food speciality stores (*shokuryō senmonten*) operated in Japan, with yearly sales of 702.31 billion yen (*Shokuseikatsu Dēta Sōgō Tōkei Nenpō*, 2009, p. 25). Food speciality stores are defined as self-service retail outlets whose range consists of over 90 per cent of food items such as alcoholic beverages, meat products, fish, dried foods, vegetables, fruits, sweets, bread, milk products, tea, coffee and tofu (*Shokuseikatsu Dēta Sōgō Tōkei Nenpō*, 2009, p. 25). Self-service food speciality stores offer a range that consists of more than 90 per cent of food items such as alcohol (*sake*), meat, fish, dried foods, vegetables and fruits, sweets, bread, rice, milk, tea, tofu and cooking utensils. As mentioned earlier, food speciality stores often operate in the food markets of department stores in the form of a shop-in-the-shop system. Among those food speciality stores are also imported food stores such as the exclusive retailer Meijiya, which was founded in 1885 in Tokyo after the Meiji Restoration (1868), when Japan had just begun to embrace other Asian and European foods. Currently, Meijiya operates 13 stores throughout Japan in major cities such as Tokyo, Kyoto, Nagoya, Sendai, Yokohama and Kobe, and a store in Amsterdam (Meijiya website, 2010). The range consists of imported food products from Europe, the United States of America and a number of Asian countries such as Thailand and Vietnam. Meijiya also offers a fine selection of alcoholic beverages such as European wines, sparkling wines, beers and whisky. Taking a stroll through the Sendai branch of Meijiya takes the visitor first to a corner with beverages such as Italian coffee and espresso products, a number of cooking herbs from different origins, and a corner with noodles and pasta in addition to pasta sauces. Fruits and vegetables are also part of Meijiya's range, as are a number of fine imported chocolates from Switzerland and Germany. Asian countries are represented with a variety of spices from Thailand, dried fruits from the Philippines and noodles from Vietnam.

Trend: fewer people strive for high-quality foods and convenience

This chapter has provided an overview of transformations and recent trends in food consumer behaviour. A number of tasks remain for future research. It will be essential to study the impacts of demographic changes on food consumer behaviour more intensively in the form of the identification of particular food products and suitable distribution channels for people living in small-sized households. In addition, this chapter has examined a diversification of food retailers and distribution strategies that cater to the need of consumers for convenient shopping possibilities, in particular for professionals and older and less mobile consumers, but also families. Here, this study has revealed that a fragmented food retail market includes the coexistence of family-owned food retailers and convenience food retailers. In this context, future research will benefit from identifying specific food products that are attractive for older consumers. A further trend of significance is the embrace of local food products. It will be vital to analyse how a demand for convenience on the one hand and for fresh foods and local foods on the other will complement each other, and to observe whether and how native and regional food products will be integrated into the mix of diverse food retailers, especially in the context of changing lifestyles, increased mobilization, and demographic change. The focus on the food retail market thus also functions as a lens for examining the current challenges and transformations that confront Japanese society.

Notes

I would like to thank the editor Parissa Haghirian for including this chapter in this edited collection on Japanese consumerism. Further, I am indebted to Eric C. Rath and Sebastian Maslow for insightful comments on earlier drafts of this chapter.

1. Consumer co-operatives (co-ops) such as the Japan Consumers Cooperative Union (JCCU) (Seikyō) were founded in the 1950s and 1960s through networks between food retailers, distributors of organic food products and consumer co-operatives, partially in response to concerns about food safety. Consumer co-operations operate retail outlets and home delivery services of non-brand food products, fresh and organic food on a communal basis to private households at lower prices than supermarkets (Cwiertka, 2006, pp. 169–70).
2. Japan is undergoing significant demographic changes. Japan's population is declining. The population of Japan amounted to 128,085 million inhabitants as of 2005. According to forecasts by the UN Population Division, the population will decline to 124,489 million people in 2020 and is expected to fall further to 118,252 million people in 2030 (BMI, 2009, p. 71). Japan's population is also ageing. Life expectancy is among the highest in the world, at 78.3 years for males and 85.3 years for females (BMI, 2009, p. 71). The number of persons aged 65 years and over is expected to continue rising until 2030. For example, according to estimates by the Japanese government, the number of females in their mid-eighties is forecast to rise to 800,000 women (Japan Statistical Yearbook, Population Pyramid). http://www.stat.go.jp/data/nenkan/pdf/z02–2.pdf (accessed 24 March 2010).

3. The Morinaga milk incident in 1955, involving arsenic contamination of milk products, was one of the first food safety scandals to attract public attention (Jussaume *et al.*, 2000, p. 218).
4. Organic foods are defined as foods that are produced without the use of chemicals, including pesticides, additives and fertilizers, or hormones given to livestock. Furthermore, organic foods are defined in that their methods of production are not environmentally harmful or damaging. A certification system of organic food products has been developed in a number of countries in order to ensure that only food products that fulfil these criteria are marketed as organic products. Source: Organic Food for Everyone: http://www.organic-food-for-everyone.com/definition-of-organic-food.html (accessed 24 March 24, 2010).
5. In that regard, it is important to distinguish between domestic food products such as *miso*, which is available nationwide with regional interpretations, and regional food products such as specific vegetables, fruits or cattle that are only cultivated and available in one particular region of the country.
6. One reason for the decline of food self-sufficiency can be seen in the decline of farm households since the beginning of the economic high-growth period in Japan. The number of farm households declined from 5.4 million in 1970 to 3.3 million in 1998 (Rath, 2007, p. 486). Correspondingly, the number of farmers has declined from 37.7 million in 1950 to 14.8 million in 1998 (Rath, 2007, p. 486).
7. According to statistics compiled by the Japan External Trade Organization (JETRO) based on data of the Ministry of Finance (MOF) for 2009, Japan imported 25.1 per cent of its food products from the United States and a share of 13.1 per cent from China, followed by 7.0 per cent from Australia (JETRO, 2010).
8. Data for other industrialized countries were as follows: Canada 145 per cent, France 122 per cent, Germany 84 per cent, Italy 62 per cent, The Netherlands 58 per cent, Spain 89 per cent, Switzerland 49 per cent, and Great Britain 70 per cent (MAFF, 2008).
9. For a detailed discussion of the *o-nigiri* in Japanese convenience stores see Whitelaw (2006).
10. Millenium Retailing Inc., Sogo Co. Ltd and the Seibu Department Stores Ltd merged on 1 August 2009, with Sogo Co. Ltd being the surviving entity. Millenium Retailing Inc. and the Seibu Department Stores Ltd were dissolved. Sogo Co. Ltd changed its name to Sogo & Seibu Co. Ltd. Source: Consolidated Financial Results for the Nine Months ended November 30, 2009, Seven & I Holdings Ltd:http://www.7andi.com/en/news/pdf/fresult/2010_0107kte.pdf (accessed 27 March 2010).
11. These data were taken from the following website: Gyōkai dōkō [Trends in the World of Commerce], http://gyokai-search.com/3-dept.htm (accessed 23 March 2010). For data on Mitsukoshi Isetan Holdings, the following website was consulted: Mitsukoshi Isetan Holdings (ed.), Annual Report 2009, http://www.imhds.co.jp/english/ir/pdf/annual_report/imhds/2009/2009_ar_e_15p.pdf (accessed 24 March 2010). Data on Japan Front Retailing were taken from the following source: Japan Front Retailing (ed.), Annual Review 2009, http://www.j-front-

retailing.com/ir/annual_review/jfrnowe02_03.pdf (accessed 24 March 2010).

References

Aeon Ltd. Website, available at http://www.aeon.info/en/index.html (accessed 26 March 2010).

Assmann, S. (2009), 'Food Action Nippon and Slow Food Japan: The Role of Two Citizen Movements in the Rediscovery of Local Foodways', in Farrer, J. (ed.), *Globalization, Food and Social Identities in the Pacific Region*, Tokyo: Sophia University Institute of Comparative Culture.

Business Monitor International (BMI) (ed.) (2009), *Japan Food & Drink Report Q1 2010* , London: Business Monitor International.

Cabinet Office, Government of Japan (ed.) (2007), Whitepaper on Birth-declining Society, First Chapter: 'Current Situation of Few Children [Shōshika no genjō]', available at http://www8.cao.go.jp/shoushi/whitepaper/w-2009-/21pdfhonpen/pdf/b1_1_01.pdf (accessed 27 March 2010).

Creighton, M. R. (1992), 'The Depāto: Merchandising the West While Selling Japaneseness', in Tobin, J. J. (ed.), *Re-Made in Japan: Everyday Life and Consumer Taste in a Changing Society*, London and New Haven: Yale University Press, pp. 42–57.

Cwiertka, K. J. (2006), *Modern Japanese Cuisine: Food, Power and National Identity*, London: Reaktion Books.

Humphries, K. (2010), 'In the Spotlight: Japanese Food Retail in Just-Food', 8 January, available at http://www.just-food.com/article.aspx?id=109350&lk=s (accessed 25 February 2010).

Fujisaki Website, available at http://www.fujisaki.co.jp/ (accessed 24 March 2010).

Ito-Yokado Co. Ltd. (2010), 'Kaisha Jōhō [Company History]', http://www.itoy-okado.co.jp/company/history.html (accessed 5 October 2010).

Japan Department Stores Association (JDSA) [Nihon Hyakkaten Kyōkai], available at http://www.depart.or.jp (accessed 24 February 2010).

Japan External Trade Organization (JETRO) (ed.) (2008), 'Nihon no shokuryō yunyū (jōi 10 kakoku) [Japan's Food Imports {10 Major Countries}]', available at http://www.jetro.go.jp/jpn/stats/trade/pdf/20052006_import_2.pdf (accessed 5 October 2010).

Japan Front Retailing (ed.) (2009), Annual Review 2009, http://www.j-front-re-tailing.com/ir/annual_review/jfrnowe02_03.pdf (accessed 24 March 2010).

Japan Times Online (2007), 'Meat Hope Chief Admits Pork Was Disguised as Ground Beef', 21 June.

Japan Times Online (2007), 'Fujiya Restarts Sweets Production after Sour Month', 2 March.

Japan Times Online (2007), 'Akafuku Hit by Fresh Food Safety Allegations', 21 October.

Japan Times Online (2008), 'Seventy-six Percent Plan to Avoid Chinese Food. "Gyoza" Contamination Takes Toll on Products' Popularity, 11 February.

Jussaume, R. A., Hisano, S. and Taniguchi, Y. (2000), 'Food Safety in Modern Japan', in Liscutin, N. and Haak, R. (eds), *Essen und Ernährung im modernen Japan [Eating and Nutrition in Modern Japan]*, Munich: Iudicium, pp. 211–28.

Lawson Inc. (2010), 'Kaisha Gaiyō [Company Overview]', available at http://www.lawson.co.jp/company/corporate/about.html (accessed 5 October 2010).

Matsumoto Kiyoshi Website, available at http://www.matsukiyo.co.jp/company/store.html (accessed 5 March 2010).

Meijiya Website, available at http://www.meidi-ya.co.jp/ (accessed 15 February 2010).

Meyer-Ohle, H. (1994), 'Wer kauft wo? Zur Einkaufsstättenwahl japanischer Konsumenten [Who Is Shopping Where? On the Choice of Retailing Outlets by Japanese Consumers]', in Deutsches Institut für Japanstudien [German Institute for Japanese Studies] (ed.), *Japanstudien*, Munich: Iudicium, pp. 171–207.

Ministry of Agriculture, Forestry, and Fisheries (MAFF) (Nōrin Suisanshō) (2008), 'Shuyō senshinkoku no shokuryō-ritsu (1960–2003) [Self-Sufficiency Rates of Major Industrialized Nations {1960–2003}]', available at http://www.maff.go.jp/j/zyukyu/zikyu_ritu/013.html (accessed 12 February 2008).

Ministry of Health, Labor and Welfare (2008), 'Chūgoku-san reitō gyōza ni yoru kenkōhigai ga kōhyō sareta hi (1 gatsu 30 nichi) ikō ni todōfuken nado ni atta sōdan /hōkoku sū ni tsuite [About Various Reports and Consultations in the 47 Prefectures of Japan since the day (30th January) that Health Casualties Caused by Fozen Dumplings Made in China Were Reported]', available at http://www.mhlw.go.jp/houdou/2008/02/h0211-1.html (accessed 5 October 2010).

Ministry of Internal Affairs and Communications, Statistics Bureau, Director General for Policy Planning (Statistical Standards) and Statistical Research and Training Institute (ed.), *Japan Statistical Yearbook*, 'Population Pyramid', available at http://www.stat.go.jp/data/nenkan/pdf/z02–2.pdf (accessed 24 March 2010).

Mitsukoshi Isetan Holdings (ed.) (2009), Annual Report 2009, http://www.imhds.co.jp/english/ir/pdf/annual_report/imhds/2009/2009_ar_e_15p.pdf (accessed 24 March 2010).

Mitsukoshi Website, available at http://www.mitsukoshi.co.jp/store/ (accessed 15 February 2010).

Mos Burger Japan, available at http://www.mos.co.jp/company/pr_pdf/pr_080118_1.pdf (accessed 9 February 2010).

Organic Food for Everyone, available at http://www.organic-food-for-everyone.com/definition-of-organic-food.html (accessed 24 March 2010).

Rath, E. C. (2007), 'Rural Japan and Agriculture', in Tsutsui, W. M. (ed.), *A Companion to Japanese History*, Oxford: Blackwell Publishing, pp. 477–92.

Schmidtpott, K. (2000), 'Heilmittel, Genussmittel, Erfrischungsgetränk. Milchkonsum in Japan 1920–1970 [A Drink for Healing, Enjoying and Refreshment. The Consumption of Milk in Japan 1920–1970]', in Liscutin, N. and Haak, R. (eds), *Essen und Ernährung im modernen Japan [Eating and Nutrition in Modern Japan]*, Munich: Iudicium, pp. 117–56.

Seven & I Holdings Ltd., available at http://www.7andi.com/en/news/pdf/fresult/2010_0107kte.pdf, (accessed on 27 March 2010).

Shibata, Y. (2007), 'Development and Problems of the Equal Employment Opportunity Law', in Tsujimura, M. and Yano, E. (eds), *Gender and Law in Japan, Gender Law & Policy Center*, Sendai: Tohoku University Press, pp. 171–87.

Shokuseikatsu Dēta Sōgō Tōkei Nenpō 2009 [Year of Food Consumption Statistics 2009] (2009), Tokyo: Sanfuyusha.

Suematsu, H. (2008), *Shokuryō jikyū-ritsu no 'naze'. Dōshite hikui to ikenai no ka? [The Purpose of the Food Self-Sufficiency Rate and Why It Must Not Be Low]*, Tokyo: Fusosha Shinsho.

Takarajima-sha (ed.) (2008), ' "Kokusan" "anshin" no tabemono ha kore da [Safe and Domestic Foods Are These]', 20 June.

Takashimaya Company (ed.) (2009), Takashimaya Annual Report, available at http://www.takashimaya.co.jp/corp/ir/annualreport/2009/fs090228.pdf (accessed 25 February 2010).

Takashimaya Company (ed.) (2009), Takashimaya Company Fact Book, February, available at http://www.takashimaya.co.jp/corp/ir/factbook/2009/book.pdf (accessed 25 February 2010).

Whitelaw, G. H. (2006), 'Rice Ball Rivalries: Japanese Convenience Stores and the Appetite of Late Capitalism', in Wilk, R. (ed.), *Fast Food/Slow Food: The Cultural Economy of the Global Food System*, Plymouth: Altamira Press, pp. 131–44.

Yoshida, R. (2008), '10 Sick after Eating Tainted "Gyoza" from China', in *Japan Times Online*, 31 January.

10
Fashion, Self, Postmodern Consumer Culture and *Sex and the City*

Aiko Yoshioka

Introduction

The American TV series *Sex and the City*, produced by HBO (Home Box Office), ran from 1998 to 2004. The programme received seven Amy Awards and attracted audiences in 200 countries. When the film *Sex and the City* was released in 2008, this worldwide audience took the opportunity to revisit the original TV drama (Beard, 2008, p. 40). In Japan, the cable TV station WOWWOW broadcast six seasons between 2000 to 2004, and each season was repeated more than 10 times.[1]

The series concerns the lives of four single women who live in Manhattan, New York: the columnist Carrie Bradshaw (Sarah Jessica Parker), the lawyer Miranda Hobbes (Cynthia Nixson), the art dealer Charlotte York (Kristin Davis) and Samantha Jones (Kim Cattrall), the manager of a PR company. The stories concern their friendships, romances and sexualities, and the film portrays the heroines 4 years after the events in the TV series. Aside from the actresses themselves, fans also paid great attention to the work of the stylist Patricia Field, who was in charge of costumes for both the TV series and the film.

Sex and the City (henceforth *SATC*) visibly infuses its audiences with notions about certain lifestyles and the aestheticization of everyday life in postmodern consumer society. Its influences bear on various phenomena of contemporary consumer culture such as celebrity culture, fan culture, globalization, the spread of fashion, and the coordination of cross-media.

Fashion and feminism have not traditionally been seen as compatible. However, it is impossible to explain the global success of *SATC* if one only applies the views of the 'second wave' feminists who stand against fashion and are negative about female consumption. It is necessary, rather, to consider the interests in popular culture developed by post-feminists, also known as 'third wave' feminists,[2] and to examine their arguments regarding femininity, female fashion and consumerism – arguments that dissent from the second wave feminists' anti-fashionism. Needless to say, it is also useful to look at social theorists' discussions of the aestheticization of everyday life and lifestyles in analysing *SATC*'s discourses around fashion, body and consumer culture.

In this chapter, I first apply feminist and social theory in order to examine *SATC*, treating it as a text that epitomizes postmodern consumer culture through its representation of lifestyles and the aestheticization of daily lives and urban culture.

SATC has, however, expanded its influence beyond multimedia TV, film, and magazines, to develop a global celebrity and fan culture through internet fan sites and weblogs, with the actress Sarah Jessica Parker – who plays the leading role – gaining the status of fashion icon. I therefore go on to examine what kinds of images Parker has constructed about herself in the Japanese media, focusing on Japanese fashion magazines, while also discussing the relationships between celebrity culture, fashion and self/body.

Finally, exploring both American and Japanese fan sites, I demonstrate how *SATC* fans interrelate with celebrity culture and fashion, and how these aspects influence their identities and daily lives.

Postmodern consumer culture and *Sex and the City*

Feminists have generally presented negative points of view regarding women, fashion and consumption. In the classic feminist work *The Second Sex*, Simone de Beauvoir states that there are two objectives behind female fashion: to display women's social status, and to satisfy female narcissism. Women tend to think they attain their own character through the way they fashion themselves. In society, women are placed in the position of sexual objects for men, and thus expose themselves to male desire. Meanwhile, as male clothes don't make men into objects to be looked at, men don't regard their outfits as reflecting their inner selves or existences (de Beauvoir, 1997, p. 371). Men, due to their occupations, 'produce, struggle, create, progress and must transcend themselves for the world and the infinite future' (de Beauvoir, 1997, p. 242); but women, who can do nothing in public, are relegated to housework and the domestic sphere, can only achieve self-recognition and explore themselves through their choice of clothes, furniture and other domestic products (de Beauvoir, 1997, p. 245). Women's gorgeous clothes are nothing but conspicuous consumption to display their husbands' wealth and social status (de Beauvoir, 1997, p. 468).[3]

Germaine Greer, the prominent voice among second wave feminist critics, also wrote that many young women occupy themselves in reading fashion magazines and copying the latest fashion models, hoping to achieve social advancement through their youth and good looks. Such a stereotype is 'the Sexual Object' of all men and women (Greer, 1971, p. 55). In addition, it is a women's job to go shopping, look through bargain sales, examine products and purchase them. Men buy things, but do not go shopping for themselves or want to spend their time on unnecessary shopping (Greer, 1999, p. 145). Greer proclaimed that 'There are a few male fashion victims; all women are victims of fashion. Men will not buy cosmetics' (Greer, 1999, p. 150).

However, these notions of second wave feminism are arguably out of date in discussions of contemporary consumer society. In the postmodern capitalist society, the division between the male sphere (production, work and city) and the female sphere (consumption, home and suburb) has become ambiguous. The protagonists of *SATC* are single women who live in the city and have high levels of disposable income. These working women are a common phenomenon, and they constitute a new and powerful market group in big cities. This kind of market group exists in Japan as well as the US. Ever since Kumiko Iwashita took up financially independent single women – *ohitori-sama* – and Takayo Yamamoto researched consumption and desire among bachelorettes older than 30, naming them *banjō* (Iwashita, 2001; Yamamoto, 2008), their presence cannot be ignored. During the sluggish 'lost decade' after the collapse of the bubble economy, these women in their thirties and forties have been the most vigorous consumers. They had gone out into society after the enforcement of the Equal Employment Opportunity Law (1986), and chose a continuing career over marriage or maternity (Shinkokyū, 2008, p. 10).

Products are no longer necessities for people simply to use: they play an important role in displaying social status and individual taste. Thus we are required to be aesthetic in order to select superior and tasteful products. Lifestyles – that is, 'patterned ways of investing certain aspects of everyday life with social or symbolic value' and 'ways of playing with identity' (Chaney, 1996, p. 44) – are seen as 'no longer based in class structures but more readily reflecting the shifts and transformations of identity and consumption within the social sphere' (Paterson, 2006,

p. 49). The once distinctively feminine economic activity of defining oneself in society through the choice of tools from a wide array of products has become relevant regardless of whether one is male or female. One judges another person's identity through observing their clothes, food, furniture, and holiday destinations, as well as their occupation. The criteria of lifestyles have come to encompass more general everyday life practices, and here again the distinction between the public male domain and the private female domain is not clearly maintained.

The four heroines of *SATC* represent aesthetic consumers in contemporary society. For them, everything they bring into their lives – whether fashions, interiors, food, their looks, physicality, dates, actions and experiences – is based on their personal choices and individual tastes. Their lifestyles, produced from daily practices, 'display their individuality and sense of style' and their own guidelines for life (Featherstone, 2007, p. 84). Mike Featherstone explains why *SATC* was successful in attracting international interest:

> Consumer culture publicity suggests that we all have room for self-improvement and self-expression whatever our age or class origins. This is the world of men and women who quest for the new and the latest in relationships and experiences, who have a sense of adventure, take risks to explore life's options to the full, who are conscious they have only one life to live and must work hard to enjoy, experience and express it. (Featherstone, 2007, p. 84)

The portrayal of four single women struggling to find eligible bachelors for dates or marriage in New York looks like a burlesque of postmodern consumer culture, in which it seems possible to say that shopping has something in common with finding a date or a marriage partner. The pleasure of shopping or having a romantic relationship involves transforming a psychic wish into physiological action (Bowlby, 1993, p. 115). Choosing a love-object is similar to selecting something in a shop; however, acquiring the love-object is bound up with matters of individual attraction, desire and choice, and thus cannot be easily satisfied (Bowlby, 1993, p. 115). Formidable heroines with sharp aesthetic eyes, they evaluate and harshly criticize the men they encounter, as if trying on clothes and checking that the sizes and colours are right. The men are under the women's gaze, and most of them are treated like dresses which women won't buy, or in which they lose interest soon after purchase. After a blind date set up by her married friends, Carrie unenthusiastically says 'He was like the flesh and blood equivalent of a DKNY dress. You know it's not your style, but it's there, so you try it on anyway.' However, bothered by the man, who is obsessed with marriage, she turns him down, saying: 'I was trying you on, you know, to see if it fits. It doesn't.' When Miranda meets an attractive divorcé with a son at a gym, she holds back from dating him, telling her ladies 'I don't wear vintage clothes, I hate flea markets, I don't collect antiques. Is it too much to ask that he not be ... I don't know, used?' After Carrie has gone through many dysfunctional relationships, she meets her old boyfriend at a high school reunion. Looking back at the past she mutters, 'Since high school, most women I know have acquired better taste in clothes, hairstyles and food. But what about in men?' The four women repeatedly fail to establish stable and fulfilling relationships with their men and Charlotte suffers a painful divorce; nevertheless, they don't compromise their way of life and never grant men control over them. Fiske points out that 'any one single act of buying necessarily involves multiple acts of rejection – many commodities are rejected for every one chosen' (Fiske, 1989, p. 26). Seeking 'the one' for themselves, the heroines learn that there are always psychic trade-offs between gains and losses: one can attain a desirable object only by paying the cost (Bowlby, 1993, p. 115). Carrie, exultant over her marriage with Big appearing in *Vogue*, plans a grand ceremony; although she gets furious and distressed when Big boycotts her smug wedding, she admits her self-righteousness and forgives him. Very independent and non-domestic Miranda takes a lesson in devotion from her family: she goes through separation from her husband Steve after he confesses his affair to her, but the two face each other, open up and overcome their crisis. Samantha, who cannot value marriage or restrained monogamy, decides to leave her boyfriend Smith in Los Angeles to start a carefree single life in New York again.

Along with fashion, another highlight of the show is New York itself, with the creator and executive director Daren Star calling the city space 'the fifth main character' (Sohn, 2007, p. 146). Both the TV series and the film introduce the audience to restaurants, cafes, bars, boutiques and beauty salons which the four heroines frequent, as would a guidebook. Sharon Zukin points out that in the 1970s and 1980s writers in New York wrote reviews of new gourmet food stores, restaurants and art galleries and took up new cultural trends. These cultural informants themselves became 'critical infrastructure' and 'provided a material base for both new cultural production and consumption' (Zukin, 1998, p. 831). This means that the information produced by the service sector intervenes in industrial production. These cultural informants, who judge products and services according to their own tastes, are able to influence consumers and manipulate lifestyles (Chaney, 1996, p. 57).

Tokyo rapidly changed into an 'informed' city in the early 1970s. The entertainment magazine *Pia* was published in 1972; thus, even before the network era, residents in Tokyo could easily get access to information about all kinds of cultural events such as films, music, plays and art. In 1980 Yasuo Tanaka wrote *Nantonaku Kurisutaru* [Somehow, crystal], portraying the urban lifestyle and love life of a female college student in Tokyo; this became a bestseller, shifting more than a million copies. From the frivolous image of main characters who spend a lot on brand products, the new word *kurisutaru-zoku* [the crystal set] was coined to refer to urban young people leading a similar lifestyle.[4] Furthermore, the 1980s saw the boom in *katarogu shōsetsu* [catalogue novels] – as the critic Minako Saitō named them. Mariko Hayashi and Yōko Mori wrote essays and serial stories on women, urban consumer culture and brand products for fashion magazines.[5] As the city transformed into an information society with the arrival of the network era, information became instantly globalized and the world, connected by the Internet, could respond immediately. The global cultural movement caused by *SATC* is indeed the product of the Internet age.

Apart from the lawyer Miranda, the *SATC* heroines' occupations locate them as new cultural intermediaries who exert control over the production of the criteria of discrimination, and thus have a powerful influence on the ways in which people consume. They are female dandies, reincarnated for the late twentieth and the twenty-first century; they are *flâneuses* (female *flâneurs*) in the metropolitan city. The lifestyles of fictional drama characters stimulate production, business and people's consumption, proving that traditionally 'feminine' culture exercises significant influence on 'masculine' industry. Since fashion is precisely a cultural industry, we recognize the four heroines in *SATC* as symbols in the postmodern consumer society, where the dichotomy between public/private and production/consumption is dissolving.

Sarah Jessica Parker/Carrie Bradshaw – body, fashion and the celebrity

SATC is a deeply fascinating TV programme; however, its huge cultural impact was dependent on its being backed up by cross-media, particularly fashion and women's magazines.[6] In the first issue of the Japanese version of *Harper's Bazaar*, published in October 2000, the then chief editor Misao Itō (who lived in New York) introduced *SATC* to the

Japanese fashion press. Since then, other magazines have followed, taking up the fashion exhibited in *SATC*. *Harper's Bazaar* featured repeated interviews with Sarah Jessica Parker; but, in Japan, magazines associated with overseas press called *mōdo-kei* [mode oriented] featuring only foreign models are less popular than Japanese fashion magazines focused on real clothes.[7] Thus, the most influential sources in the Japanese print media to promote Sarah Jessica Parker were those fashion magazines that took up the *SATC* fashion as real clothes, and modified the styles for the tastes of their own target Japanese readers. Each fashion magazine's target readers differ according to financial position, lifestyle and age (ranging from twenties to fifties). These fashion presses also set up their official sites on the Internet and provide information about various trends for the readers and the public. I now examine how the American-made *SATC* has filtered into the Japanese media, and how the unknown actor Sarah Jessica Parker has been accepted as a fashion icon and celebrity. Here it is useful to discuss the role played by Japanese magazines, and Parker's multiple star images/identities as produced by the Japanese media.

The most widespread star image of Parker is as the TV character Carrie Bradshaw herself. Unlike other well-known Hollywood stars, despite her long acting career Parker was hardly known in Japan before *SATC*, and suddenly came into the spotlight as Carrie Bradshaw with the success of *SATC*.

One of the main fashion magazines to feature articles on *SATC* is *JJ*,[8] targeted at women around the age of 20. In the October 2001 issue, *JJ* treated the *SATC* fashion trend as a purely American phenomenon, writing that 'the popular TV drama is leading American fashion' (*JJ*, 2001, pp. 194–5). However, in the October 2002 issue *JJ* changed its tone, introducing popular products from the TV series and announcing: 'You can be Sarah Jessica Parker instantly even if you haven't watched it: Take the celebrity style in Sex and the City!' At the same time, *JJ* coordinated fashion items available in Japan in order to create the Carrie style: 'Once you watch, you can tell how glamorous Carrie performed by Sarah Jessica Parker looks'; 'The Carrie style in the drama shows a lot of wonderful coordinates to copy' (*JJ*, 2002, pp. 133–5). After the Japanese cable TV WOWWOW started broadcasting *SATC* in 2000, many fashion and lifestyle magazines picked up the fashion and make-up in *SATC*. *Frau Gorgeous*[9] devoted 15 pages to the fashion of Carrie Bradshaw on 20 May 2003; the edition looks like a manual for Carrie Style, including clothes, shoes, bags, accessories, belts and a scarf. It was unusual for a Japanese fashion magazine to focus on a TV character's outfit with this intensity. The Carrie Style was no longer a peculiar American fashion phenomenon, but had been transformed into a Japanese street fashion trend through the medium of Japanese fashion magazines.

The second popular image of the star in Japanese fashion magazines is of Parker herself as a fashion icon. Drawing from photos in which she walks on the red carpet, and snapshots of her off-screen, Japanese editors suggested ways in which Japanese models could reproduce her style using the items the magazine provides. The Carrie Style, called 'a trend setter' in *SATC*, is a creation of the stylist Patricia Field; however, the clothes Parker wears off-screen and in her private life reveal her own taste and aesthetic ability. Clearly, then, Japanese fashion editors approve of Parker as a fashion icon. People evaluate stars' aesthetic sensibility as expressed in their lifestyles and fashion, above and beyond their professional skills such as acting, singing and dancing. This tendency corresponds to the fact that, in postmodern consumer culture, body and lifestyles are at the centre of people's attention. In contemporary society, self and body are reciprocal components, such that it is important to manipulate and discipline individual bodies as a means through which to express one's selfhood and lifestyle (Chaney, 1996, pp. 116–17). The self/body is a project for the audiences among the general public, and 'fashioning of the body as display of the self' (Chaney, 1996, p. 117; Finkelstein, 1991, pp. 130–1) is the most effective means of producing and negotiating one's identity in relation to society. Sarah Jessica Parker is one exponent of this among the many celebrities who use fashion to produce their star identities, thus leading to professional success.

However, the actor Sarah Jessica Parker as a fashion icon and the TV character Carrie Bradshaw are often mixed up in the Japanese fashion press. For instance, in the article 'Take after Sarah Jessica's Plus One technique: Wear remarkable dresses elegantly', *Grazia*[10] wrote 'Print dresses Sarah Jessica wears for receptions and parties. She adds extra small items to them and shows the mixed balance between sweet and cool. This contrasts with gorgeous prints'; and on the other hand, 'Put a little black dress on not only for a special day but also for Sunday brunch. We'd like to wear it on such an occasion, like Carrie played by Sarah Jessica in *SATC*' (Ōkusa, 2006, pp. 132–41).

Her third star image accentuates Parker's ordinariness and familiarity, which readers feel is incompatible with her glamorous, extreme and confident star image. *Studio Voice* chose Sarah Jessica Parker as one of its style icons in the special edition 'How to create fashion icons' in April 2004, but the image the article presents is completely different from the first and second star images.

The heroine Sarah Jessica Parker is plain, but pleasant and has a nice shape (ordinary people could reach that level with some effort). Besides I feel good about her excellent balance in her fashion taste that needed to spend cost and time. Particularly Sarah's coordinate with a blue feather stole and a pink dress on the date scene in Season 1 made me purchase a work alike of ANNA MOLINARI. (Yuyama, 2004, pp. 46–7)

The toned body and sophisticated fashion taste contribute to glamorize plain Sarah Jessica Parker. This star image, combined with ordinariness and familiarity, provokes the audiences' and readers' wishes to transform themselves. They expect that if they polished their tastes and made an effort to discipline themselves they would be able to look like her.

A critic once teased Sarah Jessica Parker about her role as the awkward bespectacled high school student Patty Green in the TV serial *Square Pegs* (1982–3), saying that 'she has a face like a shaved Staffordshire bull terrier' (Jermyn, 2006, pp. 77–8). Deborah Jermyn observes for the viewers that Parker's transformation into a style icon through taking the role of Carrie Bradshaw in *SATC* is an 'ugly-duckling-turned-swan' story (Jermyn, 2006, p. 78). Jermyn continues that, although Parker isn't a classic Hollywood beauty, she enhances herself through skill and elaborate work. Parker's ' "ordinary/extraordinary" paradigm' gives ordinary women hope and provokes public fascination with the star (Jermyn, 2006, p. 78). It is interesting to see that a similar discourse has appeared in Japan, where Japanese fans don't know about Parker's career before *SATC*. In the postmodern consumer culture, women could think that 'beauty is something that can be achieved, that it is something to be worked on … as work on femininity' (Lury, 1996, p. 135).[11]

The fourth image concerns the Sarah Jessica Parker who talks about her private life in associated magazines with an overseas press. I have already pointed out that in Japanese fashion magazines Parker cannot escape from her role as Carrie Bradshaw, and that both Parker and the role are always mixed up in the articles about her. However, reports on interviews with Parker in *ELLE*[12] and *Harper's Bazaar* represent Parker as a totally different type of person from Carrie Bradshaw; she doesn't talk about sex with other people and doesn't smoke. The most significant difference from single Carrie is that Parker leads a happily married life (Alford, 2001, p. 157; *ELLE*, 2003, p. 40). Notably, the *ELLE* interview was conducted at a time when Parker had postponed shooting the next season of *SATC* because she was expecting her first baby after 5 years of marriage to Mathew Broderick, whom she met after several relationships. Parker's real life – with her family, and as mother-to-be – is remote from Carrie's single life in which she enjoys her independence and solid female friendships and romances despite undergoing painful breakups.

However, in reviewing the articles, one notes that *ELLE* doesn't omit mention of Parker's attire, commenting that it is as fashionable as Carrie's, and that the magazine cannot close the interview without asking about Carrie's future. The photo images of Parker in *Harper's Bazaar* are as provocative and stimulating as those of Carrie. One is of Parker stretching out in a striped bikini; another shows Parker posing with a men's suit to remind the reader of Big, the love of Carrie's life; in another, Parker exposes her legs, putting on only a white shirt and black Manolo Blahnik stilettos (Carrie's trademark). Parker says 'I keep all the shoes I bought – no matter how ridiculous the heels look. Manolos are art. ... I'll tell my daughter in the future – Mum bought the first Manolo Blahnik at the little boutique Madeline Garret in 1983' (Alford, 2001, p. 158). Ultimately, both articles somehow end up by retrieving images of Carrie Bradshaw.

The fifth image is of Sarah Jessica Parker as a professional and a producer. Although this image is less familiar in Japan, some interview articles do introduce Parker's various professional activities and her passion for work. One article in *Harper's Bazaar* reveals that Parker acts as a UNICEF ambassador, is very politically minded – a Democrat – and performs in stage plays. Now she is working on an off-Broadway production, *Fuddy Meers*, as a co-producer, and simultaneously managing a film shooting (Alford, 2001, p. 156). The interview informs us that Parker is a professional with passion for her work. Since her debut off-Broadway at the age of 11, she has worked her way up to her current position over a long period of time (Alford, 2001, p. 156). 'Playing on stage is really demanding because the expectation of the audiences is very high,' but Parker sets herself a rule to act on stage once a year (Alford, 2001, p. 158). As an actor, Parker takes pride in having more experience on stage than in film and TV, and her ideal image to follow is the actor Blythe Danner. Danner took breaks for her family, but continues playing on stage and gained fame in films; Parker concludes that 'She became an excellent actor as she chose her own way. That's what it's all about. So she could be a rich person' (Alford, 2001, p. 158). Parker demonstrates her occupational pride and indomitable spirit, showing how her commitment to her job has allowed her to get over a long difficult period.

It is notable that the men's magazine *BRUTUS* selected Sarah Jessica Parker for the opening page of the special issue 'Trend Makers 2005'.

BRUTUS seems to be interested in Parker as a producer rather than as an actor. The article asks 'What is the real state of the boom that producer Sarah Jessica Parker reflects?' and interviews her about the reasons why *SATC* became a social movement.

One of the reasons for the boom is the exquisite styling by Patricia Field, who drew inspiration from fashionable New York women she saw on the street (*BRUTUS*, 2005, p. 28). Alongside Field, Parker became deeply involved in *SATC* fashion as a producer. For the first season, they purchased 80 per cent of the costume through production costs; but after the TV show was recognized they received many offers from designers (*BRUTUS*, 2005, p. 28). In the last season, 80 per cent of the clothes were on lease; so they needed only to buy the vintage materials that they could not get in any other way (*BRUTUS*, 2005, p. 28). Even famous designers realized that *SATC* functioned as a huge show window for global audiences, in which they could advertise their products.

On the other hand, Parker stresses that they didn't intend to make a merely trendy drama, but to produce an authentic TV programme. Her emphasis in the series is 'what are important for women's lives and whether they can portray these things' (*BRUTUS*, 2005, p. 28). She thinks that if the programme had played down to the audience and was artificial, lacking reality, it wouldn't have lasted, even though it might have caught people's attention for a short while (*BRUTUS*, 2005, p. 28). Female audiences commenting on *SATC* fan sites indicate that the most appealing part of the drama is watching four single women's firm and unchangeable friendships, which remain constant whatever happens to them through their fashionable lifestyles, romances and frank talks on sex. These heroines face various problems that women encounter in real life: relationships, marriage, divorce, infertility, sickness, and care for elderly. They struggle through the difficulties, but courageously carve out their own lives by supporting one another. Female viewers sympathize with heroines of this kind; thus Parker's production policy seems vindicated.

In addition to her position as producer, Parker's new job is to design products for a Japanese company. She had already gone into designing the clothing line 'Bitten' for Steve & Barry's in the US, and the Japanese brand Samantha Thavasa also appointed her as designer for the spring–summer seasons in 2007. The Japanese media reports that Parker came to Japan to promote her new bags 'Orlare' (Ryūkōtsūshin, 2007, p. 161; *SCREEN*, 2007, p. 42).

In this section I have explored Sarah Jessica Parker's various star images as reflected in the Japanese press: the TV character Carrie

Bradshaw, a fashion icon, an ordinary-looking celebrity, a married woman who cherishes her private life, and a highly committed professional actor/producer. Regarding these star images promoted by the Japanese media, we realize that, while Japanese readers consume her images as star and fashion commodities, Sarah Jessica Parker as a cultural intermediary gives impetus to cultural and economic activities. Fashion underpinned Parker's success. She seized the chance to play Carrie Bradshaw and thereby make over her previous star image and rise through the ranks of the entertainment world. Parker exploits her aesthetic taste for selecting fashion, making a project of her own body, and thereby achieved 'a social promotion' to stardom through being recognized as a 'distinguished possessor' of taste (Bourdieu, 1984, p. 251). Aesthetic bodily ability to express selfhood is also closely connected to the profession of actor. In addition, Parker opens up fresh ground, intimating that there is no boundary between work and home, or between consumption (of star/fashion commodities) and production (as a producer and designer of the same). Her vitality in taking active parts in various fields seems to prove that she is a real postmodern 'third-waver'.

Feminine pleasure – *Sex and the City* and fandom

For the second wave feminists, red lipsticks and stilettos are the symbols of women subordinating themselves to and being oppressed by men. Women who shop and dress up vainly are foolish consumers manipulated by the capitalist economy, and fashion victims who are nothing more than sexual objects for men. However, *SATC* seems to have overturned these pessimistic notions of the second wave feminists.

Female researchers of the third wave have tackled fashion and consumption, which were previously not seen as serious topics to study (Entwistle, 2000; Finkelstein, 2007; Gibson, 2000; Wilson, 2007).[13] Elizabeth Wilson insists that fashion offers us aesthetic creativity and 'acts [as] a vehicle for fantasy' (Wilson, 2007, pp. 245, 246). Fashion links 'the inner to the outer world' and works to produce the social self (Wilson, 2007, p. 246). According to Finkelstein, it makes clear the relation between subjectivity and products as signs by investigating cultural practice such as fashion. Our socialization with use of fashion including discourses, practices and values doesn't promise us to bring the stability of our subjectivity. However, fashion doesn't always exploit or degenerate people, rather gives discourses of signs that directly represent individual desire and subjectivity (Finkelstein, 2007, p. 116). Their argument is useful for an examination of the success of *SATC* and its global fandom.

Here, I focus on the relationship between *SATC* and its fans, and investigate *SATC* fans as contemporary female consumers to explore how fashion and consumption acts on their identities. For this purpose I looked into *SATC* fans' comments on the Fashion in American Fan Forum, HBO's *SATC* fan website, and the independent Japanese fan website Sex and the City Girls' Talk. Both American and Japanese fan websites obviously constitute female-dominated communities, and this shows that Sarah Jessica Parker is a popular star, particularly for female audiences.

On the American sites it is appealing for the fans that the four women in *SATC* have individual styles and express their personalities with their fashions. The fans can identify themselves with their favourite characters according to their individual tastes.

> I loved Charlotte's Elizabeth Taylor look. I'll try to find the picture. I think she looked soo pretty. (CrazyBeautiful)[14]

> Charlotte looked sooo pretty when she did that look! I love all the girls' clothes but Carrie is my fashion idol. She's so eclectic and unique and always has the perfect mix of designer, vintage and high street. I don't know who's going to set all the trends now SatC is gone. (Chazina)[15]

> I love the girls' fashion. I like most the clothes of Samantha and Miranda though. (Addison McHot)[16]

American *SATC* fans value the significant contribution to the series by the stylist Patricia Field and her staff in the costume department. In Japan, however, fans' interests concentrate on Carrie's fashion. For Japanese fans, Carrie's emblem, Manolo Blahnik high heels, are the symbol of independent working women.

The common point is that fans online exchange opinions about their chosen clothes from *SATC* as if they were chatting and turning over pages in fashion magazines in the same room. Iris Marion Young suggests that clothing serves a role in maintaining 'the bonds of sisterhood' in society: in our everyday lives women often talk about clothes and share opinions, and occasionally go shopping for clothes together.[17]

The *SATC* fans seem to enjoy this female bonding. The fan websites are full of female voices showing their interest and pleasure in clothes. One of the Japanese fans is amazed by Carrie's unconventional coordinates, and an American participant reports the influence of *SATC* on American women, noting that she witnessed a well-dressed woman in the *SATC* style in town.

> I'm careful of wearing less than three colors and match the similar materials avoiding too much doing. But Carrie wears so many colors, in addition, put on a print × a print, a check × a check and a print × a stripe. As Tamarī-san pointed it out, it really depends on individual personality and taste. ... Despite fabulous coordinates, it's impossible for me to copy everything from her! (Kaorukaze)[18]

> Beachy: You can't imagine how many times I've seen the 'influence' of film/series on women around where I live – from the shoes, dress styles, fashion trends. Last time I went to the doctor's office I saw one of the ladies wearing a black dress with a X-wide black elastic belt that she had underneath her breasts! She was wearing black Coach slides with the dress! Looked really good!! (Marlennemm)[19]

These women's voices demonstrate that women get visual pleasure from observing how other women dress and enjoy sharing their information and knowledge on fashion. Fashion, then, is not necessarily just a tool for attracting male attention.

Some fans ask questions about what brands the heroines wear, and where and how to get the products that the heroines exhibit in *SATC*. Some fans are really knowing and informative about the commodities shown in *SATC*. For example, the host of the Japanese fan site answers an inquiry made by another participant about the dark and white striped dress Carrie wore when she visited her then boyfriend Aleksandr Petrovsky (Mikhail Baryshnikov) in Paris.

> Yes, that dress is Sonia Rykiel's. It's Carrie's intentional and fashionable choice to go to Paris. And the brilliant black coat over the dress is Behnaz Sarafpour's (the former designer for Barney's New York ... Carrie is a true New Yorker!). The cream color clutch bag is Judith Leiber's (She once collaborated with Sanrio[20] to produce some Hello Kitty bags). Carrie puts the finishing touch to Chanel's hat trimmed with pearls. Looking at them, they are half American and half French. It is really clever! This expresses Carrie's feeling hesitating over going to Paris, so it's not only the script to be excellent. (Julia)[21]

Others write that they have already bought the same goods as Carrie wears. A Japanese fan in Tokyo reports that she went window-shopping in town, and saw some *SATC* goods in stock.

> I went to Le chame de fifi et fafa in Aoyama on the other day. It was a truly enchanting atmosphere. Of course I saw Lizzie Scheck's necklaces! The shop assistant there said she watches SATC as well. She showed me same necklaces as Carrie and Charlotte wore in the drama and a necklace that Mathew gave Sarah as a present. ... Another day I dropped into Isetan Department Stores and there were different sizes of horseshoe necklaces. I wonder if the number of these goods has decreased from before?!?! They looked prettier than mine (Oh my gosh!!) (Bānetto)[22]

The Japanese fan who bought the horseshoe necklace, and the American woman who wore the *SATC*-style black dress, were performers who enjoyed the visual images of Sarah Jessica Parker and took them in, imitated and copied them with their own bodies. When fictional spectacles come into people's everyday lives, the audience itself begins to negotiate with the spectacle (Sandvoss, 2005, p. 53).[23] The desirable feminine images of Sarah Jessica Parker are introjected by the viewers' consumption through their bodies (Sandvoss, 2005, p. 82; Stacey, 1994, p. 231).

Many participants of the fan sites are not people in the upper income bracket like the four women in *SATC*, who can afford designer brands and high-class fashions. They are thought to be around the age of 20 to their thirties, and popular products for them to purchase include accessories such as horseshoe necklaces in both countries and also name tag necklaces in America that are quite reasonably priced (they can even get imitations in the market). Luxurious clothes are out of their reach, so some say they usually go to Benetton and H&M to buy their clothing.

Moreover, not all fans are necessarily consumers, and in the American fan sites in particular even some passionate fans question whether they would pay for expensive brand products.

> Ginna: The price of that bag was let's say either a house or car payment – or a credit card payment!!! LOL!!! Or it would pay to feed a family of six people for three months in a country like India. (Marlennemm)[24]
>
> It just makes you really think hard about how different the world is. In a society where there are $1200 handbags there is another where $1200 would be like a year's wages. I think where you see us

going more and more 'green' we should be going more and more 'humanitarian'. Know what I mean? Did I just go really deep there? Lol. (Host_Ginna)[25]

Although many participants don't actually buy luxurious products, they are 'window-shopping' in order to consume the images and enjoy simulating what they see when they watch *SATC* on TV, as the fan who spoke out above against designer handbags says:

> Beachy: SATC was a 'nice weekly escape from the real world – that lasted for six seasons. When you really look at the series 'who could really afford the fashions, shoes, apartments, jewelry, dinners' that those girls enacted each week – What didn't the writers/producers show us?? How many times did the girls 'go without' something – like food or telephone?? SATC was 'a major Fantasy' – and we all ate it up. (Marleneemm)[26]

Many *SATC* fans switch on their TV sets weekly to enjoy half an hour's fantasy to escape from boredom in everyday life and forget the modest material condition of their real lives. The visual pleasure they derive from gazing on gorgeous attire, tasteful room interiors and costly jewellery is ascribed to femininity (Stacey, 1994, p. 97).[27] They indulge in the fantasy of 'a feminized environment of consumption' as spectacles (Stacey, 1994, p. 97). However, their financial positions don't restrict fashion-conscious fans' enjoyment of trying to be innovative: as Chaney points out, opportunities for being creative and fashionable are not limited to economically privileged groups (1996, pp. 97–8).

One of the hosts of the HBO *SATC* fan site sets out the relationship between women and fashion as follows:

> It is so true! Sex and the City really did a lot for the fashion world and showed women how they could be fabulous no matter what the occasion called for. There is nothing wrong with a woman wanting to dress well, because when you feel good about how you look, your confidence is lifted. When you feel good about yourself, you feel like you can do just about anything. (Host_Ginna)[28]

The female fans are pleased to see the *SATC* heroines selecting clothes that perfectly fit and express their personalities and charm, and enjoy dressing themselves creatively. This is an aesthetic capacity for bodily self-expression, which they admire, and they understand it as 'a skill for distinction' that can only be acquired by mature women who have had experiences and who know themselves well. In other words, the fans perceive that the four women in *SATC* are active agents who intentionally and innovatively demonstrate their personae and ways of life through their fashions. The 'pleasure of fashion' lies in 'the symbolic replay of this profoundly productive moment when subjectivity emerges' (Rabine, 1994, p. 64).

Conventionally, feminine narcissism has been ascribed negative connotations; the third wave feminists, however, reconsider this notion of narcissism, locating it as 'a source of feminine pleasure' through which self-esteem and autonomy can evolve.[29] Dressing beautifully is not merely keeping up appearances, but also has an effect on the wearer's subjectivity. Wearing clothes glamorously is to please oneself and feel confident; thus women think it empowers them to live positively and autonomously.

Conclusion

SATC is a fictional drama, which dwells upon lifestyle and the aestheticization of everyday life in postmodern consumer culture. However, the individual lifestyles and fashions that the four main characters exhibit on TV became a global cultural and economic movement involving production and consumption. The TV show, rather than designers, decided new trends, and the four heroines performed the role of cultural intermediaries while *SATC* worked as a huge show-window open to the world. In this chapter, then, we have seen the process through which celebrity culture has been shared by a global information society, has diffused into the local Japanese media and has thus exerted an influence on production and consumer activities.

We have realized that popular culture can have a significant impact on both global and local industries, such as media, manufacturing and retail. Celebrities who motivate popular culture exercise their influence on people as cultural intermediaries, and at the same time are also consumed by people as star and fashion commodities. In contemporary celebrity culture, stars are evaluated by audiences with respect to their aesthetic tastes as performers of fashions and lifestyles. Sarah Jessica Parker is a child of postmodern consumer culture and celebrity culture, and she understands that fashion is the basis of a project, carried out on her own body, through which she can power her rise to professional stardom. Moreover, Parker is not only a commodity to be consumed, but was appointed as a producer of the TV series and has been energetically involved in production in the entertainment world ever since.

In contemporary Japan, Japanese audiences have various opportunities to encounter not only Japanese and American cultural products, but also other popular Asian TV series (especially Korean TV dramas), films and music. Thus it goes almost without saying that we need to investigate the composite cultural dimensions in postmodern Japanese society in our future studies of popular culture and consumer interests.

Furthermore, fandom that accretes around celebrities *qua* agents holds the key to understanding the global cultural and economic movement represented by *SATC*. Female *SATC* fans in both the US and Japan enjoy popular culture and are themselves enthusiastic performers who take in celebrity culture in their daily lives, and practise it with their own bodies in the way that they consume fashion. They are active examiners who seek access to information about *SATC* commodities that interest them, through TV, film, magazines and the Internet. It is obvious that these fans also play active roles as knowing informants for others in the online communities.

I have no intention of recommending unreserved consumption; however, I would like to suggest that we adopt a more balanced view, which is not unduly partial to the notion of anti-fashion. Further feminist fashion study may find it fruitful to take a more balanced view, which considers the aesthetic aspects of fashion and the psychological influence of fashion on the inner self, and understands the crucial roles of gender and femininity in consumption.

What female *SATC* fans are absorbed by are the four heroines' unshakeable friendships, their romances, lifestyles and, above all, their fashions. For them, dressing beautifully is a skill that leads to distinction, and to the distinctively feminine pleasure of lifting up the spirit.

Notes

1. According to WOWWOW Customer Centre, by 2009 Season 1 had been rerun 12 times; Season 2, 14 times; and Seasons 3–6, 11 times (personal communication, 2010).
2. See Imelda Whelehan's *The Feminist Bestseller: From Sex and the Single Girl to Sex and the City* (2005, pp. 141–212) regarding the definition of the term 'third wave' and the difference between second and third wave feminists. The term 'Third wave' was first used in 1992 by Rebecca Walker, who is one of the founders of the US Third Wave Foundation. Whelehan writes that 'Third Wave feminists are young women who are the beneficiaries of a feminist education' and 'They profit from a pre-established discourse of feminism with an embarrassment of riches, in terms of theoretical and political explorations,

and their own experiences of their postmodern world – arguably more baffling and contradictory than that inhabited by early Second Wavers.'

3. This notion is shared by the second wave feminists; however, Thorstein Veblen set down this well-known view very early on. in his *Theory of the Leisure Class: An Economic Study of Institutions* (1899).

4. See Minako Saitō (2002, pp. 220–53) regarding her critique of Yasuo Tanaka's *Nantonaku Kurisutaru*.

5. For critiques of the works of Yōko Mori and Mariko Hayashi, see Minako Saitō's (2004, pp. 61–82) arguments regarding the relationship between Japanese consumer society and Japanese literature.

6. See Anna König (2006, pp. 130–43) for the influence of *SATC* on the British fashion press.

7. For a comparison of the real sales of fashion magazines in Japan, see Akira Nagae (2001, pp. 25–9) and Yano Keizai Kenkyūsho (2006, pp. 21–31).

8. See Fashion Magazine Headlines. The main readers of *JJ* are supposed to be around 20; however, it can be expected that the magazine enjoys a wider readership range, perhaps from 18 to 32 years.

9. Fashion Magazine Headlines. The target age of *Frau* is 28, and the expected readers are from 25 to 37 years old.

10. Fashion Magazine Headlines. The target age of *Grazia* is 35, but it possibly attracts readers aged between 28 and 44.

11. Taking up Janice Winship's study of English women's magazine *Options*, Lury notes that women's magazines have advocated consumption as a creative skill to construct lifestyles and to create a look that coordinates clothes, furnishings, food and make-up (Lury, 1996, pp. 132–5).

12. Fashion Magazine Headlines. The possible readers of *ELLE* range from age 23 and beyond. Targeted readers are fashionable and cosmopolitan women who are urban, interested and fashion-conscious.

13. Regarding the difference between second wave feminism and post-feminism/third wave feminism in their attitude towards fashion, see Elizabeth Wilson (2007, pp. 228–47) and Pamela Church Gibson (2000, pp. 349–62).

14. American fan website Fan Forum's Sex and the City – The SatC – Fashion: 'Cuz they wear the most beautiful dresses' (1 November 2004).

15. Fan Forum (1 November 2004).

16. Fan Forum (2 November 2004).

17. Iris Marion Young states that women enjoy touching and sensing fabrics, and female bonding through fashion, and take pleasure in fantasies of transport and transformation (1994, pp. 205–6).

18. Japanese fan website, Sex and the City Girls' Talk, 253. Re:Carrie no fasshion ni tsuite [Re: On Carrie's fashion] (12 August, 2005).

19. HBO's fan website, Sling Back: Fashion Through the Seasons in Archives in HBO Community Home (11 July 2008).

20. Sanrio is the Japanese company that produces 'Hello Kitty'.

21. See Sex and the City Girls' Talk, 232. Re: Carrie no doresu [Re: Carrie's dress] (3 July, 2005).

22. Sex and the City Girls' Talk, 217. Le chame de fifi ... (10 June, 2005).

23. Cornel Sandvoss conceptualizes fans as active agents and analyses their performance, consumption and productivity in *Fans: The Mirror of Consumption* (2005).

24. HBO's Fan Website (7 July 2008).
25. HBO's Fan Website (7 July 2008).
26. HBO's Fan Website (9 July 2008).
27. Jackie Stacey challenges traditional psychoanalytic theories of female spectatorship, focusing on the relation between Hollywood female stars and female fans in *Star Gazing: Hollywood Cinema and Female Spectatorship* (1994).
28. HBO's Fan Website (15 June 2008).
29. Based on Eugénie Lemoine-Luccioni's analysis of female narcissism observing the mother–daughter relationship, Hilary Radner suggests feminine narcissism is not initially heterosexualized. Radner challenges Freudian psychoanalysis, reconsidering female narcissism and eroticism in *Shopping Around: Feminine Culture and the Pursuit of Pleasure* (1995, pp. 35–65). Celia Lury refers to female narcissism in her analysis of women and consumption in *Consumer Culture* (1996, pp. 118–55). See also Jackie Stacey (1994, pp. 131–2).

References

Alford, H. (2001), 'Sarah Jessica Parker dokusen intabyū: shinayakana sekkusu shinboru', in Alford, H., 'Head Over Heels', Anno, R. (trans.), *Harper's Bazaar* (Japan), April: 154–9.
Bandai, E. (2003), 'Chō-rittai tokushū 30dai kara no sekushī to huku: 30dai, "sekushī" teizō-hōsoku – "Sex and the City" wa taikutsushinai jinsei no michishirube', *Frau Gorgeous*, 20 May: 36–7.
Bandai, E., Tani, H. and Tsukamoto, S. (2003), 'Chō-rittai tokushū 30dai kara no sekushī to huku: "otona" no naka no "otona" ga mamoru beki huku to komono no rūru', *Frau Gorgeous*, 20 May: 38–41.
Beard, J. (2008), 'Sekkusu to Ai to Singuru Raihu', *Newsweek Japan*, 27 August: 40.
Bowlby, R. (1993), *Shopping with Freud*, London and New York: Routledge.
BRUTUS (2005), 'Trend Makers 2005 – karera no mai būmu ga 2005nen no ryūkō o kimeru!', *BRUTUS*, 1/15 January: 28.
Chaney, D. (1996), *Lifestyles*, London and New York: Routledge.
ELLE (Japan) (2003), 'Terebidorama no 2dai sutā ga kataru watashi no puraibēto raihu: osharena mama ni natta kyaria no shōchō, Sarah Jessica Parker', January: 40–1.
Entwistle, J. (2000), *The Fashioned Body*, Cambridge, UK: Polity Press.
Fan Forum, available at http://www.fanforum.com/f199/satc-fashion-cuz-they-wear-most-beautiful-dresses-26932/ (accessed 27 February 2009).
Fashion Magazine Headlines, available at http://www.nightscape.info/fhl/ (accessed 2 May 2010).
Featherstone, M. (2007), *Consumer Culture & Postmodernism*, 2nd edn, London, Thousand Oaks, CA, New Delhi and Singapore: Sage.
Finkelstein, J. (2007), *The Fashioned Self*, Cambridge, UK: Polity Press.
Fiske, J. (1989), *Reading the Popular*, Cambridge, MA, London, Sydney and Wellington, NZ: Unwin Hyman.
Gibson, P. C. (2000), 'Redressing the Balance: Patriarchy, Postmodernism and Feminism', in Gibson, P. C. and Bruzzi, S. (eds), *Fashion Cultures: Theories, Explorations and Analysis*, London and New York: Routledge, pp. 349–62.

Greer, G. (1971), *The Female Eunuch*, New York: McGraw-Hill.
Greer, G. (1999), *The Whole Woman*, New York: Anchor Books.
HBO, available at http://boards.hbo.com/topic/Sex-City-Archives/Sling-Fashion-Seasons/200000... (accessed 19 March 2009).
Iwashita, K. (2001), Ohitorisama, Tokyo: Chūōkōron-shinsha.
Jermyn, D. (2006), ' "Bringing out the ★ in You": SJP, Carrie Bradshaw and the Evolution of Television Stardom', in Holmes, S. and Redmond, S. (eds), *Framing Celebrity: New Directions in Celebrity Culture*, London and New York: Routledge, pp. 67–85.
JJ (2001), 'L.A. chokkō serebu no ryūkō kurozetto – kininaru anohito wa nani o kattanoka', October: 194–5.
JJ (2002), 'Mitenai Watashi mo suguni Sarah Jessica Parker: Sex and the City no NY serebu sutairu o nusume!', October: 133–5.
Kitō, E., Ueda, N., Handa, N., Ibuki, M., Shimada, Y. and Haruyama, Y. (trans.) (2002), *Sex and the City: Kiss and Tell Kanzen-ban* [Sohn, A. (2007), *Sex and the City: Kiss and Tell*], Tokyo: bookmansha.
Kō, T. (trans.) (2005), *Yūkan Kaikyū no Riron – seido no shinka ni kansuru keizaiteki kenkyū* [Veblen, T. (1899), *The Theory of the Leisure Class: An Economic Study in the Evolution of Institutions*], Tokyo: Chikuma Shobō.
König, A. (2006), 'Sex and the City: A Fashion Editor's Dream', in Akass, K. and McCabe, J. (eds), *Reading Sex and the City*, London and New York: I.B. Tauris, pp. 130–43.
Lury, C. (1996), *Consumer Culture*, New Brunswick, NJ: Rutgers University Press.
Nagae, A. (2001), 'Fasshonshi kindan no jitsubai-busū o suppanuku', *Henshū Kaigi*, May: 25–9.
Nakajima, K. and Katō, Y. (trans.) (1997), *Kettei-ban Daini no Sei II Taiken* [de Beauvoir, S. (1949), *Le Deuxième Sexe: L'expérience vécue*], Tokyo: Shinchōsha.
Narumi, H. (trans.) (2007) *Fashion no Bunkashakaigaku* [Finkelstein, J. (1996), *After a Fashion*], Tokyo: Serika Shobo.
Nice, R. (trans.) (1984), *Distinction: A Social Critique of the Judgments of Taste* [Bourdieu, P. (1979), *La distinction: Critique sociale du jugement*], Cambridge, Massachusetts: Harvard University Press.
Ōkusa, N. (2006), 'Onna o intaishinai oshare no rūru otehon wa Grazia-sedai no jyoyū ni ari! – Part 1 Sarah Jessica Parker no purasu 1 teku ga otehon: daichūmoku no wanpīsu o kiru', *Grazia*, April: 132–41.
Ono, A. (2003), 'Chō-rittai tokushū 30dai kara no sekushī to huku : 30dai no "ii koi" wa shūchūryoku no sanbutsu de aru', *Frau Gorgeous*, 20 May: 48–54.
Paterson, M. (2006), *Consumption and Everyday Life*, Milton Park, UK and New York: Routledge.
Rabine, L. W. (1994), 'A Women's Two Bodies: Fashion Magazines, Consumerism and Feminism', *On Fashion*, New Brunswick, NJ: Rutgers University Press, pp. 59–75.
Radner, H. (1995), *Shopping Around: Feminine Culture and the Pursuit of Pleasure*, New York and London: Routledge.
Ryūkōtsūshin (2007), 'Barērīna reggu vs dansā reggu – omiashi taiketsu akoga-reno serebu ni semaru!', June: 160–1.
Saitō, M. (2002), *Bundan Aidoru-ron*, Tokyo: Iwanami Shoten.
Saitō, M. (2004), *Bungakuteki Shōhin-gaku*, Tokyo: Kinokuniya Shoten.
Sandvoss, C. (2005), *Fans: The Mirror of Consumption*, Cambridge, UK and Malden, MA: Polity.

SCREEN (2007), ' "Samanta Thavasa" & "Samantha Tiara" no PR de rainichi no Sarah Jessica Parker', June: 42.

Sex and the City Girls' Talk, available at http://www2.ezbbs.net/cgi/bbs?id=satc-fans-page&dd=14&p=5 (accessed 17 October 2009); http://www2.ezbbs.net/cgi/bbs?id=satc-fans-page&dd=14&p=6 (accessed 22 March 2009).

Shinkokyū (2002), 'Keizai-kishōdai – banjō shōhi', *Asahi Shimbun*, 2 September: 10.

Stacey, J. (1994), *Star Gazing: Hollywood Cinema and Female Spectatorship*, London and New York: Routledge.

Whelehan, I. (2005), *The Feminist Bestseller: From Sex and the Single Girl to Sex and the City*, New York: Palgrave Macmillan.

Wilson, E. (2007), *Adorned in Dreams: Fashion and Modernity*, 2nd edn, London and New York: I.B. Tauris.

Yamamoto, T. (2008), *Banjō to iu Ikikata – bankon bansan no 30dai ijō no jyosei*, Tokyo: Presidentsha.

Yano Keizai Kenkyūsho (2006), 'Sōryoku-chōsa Kibishii Zasshi Bunya no Kōbō: sōgō-shūkanshi josei-fasshionshi no kōbō', in Yano, K. K. (ed.), *Yano Report*, Tokyo: Yano Keizai Kenkyūsho, pp. 21–31.

Young, I. M. (1994), 'Women Recovering Our Clothes', in Benstock, S. and Ferriss, S. (eds), *On Fashion*, New Brunswick, NJ: Rutgers University Press, pp. 197–210.

Yuyama, R. (2004), ' "Sex and the City" ron – Tokyo no jyosei gyōkai pīpuru to hikaku shitemiru', *Studio Voice*, April: 46–7.

Zukin, S. (1998), 'Urban Lifestyle: Diversity and Standardisation in Spaces of Consumption', *Urban Studies*, 35(5–6): 825–39.

DVD and Film

Sex and the City (Shoebox Ver.2.0 The Complete Series) (2007), produced by Darren Star and Michael Patrick King, performed by Sarah Jessica Parker, Kim Cattrall, Kristin Davis and Cynthia Nixon, DVD, Paramount Pictures.

Sex and the City (2008), directed by Michael Patrick King, performed by Sarah Jessica Parker, Kim Cattrall, Kristin Davis and Cynthia Nixon, Humax Cinema.

11
Mobile Consumers and Consumption in Japan
Benjamin Hentschel

Introduction

The market for mobile phones in Japan is the most advanced in the world, and handsets that can access the Internet have existed in Japan for more than a decade. The main disruptive invention that triggered this development was the emergence of the Internet and the ensuing digital revolution. In Japan, however, the diffusion of the Internet followed a specific pattern, different from its Western counterparts: Internet access from mobile devices such as cell phones became more common than accessing the Internet from conventional personal computers (PCs). Although Japan did not become the fastest adopter of the latest technologies until around the mid-1990s, it is now leading innovations in the mobile market. Japanese mobile phones, however, are more than a mere portable device that exchanges data. The typical Japanese mobile phone is a high-speed gateway to the Internet and an mp3 player (including download-store), as well as offering access to electronic cash, train tickets, banks and televisions, among other things. In fact, the definition of a mobile phone is slowly shifting to that of a multimedia device that has the potential to substitute for many other devices used in everyday life. As a result, Japanese consumers have become a very specific group of end-users, who do not only utilize what technology offers but are drivers of innovation as well. Nowadays, new products and services for mobile phones are usually introduced in Japan and are then adopted by other countries, often after a few years' delay. The consumer landscape in Japan – including suppliers, mobile providers and consumers – has dramatically changed over the last few decades. This chapter will be an introduction to Japanese mobile consumers, with a focus on the major technological breakthroughs that gave rise to this specific segment of customers.

Keitai, the Japanese mobile phone

In Japanese, the term *keitai*[1] is an abbreviation for *keitai-denwa* (mobile phone), and is the most commonly used word when referring to a mobile phone device. The *keitai* often incorporates the latest cutting-edge technology, and Japanese consumers are often the first to set trends that are later adapted to other markets such as Europe or America. However, a mobile phone is much more than an aggregate of different technologies – a fact that especially holds true for the Japanese mobile consumer landscape and the *keitai*, as this section will show. According to Aguado and Martinez (2009, p. 338), a mobile phone has three distinctive characteristics. It is: (1) an 'integrated portable meta-device', (2) a 'cultural object that is connected to one's identity', and (3) a 'medium through which (cultural) content can be distributed and consumed'.

In Japan, a society that shows strong tendencies towards collectivism (Matsumoto, 1999, p. 298),[2] the mobile phone is not only a status symbol but also an expression of one's identity. For example, cell phone users in Japan often decorate their *keitai* with a variety of accessories, a practice that is essentially unique to Japanese society (Kushchu, 2006, p. 38). Japanese mobile phones are seldom seen without attached straps, mostly depicting cute character-mascots such as Doraemon or Pikachu. While this phenomenon is part of Japan's 'cute business' culture, it is common not only among the younger generation, but among adults as well (Allison, 2004, p. 39). In recent years, the handset customization business has been discovered by companies who now offer (mainly female) customers individual decoration for their *keitai* in the form of jewellery-like glittering stones (Haghirian, 2009). The service is especially famous in Shibuya, one of Tokyo's trendiest districts.

No other gadget has had a bigger impact on Japanese society than the mobile phone. The *keitai* has evolved into a device so essential that it is often referred to as a 'virtual extra appendage that people can't walk, ride or relax without' (Nagata, 2009). The *keitai* truly is a near-omnipresent device that connects end-users in Japan and transcends differences in society.

The historical development of the Japanese mobile market

In order to understand the distinctive mobile market in Japan and its unique customer base, one first has to understand how the business of cellular phones emerged in Japan. The most noteworthy advancement, which is still the driver of innovation in the Japanese cell phone market, is the evolution of the mobile Internet. In particular, the emergence of the mobile Internet redefines the need for mobile operators and content providers to understand customers' needs, and furthermore has a major influence on the advancement of the information society (Minges, 2005, p. 114). In December 1979, Japan's first mobile communications service became available to the public, although due to rigid market regulations it did not manifest any significant rate of growth (Adachi, 2001). Today, there are many cell phone providers offering their business to even the most remote of Japan's islands. Among the major players in the Japanese mobile phone market, NTT DoCoMo (henceforth DoCoMo) was the major driving force in the evolution of the mobile Internet in Japan. In the following, DoCoMo and its breakthrough mobile Internet service i-mode are introduced in more detail.

DoCoMo and the introduction of i-mode in Japan

DoCoMo's[3] roots go back to the creation of Nippon Telegraph and Telephone (NTT) in 1952. Until the 1970s, NTT held a monopoly in Japan's telecommunications market. Due to increasing calls for a competitive market environment made by the Ministry of International Trade and Industry (MITI) and US politicians, pressure mounted on the rigid telecommunications market and NTT's monopoly. When, in 1985, NTT was privatized and the market deregulated, this was a turning point in Japan's telecommunications market and NTT's monopoly (Steinbock, 2003, p. 211). In the wake of the deregulations, DoCoMo (then called Mobile Communications Network Inc.) was created as a spin-off in 1992 to operate NTT's wireless communication business (Mukund and Radhika, 2003).

In February 1999, DoCoMo launched its Internet access protocol 'i-mode'.[4] The service took off rapidly, with 33 million users only 3 years after its launch (Ishii, 2004, p. 44). DoCoMo initially made the service available on 2G handsets, calling it MOVA.[5] Only one and a half years later it was transferred to 3G technology and renamed Freedom of Mobile Access (FOMA). Despite the relatively low demand for mobile handsets a decade earlier, there were two factors that contributed to the success of DoCoMo's i-mode: (1) the deregulation of the Japanese mobile phone market, and (2) DoCoMo's manager's vision of exploring new markets through high levels of innovation (Peltokorpi *et al.*, 2007, p. 59). According to Steinbock (2005, p. 65), the introduction of i-mode was preceded by two stages of revenue growth; the i-mode service was introduced as a measure to create a third growth wave for DoCoMo. These three stages were: (1), volume growth as defined by the increase of subscribers,

(2) value growth as defined by the increase of data traffic, and (3) usage growth (i-mode) as defined by the growth of content distributed.

The introduction of i-mode and mobile Internet in Japan was very successful. In 2002, attempts were made to implement the i-mode business model in other countries, especially in Europe,[6] but these received comparatively little attention (Steinbock, 2005, p. 69). Western customers were not grasping the marketing message to the same extent as their Japanese counterparts. The i-mode phenomenon seemed to be a product that was nurtured by the demands of the unique group of Japanese consumers.

3G technology era in Japan

Compared with other industrialized countries, the introduction of 3G technology was established earlier and with more success in Japan. Whereas in other countries mobile operators struggled to generate the necessary investments in next-generation technology, Japanese operators, with DoCoMo at the fore, could successfully raise the revenue required (Weber, 2007, p. 181).

Figure 11.1 illustrates the numbers of subscriptions to 3G mobile services in selected OECD countries. Whereas in 2002 the total number of 3G mobile subscriptions was highest in Korea (17.5 million), only 5 years later the situation was reversed. In 2007, there were more than twice as many subscribers to 3G services in Japan (88 million) as in Korea (43.4 million). In Japan, subscriptions to 3G services grew steadily in the years from 2002 until 2007, with subscriptions in 2007 standing at about 10 times the 2002 levels.

Currently, there are three major mobile communication providers in the Japanese wireless communication market: DoCoMo, au (KDDI Corporation) and SoftBank. Willcom and E-Mobile both offer mobile

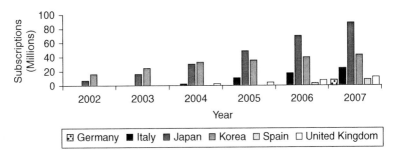

Figure 11.1   3G mobile subscriptions in selected OECD countries

Note: For ease of visualization, out of the OECD countries surveyed only the six with the highest subscriptions in 2007 were selected.

Source: OECD, 2009.

Internet access, but these have many fewer subscriptions than the three major players (Table 11.1). The diffusion of 3-G services is high among all of the three major providers, SoftBank being the highest with more than 90 per cent. This sets Japan far apart from other industrialized countries: in fact, Japan is said to be the only nation that is encountering significant growth rates in the areas of mobile marketing, physical applications and digital services, as well as in enterprise solutions experience (Funk, 2007, p. 15). On the other hand, Japan's cell phones and their users are so exceptional that Japanese companies have had little success in gaining market share abroad – hence the references to Japanese mobile phones as *galapagosu keitai* (*NYT*, 2009).[7] The obstacles that Japanese mobile providers face in going global are often cause for concern as to how the global market share of Japanese operators can be increased (Negishi, 2008, p. 514).

In the 1990s, Japanese mobile users also showed a very high tendency to use their mobile phones to send messages. As Ishii (2004, pp. 54–5) reports, in the mid-1990s there were many Japanese users of pagers who frequently exchanged messages with so-called *beru-tomo* – pager-friends that they didn't know in person. With the spread of mobile phone handsets, however, the *beru-tomo* were replaced by *meeru-tomo* (mail friends) due to the increasing popularity of mobile e-mail. In contrast to many Western markets, sending mobile mail (a fully e-mail-compat-

Table 11.1   Overview of Japanese mobile internet providers (as of FY 2009[A])

Operator	NTT DoCoMo	au (by KDDI)	SoftBank[B]	Willcom	E-Mobile
Year of establishment	1991	2000	1999	2005	1999
Logo	dōcomo	au	SoftBank	WILLCOM	ЕM
Internet service	i-mode	EZ-Web	Sky-Web	–	–
Number of subscriptions (thousands)	54,600	30,840	20,633	4,566	1,410
Market share	52%	28.7%	19.2%	–	–
3-G service	FOMA	CDMA 1X 'WIN'	SoftBank 3G	Willcom Core 3G	–
3G subscriptions (thousands)	49,040	22,720	18,654	2,600	–
3-G ratio[C]	89.8%	74%	90.4%	–	–

[A] FY 2009 ended in March 2009.
[B] Formerly known as Vodafone K.K. and J-Phone.
[C] Percentage of total subscriptions.
Source: DoCoMo (2009), KDDI (2009), SoftBank (2009), Willcom (2009), E-Mobile (2009).

ible version) is more common in Japan than using the Short Message Service (SMS) (Okazaki *et al.*, 2007, p. 165). The phenomena of *beru-tomo* and *meeru-tomo* also relate to a major aspect of virtual communication between Japanese. Ishii (2004, p. 55) relates this kind of mobile communication to a phenomenon among Japanese users, who tend to disclose their subjective self – that is, their emotional state – through pictures exclusively designed for writing mails using a Japanese mobile phone. However, the user's objective self often remains concealed, in order to avoid direct contact with his or her friends.[8] For this reason, mobile phones are a convenient mode of communication especially among the young in Japan.

Although young customers account for a large proportion of mobile consumers, they are not the only group that frequently uses the mobile phone in Japan. Easy access to the Internet via the mobile phone has led to a much larger range of customers being targeted by various businesses in Japan. In order to assess mobile consumption in Japan, mobile Internet usage patterns are discussed in the following.

Usage patterns

The introduction of the Internet had a major impact on societies all over the world. Today, most businesses can barely operate without reliable access to the network that connects their suppliers, business partners and end-users. In most industrialized countries, access to the Internet usually requires using a PC that is able to process a vast amount of data and – high-speed network access permitting – display complex web pages. In Japan, however, the main usage of the Internet has followed a completely different pattern. Despite the relative simplicity of the sites that can be displayed, accessing the Internet from mobile phones is more common than accessing the Internet from PCs (Akiyoshi and Ono, 2008, p. 293). Today, the mobile Internet in Japan is described as the 'fastest-growing mass media platform' in the world (Fujita, 2008, p. 41).

Figure 11.2 shows the ownership ratio of different devices that are able to connect to the Internet in Japan. Most strikingly, the diffusion rate of PCs has dramatically increased since the beginning of the new millennium. Whereas only half of the population had access to a PC that was able to connect to the Internet in 2000, more than 85 per cent of the population possessed an Internet-ready computer in 2008. The diffusion of mobile phones, however, was much faster. In 1999, more than half of Japan's population owned a mobile phone but fewer than half owned a PC. Nine years later, the penetration rate of mobile phones

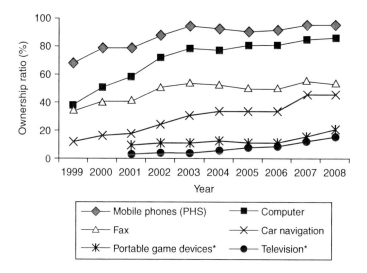

Figure 11.2 The diffusion of communication and telecommunication devices in Japan

*Device that is able to connect to the Internet.

Source: MIC, 2009a, p. 7.

in Japan reached 95.6 per cent, implying that in 2008 only one out of every 20 Japanese citizens did not possess a mobile phone. The penetration rate of PCs in the same year stood at only 85.9 per cent, thus indicating that fewer people in Japan own an Internet-ready PC than a cell phone. Also noteworthy is the increase since 2006 in televisions and portable gaming devices that are able to access the Internet (such as Sony's PSP and Nintendo's DS; McDonalds Online, 2009).[9]

While the fact that more people in Japan own a cellular phone than a PC does not itself reveal anything about usage patterns, it is nevertheless striking at first sight: it seems that the cell phone as an electronic device is more accepted as a technological element in daily life. However, as the ability to connect to the Internet from one's handset is an option that can only be activated by making a contract with one of the major providers, owning a cellular phone doesn't necessarily imply that people access the Internet. For this reason, global usage of the Internet is frequently surveyed by the WIP (World Internet Report), and the Japanese version provides some interesting insights, revealing the rate of Internet access from both PCs and mobile phones.

Figure 11.3 shows that more than 72.5 per cent of the people surveyed have access to the Internet. According to the WIP (2008) survey, however, the percentage of people who access the Internet through mobile phones was significantly higher (67.5 per cent) than the percentage of individuals who access the Internet via PC (49.3 per cent). This is consistent with the much higher ratio of ownership between mobile phones and PCs (see Figure 11.2).

The same trend becomes evident when looking at Internet access from PC and cell phones by demographic distribution; the usage rate of mobile Internet is higher than the rate of PC Internet among every surveyed demographic group (Figure 11.4). When genders are compared, a higher percentage of the surveyed male users (53.6 per cent) than female users (45 per cent) accessed the Internet by PC. Although the difference is only marginal, the opposite seems to be true when comparing mobile Internet usage. Whereas 68.4 per cent of the surveyed women

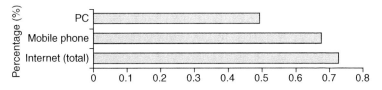

Figure 11.3   Total Internet access, access by PCs and access by mobile phones in Japan (2008)

Source: WIP, 2008.

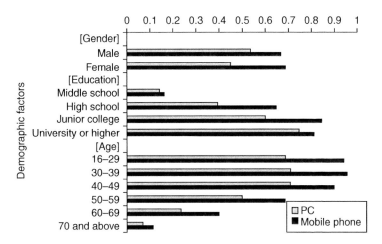

Figure 11.4   Usage of PC Internet and mobile Internet in Japan by demographic factors (2008)

Source: WIP, 2008.

access the Internet from their handsets, 66.5 per cent of surveyed men stated that they use mobile Internet. When different levels of education are compared, mobile Internet seems to be most popular among students in junior college (84.4 per cent), followed by students enrolled in universities or other higher education institutes (81.3 per cent). Internet usage by PC, however, significantly increases with level of education, being highest in this survey among university students, at 74.7 per cent. The study also implies that the usage of both PC Internet and mobile Internet decreases with increasing age.

If we reconsider the information gathered from Figure 11.3 and Figure 11.4 above, then, why is it that Japanese access the Internet more frequently from mobile devices than from PCs? First, there are many cultural factors that have led to the high demand for mobile access among Japanese Internet users. Notably, the lifestyle of a typical Japanese household is different from its Western counterpart. Comparatively little space for the members of a household and long commuting hours[10] for workers in Japan are two important factors that helped to nurture the demand for mobile Internet access rather than the use of PCs at home (Coates and Holroyd, 2003, p. 69). Furthermore, lower start-up costs, and the overall mobility and simplicity of mobile Internet in Japan, have contributed to its reaching not only highly skilled technology-oriented end-users, but the more minor groups 'such as women, the less educated and the less affluent' as well (Akiyoshi and Ono, 2008, p. 301). Consequently, mobile Internet is used regardless of age, gender or socio-economic status, resulting in a versatile market with many different customer groups in Japan.

Mobile commerce

Due to the high diffusion rate of mobile Internet in Japan, e-commerce[11] is a major channel of distribution that deserves special attention. In the case of mobile advertising, all three parties concerned derive benefits: (1) for marketing companies, reaching customers via their mobiles is a highly effective and cost-minimizing channel; (2) consumers can benefit from the free flow of information and entertainment; and (3) mobile service providers can use the platform to generate revenue (Fujita, 2008, p. 45).

Figure 11.5 illustrates usage of the Internet in Japan by customers who access the Internet by PC and by mobile phone. Most striking is the fact that sending and receiving e-mails from the mobile phone (55 per cent) exceeds the usage via PC (49 per cent). Also, digital contents

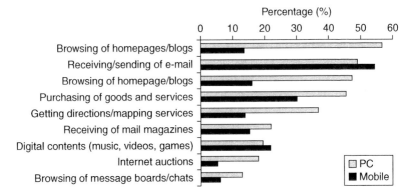

Figure 11.5   The use of the Internet in Japan in 2008
Source: MIC, 2009b, p. 64.

such as digital music, digital videos and games are consumed more on mobile devices (22 per cent) than on PCs (19 per cent). In contrast, the PC seems to remain the main platform for the browsing of company (57 per cent) and personal homepages (47 per cent), the purchasing of goods and services over the Internet (46 per cent), getting information about maps and timetables (37 per cent), and Internet auctions (18 per cent). Also, about 30 per cent of surveyed individuals indicated that they purchase goods and services through the Internet using mobile phones. Although lagging behind PC users (46 per cent), this is the second most frequent use of mobile Internet according to the survey.

This indicates that, as well as the extraordinarily high rate of e-mail usage over mobile phones, the consumption of digital goods and services is a major activity for consumers in Japan. Here again, the factors that contributed to the success of mobile Internet consumption in Japan are ease of use, portability and the easy billing system (Coates and Holroyd, 2003, p. 78).

A more detailed overview of consumption patterns is provided in Figure 11.6. Again, digital contents account for the highest rate of mobile consumption (47 per cent), whereas on the PC the consumption rate is only 19 per cent. Although lagging behind PC usage, other significant mobile consumption patterns are financial transactions (11 per cent), the purchasing of clothes and accessories (11 per cent), hobby goods (10 per cent) and books/CDs (9 per cent). The survey does, however, indicate that some goods are traditionally purchased over the Internet using a PC, such as those related to travel (22 per cent), computer goods (21 per cent) and food/drinks (24 per cent). It seems that the consumption

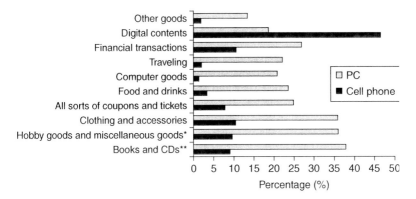

Figure 11.6 Goods and services bought/acquired through the Internet in 2008
* Digital contents not included.
** Game software, musical instruments, sport utilities etc.
Source: MIC, 2009b, p. 69.

of goods and services through the mobile Internet diffuses through all sectors and, considering the development of faster and more secure mobile browsing technologies, is an emerging field.

Digital content distribution

As outlined above, digital content is the greatest source of revenue for businesses operating in the mobile market in Japan. Following the classification used by the Digital Contents Association of Japan (DCAJ), the term 'digital content' is broken down into five main fields: video, music/voice, game, picture/text and advertisements.[12]

The total sales numbers for the five categories of digital contents distributed via mobile phones in Japan are shown in Figure 11.7. In 2004, the best-selling content type was music/voice, at 13.74 billion yen in sales. In 2008, however, this was only the second-largest seller, with revenues of 18.58 billion yen. The sales volume of digital picture/ text content for mobile phones accounted for more than 20 billion yen in the same year. In contrast to sales in 2004 (8.17 billion yen), the volume more than doubled in 4 years, making this the fastest-growing market for digital mobile phone content in Japan. In this category, comics and novels in particular became an integral part of downloadable content.[13] The latter, the so-called *keitai*-novels, have even established their own genre of talented artists – mainly young women – who write novels especially for the mobile format (Onishi,

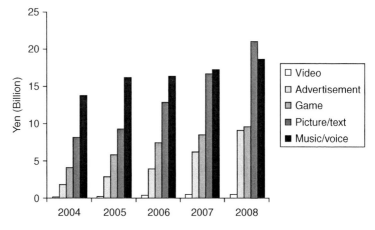

Figure 11.7   Sales volume from digital content distribution and advertisements via mobile phones in Japan (2009)

Source: DCAJ, 2009, p. 18.

2008). Among them, *Akai Ito* [Red Thread], a widely acclaimed mobile phone novel, became a hit bestseller in 2007 (Zaidan Houjin Internet Kyoukai, 2008, p. 71) and was turned into a movie and a TV series the following year.[14]

Digital text/picture is not the only growing market in the field of digital mobile content distribution in Japan. The distribution of digital game content (9.62 billion yen) and advertising (9.13 billion yen) via mobile phones both represented large sales volumes in 2008. Since 2004, the demand for digital game software distributed via mobile phones has more than doubled, and the scale of the mobile advertisement market is five times higher than in 2004 (1.8 billion yen). Although on a much smaller scale, digital video content distribution via mobile phones in Japan is also growing, with total sales of 570 million yen in 2008.

Mobile and social networks

In recent years, Social Network Sites (SNSs)[15] have become increasingly popular all over the world, especially, but not exclusively, among young people (Ellison *et al.*, 2009, p. 6). Although similar in a few functions, SNSs are fundamentally different from blogs (internet-diaries, or web-logs). The former is a medium through which people mutually inter-act in a virtual space, while the latter constitutes a medium through which people can express their thoughts and feelings while maintaining only a limited relationship with readers. However, this boundary is becoming increasingly blurred, for blogs can also be incorporated into SNSs. The motives of Japanese Internet users in accessing websites were scrutinized in a study conducted by Ishii (2008). The findings imply that Japanese consumers access SNSs mainly for self-disclosure and socialization with other individuals, whereas blogs and other websites are mainly visited in order to seek information and be entertained.[16] The most successful SNS in Japan is Mixi, an online community portal that allows users to write diaries, join friend circles, share pictures and videos, and track music listening statistics.[17] Although it is the most successful SNS among Japanese customers overall, Mixi's mobile version only ranks number two among Japanese mobile customers, coming behind competitor DeNA and their mobile-only SNS Mobage-Town (see Table 11.2).[18] These two businesses are based on the increasing popularity of so-called 'social games', free mini-games that were originally part of SNSs (*Nikkei MJ*, 2010b, p. 7). Mobage-Town combines SNS, mobile gaming and digital identity with an avatar system. The business model centres on ad-driven revenue and the optional purchase of Moba-Gold (the platform's virtual currency) with real money by the users. The mobile SNS's success is further based on the system that benefits DeNA, advertisers and customers, who share the revenue derived from user-generated content (Breckenridge, 2007, p. 11). The third major player in Japanese mobile SNSs is GREE, a mobile gaming service that ranked number five[19] among the keywords most searched through the mobile edition of the search engine Yahoo Japan (2009) in 2009.

Table 11.2 Rate of active usage of mobile SNSs in Japan (July 2009)

Place	Name (English)	Name (Japanese)	Percentage
1	*Mobage*-Town	*Mobage*-taun	48%
2	Mixi Mobile	Mixi *mobairu*	47%
3	GREE (includes au one GREE)	GREE	42%
4	*Keitai* Womens Park	*Keetai uimenzu paaku*	17%
5	Log Friend	*Logu tomo*	10%

Note: For the survey, users were asked how often they use different mobile SNSs. The percentage of usage was derived by combining the numbers of those who answered 'always' and 'occasionally'.
Source: MobileMarketing (2009).

Younger consumers in particular are the main target audience of these SNS mobile services. They have seen a huge increase in popularity in recent years, as demonstrated by the example of GREE. Whereas the page views (PVs) of GREE from mobile devices were less than 0.4 billion per month in 2007, they had reached 10 billion PVs by January 2009 (GREE, 2009). Its competitor Mixi also reported twice as much access to its portal site created for mobile devices as to the usual web-optimized version (METI, 2009).

The trend is confirmed by the growth rate in page views of the mobile-only SNS Mobage-Town, established by the Japanese company DeNA. The company confirms an increase in PVs from mobile devices in the year between October 2008 (15.5 billion PVs) and November 2009 (32.8 billion PVs), ultimately culminating in twice as many PVs at the end of the surveyed period. In contrast, GREE's PVs from PCs did not significantly increase from January 2007 (0.04 billion) to January 2009 (0.13 billion).

Mobile SNSs such as Mobage-Town have been one of the success stories for Japanese companies in recent years. The exploitation of the latest technological systems, paired with intelligent marketing (Figure 11.8) and the awareness of unique communication patterns among Japanese customers (Ishii, 2004, p. 54), are factors that have contributed to the maturation of mobile SNSs in Japan. Consequently, the potential in the market for mobile social applications is expected to grow, and is often seen as a bright opportunity for business in the future (Cnet Japan, 2009).

Figure 11.8   Still from Mobage-Town TV commercial
Source: DeNA, 2009c.

Unique aspects of mobile consumerism in Japan

So far, this chapter has introduced the *keitai* as the mobile phone specific to Japanese customers, set out the historical developments in the Japanese mobile market, and explored patterns of usage from a consumer perspective. The following section introduces some practical applications of the advanced technology found in almost every *keitai*. The capabilities of those very advanced mobile handsets are incorporated to make payment processes cheaper and more convenient, and facilitate a direct channel between companies and consumers.

Mobile phones in Japan are equipped with numerous functions. An overview of the functions available on a standard Japanese handset is given in Table 11.3. The vast number of functions that come with even a standard cellular phone in Japan exemplify the innovation-driven supply side in the Japanese mobile market. However, the strong functioning of the market in Japan is not only due to efforts made by handset producers and network providers, but is also driven from the consumers' side. According to Chen and Watanabe (2007, p. 37), the success of new functionalities in Japanese mobile phones is enabled to a large extent by Japanese mobile phone subscribers' high rate of adaptability to new innovative features.[20]

In what follows, three of these functions and their application in daily life will be introduced in detail. These are the mobile payment system *osaifu keitai*, mobile banking, and marketing initiatives for the mobile user.

Osaifu keitai – the mobile phone wallet

The *osaifu keitai* – or mobile wallet – is a wireless payment system readily accepted in many major stores in Japan. The *osaifu keitai* system makes use of Sony's FeliCa[21] IC (integrated circuit) card. Sony's FeliCa card was developed with the intention to 'make daily living easier and more convenient' (Sony, 2010a). The system consists of the FeliCa IC card and a receiver that is able to process the information sent by the card. The system enables fast processing of payments by simply hovering one's FeliCa card over the receiving unit. Today, Sony's FeliCa system is a de facto standard in Japan and abroad. In Japan, the card is already used for a variety of applications, including e-money, boarding passes, Internet credit services, access control, point card systems and train tickets.[22] Outside Japan, the FeliCa system is used for ID cards in Finland's universities, and Hong Kong's popular Octopus card, to name a few (Sony, 2010b).

Table 11.3   Standard functions of a Japanese cellular phone in 2010

Function	Description
Internet connectivity	Sending/receiving normal e-mail. Also, access to sites formatted especially for mobile phones in order to surf, shop, and download coupons or look up train timetables.
High-tech digital camera	Mobile phones are able to take high-resolution pictures for storage, multimedia-mails or other personal use. In some cases the quality is as good as a commercial digital camera at the amateur level.
Barcode reader	Enables the user to read 2-D matrix barcodes. These barcodes are frequently used in marketing campaigns in order to quickly pass on a link to a mobile site for further information.
Mobile FeliCa	Licensed by all three major operators in Japan (DoCoMo, au and SoftBank), Mobile FeliCa is a mobile port of the FeliCa system developed by Sony, which allows the consumer to purchase goods by cellular phone using electronic money. The service is called *osaifu keitai* (wallet mobile phone).
Mobile suica	As part of the *osaifu keitai*, consumers can turn their cellular phone into a *suica* card, which is used for paying fares on the railroad network operated by Japan Railways (JR) East.
1seg (wansegu)	Digital audio/video data terrestrial broadcasting system that turns the handset into a mobile television.
MP3/MP4 player	Integrated MP3 audio and MP4 video player as well as the facility to download content (songs, videos etc.).
Applications	A wide range of applications developed for each carrier is available. Those applications enable users, for example, to read e-books/manga, access and manage bank accounts, learn languages, or see up-to-date TV guides on their cell phones.
Mobile games	Portage of popular games from the 8- and 16-bit video game era as well as original content. Consumers pay either once per download, via monthly subscription and/or data transferred to/from the Internet. Increasingly, mobile phones are able to run 32-bit games, such as Sony's PlayStation video games.
GPS	Access to Global Positioning System (GPS) data in order to give directions or local guidance.

Source: Author.

Today the FeliCa card is implanted in almost every handset in Japan, recognizable by its distinctive logo (Figure 11.9). DoCoMo (2010b) had already started to incorporate Sony's FeliCa system into their handsets[23] in 2004, naming the service *osaifu keitai* (mobile wallet). Today, every major telecommunication provider in Japan provides the *osaifu keitai* service.[24]

One of the most useful applications of the *osaifu keitai* system is its linkage with the smart cards used to pay fares for trains operated by Japan Railways (JR), Tokyo Metro, and other local transportation companies. Since its launch in 2006, passengers can also use the *keitai* version, the so-called mobile *suica*. Mobile *suica* can function as both an individual ticket and a full commuter pass for passengers on Japan's transportation networks.[25] By the use of mobile *suica*, the payment process at ticket machines becomes redundant and the pace of processing through the gates speeds up, a circumstance that is particularly favourable during rush hours at overcrowded train stations in major urban centres throughout Japan.

Mobile banking

Although mobile banking is not new, it is often seen as an alternative way of processing transfers from or to a bank account at banks that also have local branches. In Japan, however, the concept of mobile banking

Figure 11.9   Osaifu keitai logo on the back of DoCoMo's P-03B model
Source: DoCoMo, 2010a.

has been taken a step further. In 2008, the Bank of Tokyo Mitsubishi UFG (henceforth MUFG) and KDDI Corporation (au) established Jibun Ginko (personal bank, henceforth Jibun Bank) as a 50–50 joint venture. Jibun Bank is the first fully fledged mobile bank in Japan, meaning that all operations are conducted with the *keitai* and exploit the existing mobile Internet infrastructure. Furthermore, the mobile bank has no physical branches in Japan.[26] Instead, customers can choose a virtual branch named after one of seven colours (the blue branch, red branch, yellow branch, etc.).

Although the mobile bank service works with most *keitai* purchased from one of the three major Japanese mobile telecommunications operators (i.e. DoCoMo and SoftBank),[27] au customers have more options available than customers with DoCoMo or SoftBank. They can access the virtual bank via a programme called *jibun tsuuchou* (personal bankbook; see Figure 11.10), and also enjoy the convenience of making money transfer orders by simply entering the recipient's (au) mobile phone number.

The establishment of a mobile phone bank accompanies the overall trend for easy-to-use applications integrated into the appliances of daily life. Due to the rigid opening hours of many banks in Japan, Internet banking used to be the only alternative for 24-hour money transfers. The Jibun Bank banking model offers a fast and easily accessible way to pay for utility bills or to transfer money. By the end of March 2010, only 2 years after its establishment, a total of 946,000 bank accounts had been opened (JibunGinko, 2010c, p. 14).

Mobile marketing

In Japan, companies have launched numerous campaigns via the *keitai* that either partly involve the end-user's mobile phone (cross-media

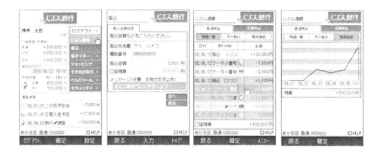

Figure 11.10   Jibun Bank's mobile phone interface
Source: JibunGinko, 2010a.

campaigns) or are specifically directed towards the end-user. McDonalds, Honda and Axe (also known as Lynx) have initiated some of the most innovative mobile marketing campaigns in recent years, and these are introduced in what follows.

McDonalds mobile coupons

McDonalds is one of the most prominent companies advertising via the mobile phone in Japan. The low-price American fast food chain attracts customers not only with its selection of 100 yen products (the Japanese equivalent of the $1 menu), but also with weekly mobile coupons delivered directly to the customer's handset. These mobile coupons give discounts on a selection of products and are available anytime after registration as a member of McDonalds' mobile site.

Customers can choose to purchase products by showing the cashier the mobile coupon downloaded to their mobile phone (*miseru* coupons), or use so-called *kazasu* coupons (contactless coupons). While *miseru* coupons are basically a digital version of the printed coupons that were previously distributed, the *kazasu* coupon system unifies McDonalds' mobile content distribution channels and Sony's FeliCa e-money chips, which are installed in most Japanese handsets (Figure 11.11). The *kazasu* coupon system was first introduced in 2008 and was the first of its kind. After registration via their mobile phone, customers can choose their meals, use available coupons, and pay with their *keitai* by transferring the data wirelessly to a FeliCa reader device installed near every McDonalds counter in Japan. Also, with the aid of the *kazasu* coupon system, the fast food giant is able to ana-

Figure 11.11 McDonalds *miseru* coupons and *kazasu* coupon system
Source: Haghirian, 2009, McDonalds Online, 2010.

lyse purchases made by its customers and can further improve mobile campaigns utilizing customers' behavioural data. McDonalds' mobile coupons – and the *kazasu* coupon system in particular – are a powerful customer relationship management tool, which reinforces a new kind of consumer communication and ultimately strengthens the customer base.

Honda's keetai *traveller*

Another example of how to use the mobile communication channel to reach end-users is a campaign launched by the Japanese car manufacturer Honda: the *keetai* traveller (henceforth *ke-tra*). Due to the lasting recession and the current reduction in young people buying cars in Japan, Honda's marketing experts decided to use the *keitai* as a marketing tool through which the younger generation can be addressed. The result is a fun mobile phone game with the aim of reinforcing consumers' brand loyalty and promoting future relationships with Honda's customers.

The interface of the *ke-tra* mobile game is depicted in Figure 11.12. Every player has a so-called movatar (abbreviation for mobile avatar) that virtually hitchhikes through Japan on other people's *keitai* handsets and brings home *omiyage* (souvenirs) from other areas where it has been. As players interact with each other through their movatars, Honda's *ke-tra* application adds a community dimension to its marketing initiative by simultaneously stimulating the users' wanderlust (Japanese *boukenshin*).

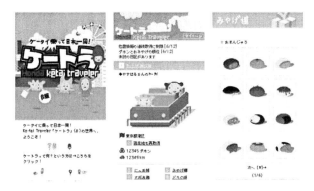

Figure 11.12 Honda's *Ke-tra* mobile site
Source: NikkeiBP Online, 2009.

Axe Wake-Up Call, Inc.

Prominent among the many innovative mobile promotions of recent years is Axe's campaign to promote use of its body spray cosmetics among Japanese men. The aim was to raise the frequency of use of Axe products in Japan, where men use body sprays much less, on average, than in Western countries. Axe Wake-Up Service Inc. – the name of the Japan-only multichannel[28] promotion – was launched in 2007 and heavily integrated with mobile phones in Japan. Upon registration via the PC site, users were asked to choose their Axe-Angel, one of several attractive young girls[29] who would give the user a morning wake-up call via the mobile phone, and further remind him to use his Axe deodorant. The more a customer used the service, the friendlier his personal Axe-Angel would become and vice versa, adding a further incentive to use the service frequently. The campaign achieved a rarely seen level of communication between the brand and its customers, and successfully raised the frequency of Axe deodorant usage among Japanese men (AME, 2009).

The impact of smart phones in Japan

The convergence of mobile phones, consumer electronics and electronic cash will continue to advance. A highly discussed field is the introduction of real browsers in Japanese mobile phones, instead of c-HTML-facilitated i-mode browsing. Miyazaki (2010, p. 7) predicts that competition with respect to real-browsing-enabled mobile devices will become increasingly important in the coming years. A first step towards this new age of mobile browsing was the introduction of Apple's i-Phone in the Japanese market in 2008, and the first mobile phone operating with Google's Android operating system in 2009 (Hisashi, 2010). All the three major mobile phone companies in Japan – DoCoMo (2010c), au (2010) and SoftBank (2010) – distribute a number of so-called smart phones, that is, mobile phones running an operating system with advanced functions. In contrast to conventional Japanese handsets that are able to connect to Internet sites specifically designed for mobile access, next generation mobile phones are able to display Internet sites as seen on a desktop or notebook computer.

However, when smart phones like the iPhone first hit the Japanese market, they weren't seen as such a big revolution in mobile computing as they were in many Western countries. Companies like Apple were trying to revolutionize a market that was much more advanced than its Western counterparts. Consequently, their impact on consumer behaviour and initial sales wasn't as high as in Western markets (*WSJ*, 2008). Despite the simple design and the intuitive touch screen, the iPhone, for example, could not exceed the vast range of functionalities of a standard Japanese handset. In fact, the opposite was true: it lacked some features that Japanese customers were used to[30] and was not fully integrated into many of the mobile marketing models in Japan.[31]

As providers increase their stocks of smart phones, Japanese customers are becoming more familiar with the functionalities and advantages of these next-generation mobile phones. Yet, despite Apple's iPhone having a share of almost 73 per cent among smart phone users in Japan, only one in 20 consumers actually owned the device in 2009 (MMRI, 2009). This figure shows the predominance of Apple in the emerging smart phone market in Japan, but also underlines the fact that the mobile market is still dominated by the classical Japanese *keitai*.

Summary and outlook

The mobile phone penetrates all aspects of daily life in Japan. As well as the basic function of voice/text messaging, a large number of customers consume digital media, engage in SNSs directly from their handset, and use the handset as a proxy for expressing their individuality – to name just a few of the activities supported by the *keitai*. Whereas DoCoMo was for a long time the unsurpassed market leader, the market for mobile communication in Japan is becoming more diversified as new players enter and next-generation products challenge established successful models such as i-mode. In addition, portable devices other than mobile phones are now able to connect to the Internet. As one of the most advanced markets in the world for mobile phones and their services, Japan's mobile landscape is both a forerunner for global trends and loyal to its own special customers and their needs. The many useful applications of the *keitai* and the innovative business-to-consumer marketing models have become an integral part of digital mobile life in Japan. Future developments are hard to predict, and the outlook can only be sketched.

Although the evolution of wireless technology is somewhat linear and therefore easy to predict, the impact of consumer behaviour is not. Bohlin *et al.* (2007, p. 239) foresee that, as well as the next level in data transmission (4G), 'the future will be shaped by the increasing integration and interconnection of heterogeneous systems.' The Japanese government also seems to embrace this development, as it promotes 'u-Japan', an information society where people are connected every-where and at all times using a wide variety of different devices. In this sense, usage of mobile devices other than cell phones that are able to access the Internet will increase. The tendency is already visible in Figure 11.2, which shows a remarkable increase in Internet-ready gam-ing devices, car navigation systems and even televisions in recent years. There has also been an increase in consumers who access the Internet by using pocket-sized wireless routers connecting a variety of mobile devices (among them laptops, smart phones and portable gaming devices) to the Internet. The *Nikkei MJ* (2010a) surveyed this phenom-enon and found that an increasing number of people in Japan purchase goods through online mail-order companies or auctions using both their smart phones and their laptops, naming this emerging customer group the 'neo-mobiler'.

Despite the tendency of mobile phones to be packed with an increas-ing number of functions, it is not clear whether additional functions (such as the ability to watch TV via the 1seg service) can generate suf-ficient revenue streams to successfully substitute the original purpose of a device for communication (Urban, 2007, p. 50). A catchphrase fre-quently heard over the last few years is the emergence of and opportuni-ties for user-generated content (UGC). As such, users of websites, rather than the company itself, create content and add value (OECD, 2007).[32] The system has already been successfully transformed into diverse busi-ness models on the Internet, such as Wikipedia, YouTube, and SNSs like Facebook or Mixi. While there are profitable mobile services based on UGC-facilitated business models in Japan (most notably Mobage-Town and the mobile version of Mixi), there are new models of user participa-tion that will enter the highly competitive market in Japan. In particu-lar, the new Japanese venture X-Ing World plans to take the approach of user participation a step further and will let its customers own a whole business in a virtual 3D world, modelled after the real Japanese archi-pelago and its mega-cities, that is accessible via conventional brows-ers on PCs as well as through special mobile handsets (X-Ing World, 2009). In whatever direction the Japanese mobile market evolves, it will remain a hypercompetitive arena that deserves special attention not only from inside Japan, but from international players as well.

Notes

1. In Japanese, the abbreviation *keitai* for *keitai-denwa* is also often written as *keetai*, corresponding to its phonetic characteristics (Okuyama, 2009).

2. Matsumoto (1999, p. 298) reminds us that culture is not a static entity. He emphasizes the fact that, according to many studies, Japanese people are no more collectivist than Americans. This perception is associated with a change in culture, especially among young people in Japan. Technological breakthroughs such as the cell phone are said to have partly facilitated this cultural change.

3. The name DoCoMo originates from the first letters of the phrase 'Do communications over the mobile network'. The Japanese word *docomo* further translates into 'anywhere', hence referring to the company's aim to provide the service free of boundaries (DoCoMo USA, 2009).

4. In contrast to the circuit-switched voice system, i-mode is packet-switched, which means that the customer is always online but essentially pays for data packets transmitted rather than for transmission time. Also, i-mode-accessible websites are built using c-HTML (a simplified and 'compact' version of hypertext mark-up language (HTML)) and CompuServe's graphical interface format (GIF) for images.

5. The transition from 2G to 3G technology should not be confused with the transition from voice to data transmissions. The fact that i-mode was initially launched on 2G devices supports the argument that it was not the change in networks, but the change of the application, that was the most critical change for the end-user (Steinbock, 2005, p. 67).

6. Among the European providers were E-Plus (Germany), Bouygues Telecom (France), KPN Mobile (The Netherlands), and BASE (Belgium).

7. The name *galapagosu keitai*, or 'Galápagos cell phone', stems from the comparison of Japanese mobile phones with Charles Darwin's experience when he first visited the Galápagos Islands: an encounter with exotic species that could not be found anywhere else.

8. This phenomenon of the disclosure of subjective but not of objective information can also be seen when surveying Japanese websites and Social Network Sites (SNS). On one of the biggest message boards (2chn), people write a great deal of subjective information but usually don't sign in with a specific user name, making them *na-nashi* (without name). This is also true for Mixi, the biggest social network in Japan, where users rarely disclose their real name but engage energetically in online activities such as writing a blog.

9. In fact, the American fast food chain McDonalds has offered Nintendo DS users in Japan free WiFi access and also distributed demos and special digital content created by McDonalds for famous video games (such as Dragon Quest and Pokémon) since 2009. By using a platform that is famous among both kids and adults in Japan, McDonalds is also able to distribute quizzes, nutrition information and special discount coupons (McDonalds Online, 2009).

10. In contrast, Beck and Wade (2003, p. 137) argue that the reason why text-based services in Japan have become increasingly popular is not necessarily related to the Japanese commuting phenomenon. Rather, they state that the success of mobile Internet (and especially DoCoMo's success with i-mode) is connected to human psychology: the more busy people become, the more in-between time has to be filled, be it during long commutes, between appointments, or while queuing.

11. Takeshi Natsuno, managing director at DoCoMo, refers to electronic commerce conducted by mobile phone as 'real commerce', indicating the next step of e-commerce and simultaneously distinguishing the term from 'normal' e-commerce that is bound to the use of a computer (Steinbock, 2005, p. 73).
12. In the DCAJ report (2009, p. 18), mobile advertising was included in the field of digital picture/text media, but was listed separately next to the list of revenues by distribution of mobile picture/text contents.
13. Despite the small screen on which such novels have to be read, the portability and easy access on the cell phone make it attractive, especially during packed commutes in Japan. One university student recalls: 'You can read whenever you have a spare moment, and you don't even need to use both hands' (Wired, 2005).
14. See also http://www.akai-ito.jp/
15. Social Network Sites are defined as 'web-based services that allow individuals to (1) construct a public or semi-public profile within a bounded system, (2) articulate a list of other users with whom they share a connection, and (3) view and traverse their list of connections and those made by others within the system' (Boyd and Elison, 2007).
16. For a typology of communicative behaviours among Japanese students, see Ogasahara (2006).
17. The 2009 financial crisis has taken its toll on mixi.jp; the company expects a decline in profits in the region of 15 per cent. It has therefore introduced plans for thorough changes to increase revenue again (Kashiwagi, 2009).
18. Mobage-town, also called mobage, is a famous Japanese portal site that also functions as a SNS. Users can write blogs, mini-mails (e-mails), join and talk in chat rooms, maintain diaries, talk on message boards, write novels with the possibility of becoming published, and find friends in shared interest communities (DeNA, 2009a).
19. Other rankings were: (1) Mixi, (2) 2channel, (3) Mobage-Town, (4) YouTube.
20. For example, Chen and Watanabe (2007, pp. 39–40) highlight the introduction of mobile phones with integrated cameras by DoCoMo and au (by KDDI) in mid-2002. Their research shows that it was this event that marked a major positive turning point in the learning capability of customers.
21. The name FeliCa stems from the English words 'felicity' and 'card'.
22. For further reference, a few of these cards are: Edy's bitWallet cards (e-money), All Nippon Airways (ANA) and Japan Airlines (JAL) boarding passes, *kesaka* cards (access control systems), Seven-Eleven's *nanaco* card (point card system), Japan Railways' (JR) *suica* card and Tokyo Metro's *pasmo* card (train tickets).
23. Advances in technology are also often associated with an increase in crime. This might especially be the case for the mobile payment system *osaifu keitai* in Japan (Whitehead and Farell, 2008). One reason, however, why new technological breakthroughs receive more positive reactions from the consumers' side in Japan is the so-called *anshinkan*, the ability of Japan's mobile phone carriers to make the customer feel secure when using the service (Weber and Wingert, 2006, p. 326).

24. Although trademarked by DoCoMo, the term *osaifu keitai* is used when referring to the mobile phone wallet service in general. The *osaifu keitai* service is also called EZ FeliCa (au), S! FeliCa (SoftBank) and Willcom IC Service (Willcom).
25. Transportation smart card services differ by region in Japan and are often incompatible. However, great effort is being undertaken to make regional systems compatible throughout Japan at the time of this chapter's publication.
26. The free service is, however, advertised and promoted within the local branches of MUFG, where applications can be made in person.
27. Jibun Ginko does work with most of the *keitai* handsets from major providers in Japan. Customers under contract with E-Mobile or Willcom, and those who possess an iPhone 3G, cannot open an account at Jibun Bank as of May 2010 (JibunGinko, 2010b).
28. The service was promoted using a wide variety of different media, such as print, television, mobile phones, and a promotion website.
29. The Axe-Angels were real girls. When receiving a wake-up call, however, the customer listened to one of their many voice recordings.
30. The iPhone (as of early 2010) has no infrared port and thus does not allow the exchange of phone numbers via infrared, a common practice among mobile users in Japan. Also, although technically supported for Google's Gmail and Yahoo!'s mail service, the iPhone does not host the same convenient push e-mail functionality for regular Japanese cell phone e-mail addresses. Furthermore, it lacks additional functions such as the 1seg terrestrial TV broadcast service.
31. To name only a few examples, the mobile coupons distributed by McDonalds don't work with an iPhone, and neither do the forms of electronic cash in Japan such as mobile *suica*.
32. The OECD (2007, p. 4) defines user-generated content (or UCC, user-created content, as they term it) according to three criteria: (1) content made publicly available over the Internet, which (2) reflects a certain amount of creative effort, and (3) is created outside professional routines and practices.

References

Adachi, F. (2001), 'Wireless Past and Future – Evolving Mobile Communications Systems', *IEICE Trans. Fundamentals*, E84-A(1): 55–60.

Aguado, J. M. and Martinez, I. J. (2009), 'Mobile Media Implicit Cultures: Towards a Characterization of Mobile Entertainment and Advertising in Digital Convergence Landscape', *Observatorio (OBS*) Journal*, 8: 336–52.

Akiyoshi, M. and Ono, H. (2008), 'The Diffusion of the Internet in Japan', *The Information Society*, 24: 292–303.

Allison, A. (2004), 'Cuteness as Japan's Millennial Product', in Tobin, J. (ed.), *Pikachu's Global Adventure – The Rise and Fall of Pokémon*, Durham, NC: Duke University Press, pp. 34–9.

AME, Best Brand Loyalty Marketing Campaign – Winners (2009), available at http://www.media.asia/Awards/AME/award_winner_H.html (accessed 5 May 2010).

AU (2010), AU Smartphone Lineup 2010, available at http://www.au.kddi.com/seihin/#smartphone (accessed 23 March 2010).

Beck, J. C. and Wade, M. E. (2003), *DoCoMo: Japan's Wireless Tsunami*, New York and Atlanta: American Management Association.

Bohlin, E., Burgelman, J.-C. and Casal, C. R. (2007), 'The Future of Mobile Communications in the EU', *Telematics and Informatics*, 24: 238–42.

Boyd, D. M. and Ellison, N. B. (2007), 'Social Network Sites: Definition, History, and Scholarship', *Journal of Computer-Mediated Communication*, 13(1): article 11, available at http://jcmc.indiana.edu/vol13/issue1/boyd.ellison.html

Breckenridge, J. (2007), 'Handset Publishing: Just a Japanese Phenomena?', *Seybold Report*, 7(24): 10–12.

Bucci, O. M., Pelosi, G. and Selleri, S. (2003), 'The Work of Marconi in Microwave Communications', *Antennas and Propagation Magazine*, IEEE 45(5): 46–53.

Chen, C. and Watanabe, C. (2007), 'Competitiveness through Co-evolution between Innovation and Institutional Systems – New Dimensions of Competitiveness in a Service-oriented Economy', *Journal of Services Research*, 7(2) (October 2007 – March 2008): 27–55.

CNet Japan, 'Mixi, mobage, facebook no soosharu apuri ga motarasu kyodai bijinesu chansu [Mixi, Mobage and Facebook Provide a Huge Business Chance as Social Applications]', available at http://japan.cnet.com/news/media/story/0,2000056023,20404393–3,00.htm (accessed 12 December 2009).

Coates, K., and Holroyd, C. (2003), 'Japan and the Internet Revolution', Hampshire: Palgrave MacMillan.

DCAJ (Digital Contents Association Japan) (2009), 'Dejitaru kontentsu no shijou kibo to kontentsu sangyou no kouzouhenka ni kansuru chousa kenkyuu [Study about the Scope of the Digital Contents Market and the Structural Change of the Contents Industry]', available at http://www.dcaj.org/report/index.html (accessed 15 March 2010).

DeNA (2009a), 'Mobage-Town', available at http://www.dena.jp/en/services/mobileportal.html#mbg (accessed 12 December 2009).

DeNA (2009b), 'Getsuji suii no go houkoku (Heisei 21nen 11gatsu do) [Report of Monthly Transitions {November 2009}]', available at http://www.c-direct.ne.jp/public/japanese/uj/pdf/10110213/20091203180357.pdf (accessed 12 December 2009).

DeNA (2009c), 'Saabisu shoukai movie [Service Introduction Movie]', available at http://www.dena.jp/services/mobileportal.html (accessed 12 December 2009).

DoCoMo (2009), 'NTT Docomo Annual Report 2009', available at http://www.nttdocomo.co.jp/english/corporate/ir/binary/pdf/library/annual/fy2008/docomo_ar2009_e.pdf (accessed 12 December 2009).

DoCoMo (2010a), 'SMART Series P-03B', available at http://www.nttdocomo.co.jp/product/foma/smart/p03b/gallery.html (accessed 5 May 2010).

DoCoMo (2010b), 'Glossary: O-saifu keitai', available at http://www.nttdocomo.com/glossary/o/Osaifu-Keitai.html (accessed 5 May 2010).

DoCoMo (2010c), 'Smartphone Lineup 2010', available at http://smartphone.nttdocomo.co.jp/ (accessed 23 March 2010).

DoCoMo USA (2009), 'Company Information', available at http://www.namikiteru.com/en/company/index.html (accessed 10 December 2009).

Ellison, N. B., Lampe, C. and Steinfield, C. (2009), 'Social Network Sites and Society: Current Trends and Future Possibilities', *Interactions*, January–February: 6–9.

E-Mobile (2009), 'E-Mobile Corporate Guide', available at http://www.emobile.jp/corporate/pdf/eMobile.pdf (accessed 12 December 2009).

Fujita, A. (2008), 'Mobile Marketing in Japan', *Journal of Integrated Marketing Communications*, 41–6.

Funk, J. L. (2007), 'Solving the Startup Problem in Western Mobile Internet Markets', *Telecommunications Policy*, 31: 14–30.

Funk, J. L. (2009), 'The Emerging Value Network in the Mobile Phone Industry: The Case of Japan and Its Implications for the Rest of the World', *Telecommunications Policy*, 33: 4–18.

GREE, 'Mobairu han GREE no gekkan akusesu-suu ga 100 oku PV wo toppa [The Monthly Number of Accesses to GREE's Mobile Version Exceeded 10 Billion Page Views]', available at http://www.gree.co.jp/news/press/2009/0302.html (accessed 12 December 2009).

Haghirian, P. (2009), 'Marketing trends in Japan: Tokio gibt den Takt vor [Marketing Trends in Japan: Tokyo Sets the Rhythm]', *Manager Magazin Online*, 16 July, available at http://www.manager-magazin.de/it/artikel/0,2828,636045-3,00.html (accessed 26 March 2010).

Hisashi, K. (2010), 'iPhone ga kirihiraki aratana sumaatofon shijou [The iPhone Opened up a New Smartphone Market]', *Senden Kaigi* [Marketing and Creativity], 758: 72–3.

Ishii, K. (2004), 'Internet Use via Mobile Phone in Japan', *Telecommunications Policy*, 28: 43–58.

Ishii, K. (2008), 'Uses and Gratification of Online Communities in Japan', *Observatorio (OBS*) Journal*, 6: 25–37.

JibunGinko (2010a), 'Jibun tsuuchou (appri) [Personal Bankbook (application)]', available at http://www.jibunbank.co.jp/pc/guidance/service/jibun-tutyo_app/ (accessed 5 May 2010).

JibunGinko (2010b), 'Kouza kaisetsu [Account Set Up]', available at http://www.jibunbank.co.jp/pc/guidance/account/ (accessed 5 May 2010).

JibunGinko (2010c), 'Zaimushohyou no gaiyou – heisei 22 nen [Summary of Financial Statements – 2009]', available at http://www.jibunbank.co.jp/pc/corporate_profile/financial_information/statement/statement_20100427.pdf (accessed 5 May 2010).

Kashiwagi, A. (2009), 'Mixi Faces Challenges as Competition Grows', *Japan Times Online*, 24 June, available at http://search.japantimes.co.jp/cgi-bin/nc20090624a2.html (accessed 12 December 2009).

KDDI (2009), 'KDDI Annual Report 2009', available at http://www.kddi.com/english/corporate/ir/library/annual_report/ebook/2009/index.html#01 (accessed 12 December 2009).

Kushchu, I. (2006), 'Foreign National's Perspectives on Japanese Mobile Society – Final Report', available at http://www.moba-ken.jp/wp-content/pdf/final_Ibrahim.pdf (accessed 26 March 2010).

McDonalds Online (2009), 'Makku de DS', available at http://www.mcdonalds.co.jp/ds/index.html (accessed 2 December 2009).

McDonalds Online (2010), 'Keitai Coupons', available at http://www.mcdonalds.co.jp/fanclub/mcd/kazasu_coupon/application.html (accessed 5 May 2010).

Matsumoto, D. (1999), 'Culture and Self: An Empirical Assessment of Markus and Kitayama's Theory of Independent and Interdependent Self-construals', *Asian Journal of Social Psychology*, 2: 289–310.

METI (2009), Results of 'Research in IT Utilization in Japan 2008' (E-Commerce Market Survey), available at http://www.meti.go.jp/english/press/data/20091014_01.html (accessed 3 November 2010).

MIC (2009a), 'Heisei 20 Nen Tsuushin riyou doukou chousa no kekka [Results of the Communication Trend Survey in 2008]', available at http://www.soumu.go.jp/johotsusintokei/statistics/data/090407_1.pdf (accessed 29 November 2009).

MIC (2009b), 'Heisei 20 nen tsuushin riyou doukou chousa houkokusho [Report of the Communication Trend Survey in 2008]', available at http://www.soumu.go.jp/johotsusintokei/statistics/pdf/HR200800_001.pdf (accessed 29 November 2009).

Minges, M. (2005), 'Is the Internet Mobile? Measurements from the Asia-Pacific Region', *Telecommunications Policy*, 29: 113–25.

Miyazaki, S. (2010), 'Mazu keitai tanmatsu ni miryoku wo [First, We Need Appealing Smart-phones]', *Nikkei Rytsuu Shinbun* [Nikkei Marketing Journal], 13 February.

M M Research Institute (MMRI) (2009), News Release 22 April 2010, available at http://www.m2ri.jp/newsreleases/main.php?id=010120100422500 (accessed 5 May 2010).

MobileMarketing (2009), 'Mobairu SNS burando chousa [Survey of Mobile SNS Brands]', 16 September, available at http://mobilemarketing.jp/commonimages/20090916press.pdf (accessed 12 December 2009).

Mukund, A. and Radhika, N. (2003), 'DoCoMo – The Japanese Wireless Telecom Leader', *ICMR Case Collection*.

Nagata, K. (2009), 'Cell Phone Culture Here Unlike Any Other', *The Japan Times Online*, 2 September, available at http://search.japantimes.co.jp/cgi-bin/nn20090902i1.html (accessed 25 March 2010).

Negishi, M. (2008), 'Mobairu jouhou akusesu konjaku: Jouhou no shouhi-shashuken no yukue [Mobile Information Access, Past and Present: Direction of Information Consumer Sovereignty]', *Jouhou chishiki gakkaishi [Japan Society of Information and Knowledge]*, 18(5): 512–5.

NikkeiBP Online (2009), Trend Forecast – 21 August 2009, available at http://trendy.nikkeibp.co.jp/article/pickup/20090820/1028329/?P=4 (accessed 5 May 2010).

Nikkei MJ (2010a), *Nikkei Ryutsuu Shinbun* [*Nikkei Marketing Journal*], 29 January.

Nikkei MJ (2010b), *Nikkei Ryutsuu Shinbun* [*Nikkei Marketing Journal*], 10 February.

NYT (2009), 'Why Japan's Cellphones Haven't Gone Global', *New York Times Online*, 19 July, available at http://www.nytimes.com/2009/07/20/technology/20cell.html?_r=1 (accessed 12 May 2009).

OECD (2007), 'Working Party on the Information Economy – Participative Web: User-Created Content', available at http://www.oecd.org/dataoecd/57/14/38393115.pdf (accessed 23 March 2010).

OECD (2009), *OECD Communications Outlook 2009*, Paris: OECD Publishing.

Ogasahara, M. (2006), 'Onrain komyuinitiruikei wo mochiita riyou to man-zoku bunseki: Nichi-kan gakusei deeta wo mochiita riyoukoudou no shinsaku tansaku-teki kenkyuu [Uses and Gratification Research Using a Typology of Online Communities: An Exploratory Study on Japanese and Korean Students' Communication Behavior in Online Communities]', *Nihon shakai jouhou gakkai gakkaishi [The Japan Association for Social Informatics]*, 18(2): 21–37.

Okazaki, S., Katsukura, A. and Nishiyama, M. (2007), 'How Mobile Advertising Works: the Role of Trust in Improving Attitudes and Recall', *Journal of Advertising Research*, June: 165–78.

Okuyama, Y. (2009), 'Keetai Meeru – Younger People's Mobile Written Communication in Japan', *Electronic Journal of Contemporary Japanese Studies*, 25 February, available at http://www.japanesestudies.org.uk/articles/2009/Okuyama.html (accessed 5 May 2010).

Onishi, N. (2008), 'Thumbs Race as Japan's Best Sellers Go Cellular', *The New York Times Online*, 20 January, available at http://www.nytimes.com/2008/01/20/world/asia/20japan.html (accessed 25 March 2010).

Peltokorpi, V., Nonaka, I. and Kodama, M. (2007), 'NTT DoCoMo's Launch of I-Mode in the Japanese Mobile Phone Market: A Knowledge Creation Perspective', *Journal of Management Studies*, 44(1): 50–72.

SoftBank (2009), 'SoftBank Annual Report 2009', available at http://www.softbank.co.jp/en/irinfo/shared/data/annual_report/2009/softbank_annual_report_2009_001.pdf (accessed 12 December 2009).

SoftBank (2010), 'SoftBank Smartphone Lineup 2010', available at http://mb.softbank.jp/mb/product/X/lineup.html (accessed 23 March 2010).

Sony (2010a), 'What is FeliCa?', available at http://www.sony.net/Products/felica/abt/index.html (accessed 5 May 2010).

Sony (2010b), 'FeliCa in Use', available at http://www.sony.net/Products/felica/csy/index.html (accessed 5 May 2010).

Steinbock, D. (2003), 'Globalization of Wireless Value System: From Geographic to Strategic Advantages', *Telecommunications Policy*, 27: 207–35.

Steinbock, D. (2005), *The Mobile Revolution: The Making of Mobile Services Worldwide*, London; Sterling: Thanet Press.

Tilson, D. and Lyytinen, K. (2006), 'The 3G Transition: Changes in the US Wireless Industry', *Telecommunications Policy*, 30: 569–86.

Urban, A. (2007), 'Mobile Television: Is It Just A Hype Or A Real Consumer Need?', *Observatorio (OBS*) Journal*, 3: 45–58.

Weber, A. (2007), 'The Convergence of Mobile Data Phones, Consumer Electronics, and Wallets: Lessons from Japan', *Telematics and Informatics*, 24: 180–91.

Weber, A. and Wingert, B. (2006), ' "i-mode" in Japan: How to Explain its Development', in Preissl, B. and Müller, J. (eds), *Governance of Communication Networks: Connecting Societies and Markets with IT*, Heidelberg; New York: Physica-Verlag, pp. 309–32.

Whitehead, A. and Farrell, G. (2008), 'Anticipating Mobile Phone "Smart Wallet" Crime: Policing and Corporate Social Responsibility', *Policing*, 2(2): 210–17.

Willcom, 'Subscriber Statistics' (2009), available at http://www.willcom-inc.com/en/company/subscriber/2009/index.html (accessed 2 December 2009).

WIP (2008), 'World Internet Report Japan. 2008 Nen intaanetto riyou ni taisuru jittai chousa [The 2008 Field Survey about the Usage of the Internet]', available at http://www.soc.toyo.ac.jp/~mikami/wip/year2008.html (accessed 5 December 2009).

Wired (2008), 'Cell Phones Put to Novel Use', *Wired Magazine Online*, 18 March, available at http://www.wired.com/gadgets/miscellaneous/news/2005/03/66950 (accessed 25 March 2010).

WSJ (*Wall Street Journal*) (2008), 'Apple's Latest iPhone Sees Slow Japan Sales', *The Wall Street Journal Online*, 15 September, available at http://online.wsj.com/article/SB122143317323034023.html?mod=2_1571_topbox (accessed 5 May 2010).

X-ing World (2009), 'X-ing World Pamphlet'.

Yahoo Japan (2009), 'Mobairu kensaku ranking [Mobile Search Ranking]', available at http://searchranking.yahoo.co.jp/ranking2009/vertical.html (accessed 13 December 2009).

Zaidan Houjin Internet Kyoukai [Internet Association Japan] (2008), 'Internet Hakusho 2008 [Internet White Paper 2008]', Tokyo: Impress R&D.

Index

masculinity, 121, 125, 132, 141, 152, 157, 197
mass culture, 148, 149
Matsushita, 41
McDonalds, 42, 213, 225–6, 230, 232
media mix, 83–5, 147, 151, 156
Meiji Restoration, 31, 179
men's leggings, 134
merit-based pay, 128–9
METI, 32, 44, 50, 220
metrosexual, 97
microwave, 75
middle class, 4, 7, 9, 13, 26, 112–13, 118
middle-class, 7, 14, 112, 114–15, 118, 147, 152
milk, 43, 55, 165, 169–70, 179, 181
Ministry of Finance, 5, 50, 181
miso, 166, 169, 181
Mitsubishi, 43, 129, 224
Mitsukoshi, 177, 181
Mixi, 219–20, 229–31
mobile banking, 221, 223
mobile game, 226
mobile mail, 211
mobile marketing, 211, 225, 228
mobile operators, 209–10
mobile phone novel, 218
mobile phones, 73, 82, 96, 207–8, 211–14, 216–17, 218, 221, 227–32
mobile *suica*, 223, 232
money transfer, 224
monopoly, 41, 209

Nagoya, 42, 67, 80, 177, 179
narcissism, 186, 201, 204
national culture, 18
NEET (Not in Education, Employment, or Training), 94, 96
neo-mobiler, 229
new rich, 12, 28, 108–9, 111, 113, 116, 118, 119
New Zealand, 45–6
Nintendo, 213, 230
North Korea, 130

obligation, 24, 178
office ladies, 115
oil crisis, 8, 19

old old age, 96, 99, 105
omiyage, 178, 226
online retail, 105
online shopping, 82, 102–3, 105, 177
onsen, see hot springs
organic food, 11, 82, 171, 173, 180–1
osaifu keitai, 221, 223, 232
Osaka, 8, 41, 113, 150, 158, 177
otaku, 12, 146–8, 151–9
overcrowded train, 223

Panasonic, 41, 72
parallel market, 113
parasite singles, 9, 12, 93–8, 102, 106
parenthood, 167–8
part-time work, 11, 129, 168
payday lending, 50
pension benefits, 111
pension payments, 68
pensioners, 67
pleasure, 4, 7, 99, 151–2, 154, 188, 196–8, 201–3
point cards, 178
Pokemon, 156
post-industrial economy, 122
post-war, 3–5, 7, 21, 108, 110–11, 115, 129–30, 150
postindustrialism, 7
poverty, 4, 130
price sensitivity, 24–5, 28
price-value relationship, 10, 112
Prime Minister, 39, 42, 53–4
product quality, 21, 23, 34
product safety, 32, 35, 39–40, 43
product selections, 81
psyche changing, 11
purchasing power, 3, 12, 65, 67, 69, 70, 108, 123
pure consumers, 152

recession, 10, 18, 25, 28, 36, 114, 156, 226
red comics, 148, 150, 154
relationships, 37, 44, 82, 154, 186, 188–9, 194–5, 226
restaurants, 97, 100, 165, 170, 176, 178, 189
retail law, 10